THE POITIER EFFECT

The Poitier Effect

*Racial Melodrama and
Fantasies of Reconciliation*

S HARON W ILLIS

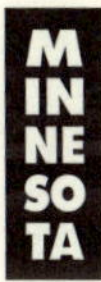

UNIVERSITY OF MINNESOTA PRESS
MINNEAPOLIS · LONDON

An earlier version of chapter 2 was published as "Race as Spectacle, Feminism as Alibi: Representing the Civil Rights Era in the 1990s," in *Keyframes: Popular Cinema and Cultural Studies,* ed. Matthew Tinkcom and Amy Villarejo (New York and London: Routledge, 2001). Portions of chapter 3 were published as "The Politics of Disappointment: Todd Haynes Re-writes Douglas Sirk," *Camera Obscura* 54 (2004); reprinted by permission of Duke University Press.

Lyrics from "The Glory of Love" copyright 1936 Billy Hill, first recorded by Benny Goodman. Lyrics from "Compared to What" by Gene McDaniels. Lyrics from "The Revolution Will Not Be Televised" by Gil Scott-Heron, 1970.

Published by the University of Minnesota Press
111 Third Avenue South, Suite 290
Minneapolis, MN 55401–2520
http://www.upress.umn.edu

Library of Congress Cataloging-in-Publication Data
Willis, Sharon.
    The Poitier effect : racial melodrama and fantasies of reconciliation /
        Sharon Willis.
    Includes bibliographical references and index.
    ISBN 978-0-8166-9284-2 (hc : alk. paper)
    ISBN 978-0-8166-9285-9 (pb : alk. paper)
    1. Poitier, Sidney—Criticism and interpretation.
    2. African Americans in motion pictures.
    3. Race in motion pictures.   I. Title.
    PN2287.P57W55   2015
    791.4302′8092—dc23
    2014040584

Printed in the United States of America on acid-free paper

The University of Minnesota is an equal-opportunity educator and employer.

20 19 18 17 16 15   10 9 8 7 6 5 4 3 2 1

CONTENTS

PREFACE

This project originates, I believe, in my childhood television viewing. From the late 1950s, television began increasingly to capture the escalation of violent white response to integration efforts and peaceful protest. Television news delivered the spectacle of police reinforcing the hysterical violence of white citizens. Their collusion with the Ku Klux Klan was often pretty clear, and this multiplied the fearsomeness of the spectacles TV captured, as the police surged forth—cheered on by white crowds, if not mobs—in brutal attacks on African American men, women, and children engaged in peaceful protests and occupying ordinary public spaces. During the same period, of course, black students (of college and high school age, and eventually elementary school age) were subjected to relentless threats of violence and to vicious heckling by terrifyingly huge white crowds as they attempted the simple act of enrolling for classes. Perhaps most terrifying of all, to this child spectator, were the repeated images of white adults verbally and physically assaulting black schoolchildren. These traumatic spectacles regularly emerged on television, all the more disturbing for their "liveness."

White men indicted for murder flaunted the protocols of courtroom behavior, and white judges and juries easily acquitted aggressive and insolent defendants, however compelling the evidence against them seemed to be. The agencies and institutions meant to guarantee justice and equality and opportunity, like schools, reacted with terrifying aggressive force.

Where was safety, and who protected it? This question emerged for me in TV coverage of the discovery of the bodies of voter registration workers James Earl Chaney, Michael Schwerner, and Andrew Goodman from the Congress of Racial Equality (CORE) in 1964. The local African American registration worker and the two northern white organizers went missing on June 21, 1964, in Neshoba County, Mississippi. Their remains were not found until August. Most chillingly memorable were the images television delivered of the hearing that followed, where the white men indicted for their murders—among them law enforcement officers—were joking together, smirking, and snacking in the courtroom.

In this media environment, and the images of violence and turbulence it registered, Sidney Poitier emerged as a figure of dignity, discipline, and reconciliation. An icon constructed in the thick of the civil rights struggle, he almost immediately became iconic of the period as well. As his star power became spectacularly and definitively established by his Academy Award for Best Actor for his role in *Lilies of the Field,* released in 1963, he was certainly no ordinary celebrity. His image was already conscripted into thoroughly compensatory scenarios in which racial difference remains manageable—and consumable—and reconciliation almost effortlessly achieved. It really is not possible to imagine his Academy Award for this role or, for that matter, the film's own nomination for Best Picture as anything other than compensatory.

This slender film's imagining that an itinerant black handyman gladly spends months doing the bidding of a group of German nuns who want to build a chapel in the Southwest could not possibly register as anything other than a monument—slight though it was—to white wishfulness. It extended to an extreme of implausibility the persistent white fantasy that black people are waiting patiently for us to "come around," and wishing us well into the bargain. Coming, as it did, just after the extremely volatile year 1963, Poitier's award seems to have secured him the dubious cinematic task of representing and assuring racial reconciliation. He continued to embody that benign fantasy at the cinema and on television, as his films were recycled on the networks.

Writing this preface in August 2013, amid a spate of media commemorations of the March on Washington's fiftieth anniversary and just after the release of Lee Daniels's *The Butler* (number one at the box office the first weekend of its national release), I am struck to see that it does not seem at all a distortion (or an artifact of my personal childhood memories) to consider that our collective memories of this period are embodied in TV images. TV *is* our memory—both subjective and shared. Very much echoing the "Forrest Gump" approach to history, *The Butler* offers us two parallel tracks through the history of the civil rights and black power movements: a father's and his son's. Their different perspectives on civil rights activism lock Cecil Gaines, who works as a butler in the White House, and his son, Louis, into an oedipal struggle that pushes the film into a parallel structure that imposes rigid constraints on its very editing.

Cecil Gaines's Forrest Gump narrative places him in close proximity to the deliberations, speculations, negotiations, and even revelations of presidents, from Eisenhower to Reagan; his presence at crucially decisive moments offers the spectator a window on the "private" presidential views that often radically conflicted with the public pronouncements. Louis, his activist son, even more like the Forrest Gump character than his father, implausibly shows up at virtually every crucial historical juncture from 1960, when, as a student at Fisk University, he participates in the Nashville lunch counter sit-ins. Subsequently, we find him on the Freedom Rider bus that was firebombed en route from Atlanta to Alabama on May 14, 1961; in Birmingham being attacked by police with dogs and fire hoses in May 1963; in Selma for the marches to Montgomery in March 1965. Later, we find him in Martin Luther King Jr.'s motel room just prior to King's assassination, and still later he quits the Black Panther Party just before the FBI begins its assassination campaign against the group.

Each of his appearances offers the occasion for a montage of contemporary TV news footage along with iconic still images. But equally important, the television images function as a regular switch point between the worlds the father and son inhabit. Repeatedly, *The Butler* cuts between a scene in which the Gaines parents and their friends, or the staff in the White House, watch the news (history in the making) and a sequence that shows Louis and his activist colleagues taking in the same images. This film's rigid parallel structuring invites us to imagine that the father's and son's interpretations of the escalating protests and the violence they evoke from white mobs and authorities alike increasingly diverge as the oedipal battle escalates. But equally important, as this film remembers it, this was a period in which, however divergent the political views of American spectators, everyone was on the "same page," so to speak, because there were only three broadcast networks. These close competitors, understandably, were in the same places at the same times, and so were delivering remarkably similar coverage, shaping remarkably similar images. Poitier's image circulated among these, both in cinema and on TV. That image persists with remarkable tenacity. It surfaces again and again in the films I consider here, just as it emerges once again, as a focal point for polarization and conflict rather than racial or generation accommodation, in a decisive argument between the butler and his son. It surfaces again and again in the films I consider just as it emerges once more in *The Butler*, in a decisive argument—one that will result in a definitive break—between Cecil Gaines and his Black Panther son. This film deploys Poitier's image, then, as a kind of shorthand for polarization and conflict, perpetuating—rather stunningly—the Poitier effect's afterlife in our contemporary moment.

Introduction

Racial Pedagogy and the Magical Negro

As a figure circulating in American popular culture and collective memory, the legendary actor Sidney Poitier has been strikingly significant in his durability. He keeps coming—or returning—to mind, it seems, as a handy trope for imagining conciliatory interracial encounters. His iconic efficacy has been uncannily enduring, and its appeal remains far from exclusive to white Americans. He operates as an organizing presence in a surprising range of discourses about race in the twenty-first century that, among other things, has seen the election of the first African American president of the United States.

For example, two cultural commentators have recently organized imaginative reconstructions of the primal moment in President Barack Obama's history, his parents' interracial marriage, by invoking *Guess Who's Coming to Dinner*. In *What Obama Means . . . for Our Culture, Our Politics, Our Future*, Jabari Asim, cultural critic and editor in chief of *The Crisis*, the journal of the NAACP, adumbrates a history of precedents in African American cultural and intellectual leadership, as well as in popular media, that he credits with providing a foundation for Obama's success.[1] Among Obama's figurative "ancestors," in the somewhat rapid genealogy he constructs, Poitier emerges as a key figure and a repeated point of comparison. For Asim, perhaps, Obama's singularity seems to recall Poitier's own. In a *New York Times* op-ed column titled "Guess Who's Coming to Dinner" (November 1, 2008), Frank Rich also compares Obama to Poitier's character, and ponders the fact that in 1959 Obama's parents, like the young couple in the film, met at the University of Hawaii. Weirdly, he seems to be imagining Obama both as a reincarnation of the Poitier figure and as his heir. For both writers, interestingly, the comparison of Obama to Poitier hinges on the quality of poise and "calm" that they share. In a more recent compelling essay, "Fear of a Black President," journalist and *Atlantic* magazine editor Ta-Nehisi Coates argues that Obama has had to act as an educator on race and racism in America. Indeed, he suggests that only in the posture of a teacher can Obama speak effectively about race. Equally interesting, however, is his argument that Obama has had to be "twice as good and half as black" to succeed politically. There could hardly be a better formula for describing the narrow bandwidth that Poitier's characters have been constrained to inhabit.[2]

To consider another closely related example: in his 2010 novel *Sag Harbor*, Colson Whitehead twice invokes Poitier, but to pointedly different effects. In an early scene, the narrator evokes the sotto voce comments he regularly overhears at the white-dominated social events to which his private school friends invite him. He becomes used to hearing, "'Who's that?' 'Whisper whisper a friend of Andy's from school.' 'So regal and composed—he looks like a young Sidney Poitier.' 'Whisper whisper or the son of an African diplomat!'"[3] Poitier appears as a kind of specter haunting the young narrator among white strangers. It is as if, in their eyes, the actor serves as template for—or the measure of—safely desirable, upright middle-class black masculinity. Interestingly, Whitehead emphasizes composure in distilling the characteristics that provoke this repeated comparison, and the narrator himself is *composed*, for these white people, in the actor's remembered image.

But later, Poitier returns in an altogether different guise. "I had a thing about stealing," the narrator begins, recounting an episode in which he resisted his white friends' urging that he join them in shoplifting from a local market. "But before I could even think about it," the narrator reports, "I heard Sidney Poitier's voice in my head and in that crisp, familiar, so-dignified tone, he declared, 'They think we steal, and because they think we steal, we must not steal'" (123). "Stealing, Sidney Poitier said, was for the white kids. Let them pull their petty crimes if they wanted—we were made of better material" (124). In this iteration, Poitier has become the superego, the internalized voice of black "righteousness," to use the narrator's term for his own satisfaction in rising above temptation. This voice anticipates and displaces white surveillance, supplanting that authority with its own. Interestingly, as he passes from white discourse into the narrator's inner monologue, Poitier transmutes from pure image into active voice. Equally important, in the narrator's revealing appropriation, Poitier becomes a figure for double consciousness as the superego of the race.

But he is also a figure, as Whitehead shows, of at least a double address; for both black and white subjects he embodies a black moral authority, though differently inflected. This authority has it roots in Poitier's career arc across the period of the civil rights movement from the 1950s through the 1960s, during which he comes back again and again, always pretty much the same. His many returns add up to a brilliant pedagogical career as he evolves through the 1950s and 1960s from recalcitrant student in *Blackboard Jungle* (Richard Brooks, 1955) to accomplished teacher in *To Sir, with Love* (James Clavell, 1967). In fact, he seems permanently compelled to teach: key roles show Poitier instructing white people whether or not he is actually playing a teacher. In *The Defiant Ones* (1958), he teaches his white companion to identify the calls of wildlife and to make a poultice from mud before finally delivering the film's decisive lesson about racial equality understood as friendship. In the 1962 film *Pressure Point* (Hubert Cornfield), he appears as a postwar psychiatrist wrestling to control his outraged response to the racist invective of his patient, a young fascist (played by an oddly convincing Bobby Darin). Elaborating postwar America's popular fascination with the "authoritarian personality," this film turns its therapeutic case history into a teaching moment as well. Its story is framed as a flashback that Poitier's character presents as an object lesson in the early 1960s to a young white colleague (Peter Falk) who is struggling to treat an angry black teenager. This false analogy between the adult white Nazi and the black youth produces the kind of stunningly unbalanced equation that governs so many of the actor's films.[4]

Poitier's teaching career culminates in 1967. In *To Sir, with Love* he returns to an actual classroom, thus inverting his role in *Blackboard Jungle*, and educates his working-class London students to tolerate difference as largely a question of good manners; in *In the Heat of the Night* (Norman Jewison) he teaches forensics and civics to Rod Steiger's redneck Mississippi sheriff; in *Guess Who's Coming to Dinner* (Stanley Kramer) he guides Spencer Tracy's

character to embrace his own liberal principles. In his Oscar-winning performance in *Lilies of the Field* (Ralph Nelson, 1963), Poitier also does a lot
of teaching, notably tutoring the German nuns in English. Perhaps most
spectacularly, in *A Patch of Blue* (Guy Green, 1965) he teaches an impoverished and abused blind white girl basic life skills and fights for her right to
equal access to education.

These films track shifting popular—and professional—conceptions of
the causes and remedies for racism. As white discourse reconceives racism,
translating its solution from the therapeutic to the pedagogical realm of the
classroom, it fashions the problem as a matter of ignorance that requires
the reeducation of backward members of the white community. For the
liberal cultural producer, intellectual, or politician, white culture splits into
"good" and "bad" elements; progressive politics needs to educate the ignorant, backward racists against whom it defines its own enlightened position. Yet popular culture remains intent on visualizing the salutary effects
of this pedagogical enterprise at the level of the individual encounter. In
the move away from the therapeutic iconography that characterized his
early social problem films, the pedagogical scenarios that multiply through
Poitier's films suggest that whites cannot seem to transmit what they learn:
each white person needs private tutoring in race relations. With startling
consistency, his black mentor arrives by accident to enlighten white people,
often by reminding them of what they already know. Having accomplished
his task, by means that remain obscure or mysterious, the mentor disappears. He has only been passing through. But though these figures clearly
relate to the long-standing trope of the "magical Negro," they operate
differently. Black characters in American cinema have been watching, encouraging, and applauding white people, and generally wishing them well,
at least since *The Birth of a Nation*. Poitier, however, set a new standard of
more active intervention.

His iconic roles remain crucially distinct for their emphasis on pedagogy
rather than on sacrifice or magical intervention. And around this construction of the black man as teacher, they also establish a set of visual codes for
these pedagogical encounters, codes that have retained surprising traction
into our contemporary moment. His characters redefined the "magical
Negro" into a paragon of respectability whose mission was to educate well-
intentioned white people to understand and accept racial equality. The

success of this project depended on his nonthreatening goodwill and his eager and patient pedagogical impulses. It also depended on his white pupils not having to work or think to win his approval. This is why the Poitier effect seems to remain so satisfying to repeat.

But Poitier also embodied significant appeal for black audiences during the civil rights period, as we will see. Kasi Lemmons offers a prolonged, and relatively affectionate, look at his force in African American popular culture in *Talk to Me* (2007), where he figures in the film's amusing examination of black cultural politics of style. Her film pays close attention to the ways that black style often opposed notions of "respectability" to "authenticity," where Poitier functioned as shorthand for "inauthenticity." Though that appeal is ambivalent, ambiguous (as it seems to be for Whitehead)—even conflicted—Poitier's characters' restrained responses to white people's bad behavior and ignorance provided a vision of racial reconciliation and reciprocal respect. But these interracial encounters never told the story of the past that produced them, or of the future that they could construct. And this very structure helps to guarantee the persistent traction of the Poitier figure. This traction seems related to his capacity to embody a moral authority that derives from his "innocence," an innocence that is also rooted in his detachment from history.

The Poitier effect is symptomatic of enduring fantasies that shape popular white-authored representations of race. It represents a dream of achieving racial reconciliation and equality without any substantive change to the "white" world or to "white" culture, and, especially, to white privilege. This story of change without change conforms smoothly with fantasies of "color blindness," imaging a world where difference makes no difference. As it repeats stories of rapid, magical, seamless transformations of white consciousness—where we never really see what difference this change is going to make, the Poitier effect is bound to reassure. The Poitier effect, I want to argue, functions as a defense, or a compensatory gesture, averting or deflecting the possibility of a kind of critical thinking that would involve a serious reciprocal interracial exchange, instead offering a fantasy of racial understanding and "assimilation" that requires no effort on the part of white people.

While Poitier became iconic as the embodiment of fantasies of interracial "understanding" within the civil rights period, subsequent iterations of the figure he repeatedly played and the scenarios he anchored made him iconic of the period as well. This book tries to account for his singular cinematic career in the civil rights era and its emergence as a central archive for subsequent representations produced by filmmakers who grew up in the period, as well as for our current collective memory of that period. And, indeed, the surprising success of Tate Taylor's 2011 screen adaptation of Kathryn Stockett's 2009 novel *The Help* offers a virtually unreconstructed version of the Poitier effect's terms. But this recycled trope of beneficent black pedagogy comes smuggled in a scenario that assigns Poitier's role to black *women*. One way of accounting for the stubborn durability of this archive relates to its emergence at a watershed moment in which Poitier's ascendance to stardom coincided quite precisely with the civil rights movement. This coincidence produced a set of foundational protocols for fictions of interracial bonding that became frozen into a kind of formulaic straitjacket for later racial melodramas.

Melodramatizing History

Not surprisingly, these stories of epiphanies and radical transformation through intimate pedagogical exchange show themselves especially hospitable to and compatible with the conventions of melodrama. As film scholar Thomas Elsaesser has argued, melodrama seems particularly adapted to moments of social and cultural crisis. Its persistence, he contends, "might indicate the ways in which popular culture has not only taken note of social crises and the fact that the losers are not always those who deserve it most, but has also resolutely refused to understand social change in other than private contexts and emotional terms."[5] Poitier's films of this period present circumscribed—if not hermetic—worlds that produce symptomatic environments. Heavily interiorized, even their exterior spaces seem limited and enclosed. Social pressures register on an interior landscape, coded as domestic and familialized, even if the field of play extends to a small town or neighborhood. Their dramas unfold in isolated environments, where cultural and social conflicts and contradictions become displaced onto individualized, private negotiations. Such conclusions as these films produce arrive through affect and intimate exchange. Like their protagonists, Poitier's films construct social issues to be managed somehow psychologically and, more specifically, pedagogically.

Speaking of U.S. film melodrama, especially as crafted by directors such as Douglas Sirk and Nicholas Ray, Elsaesser writes that it "is iconographically fixed by the claustrophobic atmosphere of the bourgeois home and/or the small town setting, its emotional pattern is that of panic and latent hysteria, reinforced stylistically by a complex handling of space in interiors . . . to the point where the world seems totally predetermined and pervaded by 'meaning' and interpretable signs" (62). Poitier-centered melodramas reduced the scope of the civil rights movement, and the turbulence surrounding it, to a manageable form in a tightly circumscribed terrain where meaning promised to emerge from private negotiations. And they seemed to respond, however inadequately, directly to white hysteria about racial integration. But the task of stabilizing whiteness by reinforcing its boundaries through the embodiment of blackness bears emphatic repetition, it seems. Over and over, Sidney Poitier's films take up this project, frequently resorting to elisions and reversals—traumas or epiphanies—to structure their strained plots.

Film theorists have long noted melodrama's peculiar relation to history, which the form tends to evoke only to displace or diffuse it into private crisis. Christine Gledhill argues that "melodrama touches the socio-political only at that point where it triggers the psychic, and the absence of causal relations between them allows for a short-circuiting between melodramatic desire and the socially constructed world."[6] Through this "short-circuiting," she argues, melodrama "acknowledges demands inadmissible in the codes of the social, psychological or political discourse. If melodrama can only end in the place where it began, not having a programmatic analysis for the future, its possibilities lie in this double acknowledgment of how things are in a given historical conjuncture, and the primary desires and resistances contained within it" (38). "Melodrama's challenge," for Gledhill, "lies not in confronting how things are, but rather in asserting how they should be" (21). Significantly, in this form, assertion displaces analysis or argument.

Geoffrey Nowell-Smith argues that melodrama only poses problems that "are always to some extent resolved." "Melodrama achieves its putatively 'happy end' . . . only at the cost of repression," he contends, precisely because "the laying out of the problems 'realistically' always allows for the generating of an excess which cannot be accommodated."[7] In the scenarios that govern Poitier's films, and those later marked by his iconic legacy, we often confront foregone conclusions, forced resolutions, and gaps in causality that deliver us, like the characters, from history.

Steve Neale's account of melodramatic form also emphasizes its uneasy relation to history: "Marked by chance happenings, missed meetings, sudden conversions, last-minute rescues and revelations, *deus ex machina* endings," melodramas privilege effect over cause, "the extraordinary over the ordinary." In the world of melodrama, Neale contends, causal succession and logic give way to events and developments that remain "unmotivated (or undermotivated) from a realist point of view," and "such preparation and motivation as does exist is always 'insufficient.'"[8] In the gap between effect and cause, melodrama introduces the affective glue of pathos. Such recourse to pathos may become especially crucial as melodrama confronts intense social conflict or historical trauma.

In *Playing the Race Card*, film scholar Linda Williams presents a sustained exploration of the centrality of melodrama to popular ideologies of race in the United States. She enjoins us to understand melodrama "not as an aberration, archaism, or excess, but as the fundamental mode by which American mass culture has 'talked to itself' about the enduring moral dilemma of race."[9] Far from being a "detour," she contends, the subject of race seems to be "a more direct route to the heart of melodrama itself," since "in racial melodrama we discover the generation of 'moral legibility' (Brooks, 1995) through the spectacle of racialized bodily suffering" (xiv). Beginning with *Uncle Tom's Cabin*, then, and proceeding across a series of nineteenth-century incarnations of racial melodrama and the minstrelsy to which it is closely bound, Williams traces the melodramatic impulse through its vigorous twentieth-century reworkings in cinematic landmarks like *The Birth of a Nation* (D. W. Griffith, 1915), *The Jazz Singer* (Alan Crosland, 1927), and *Gone with the Wind* (Victor Fleming, 1939), and beyond these to the contemporary moment, exploring "the logic of racial victimization and vilification that fuels them" (xv).

Demonstrating that melodrama has remained a central framework for the processing of racial fantasy, in both its regressive and progressive tendencies, Williams insists that we cannot dismiss its efficacy for cultural analysis of racial negotiations. Of central interest to the texts under consideration in this project is Williams's claim that "as the very logic of the excluded middle, melodrama cannot tell the story of the middle ground"

(307). Is it possible that the very appeal of melodrama as a site of interracial negotiations lies in its capacity to raise questions that it can only block? Equally important, Williams concludes by expressing her doubt "that it will be possible for popular culture to break with melodrama's obsession with past injury as a way of establishing moral legitimacy." "Until we grasp the full extent of the melodramatic imagination of race, and all of our susceptibilities to it," she concludes, "we will continue to be, like Harriet Beecher Stowe, in a profound state of denial as to what we are about" (310).

Part of the appeal of racial melodrama may be precisely its ambivalence, and the ambivalence it encourages in the spectator. As our desires and identifications circulate through melodrama's staging, across the relays of characters, spaces, situations, and scenes, visual and acoustic lures sustain complex fantasies in which it is difficult—if not impossible—to disaggregate masochism from sadism, or sympathy from aggression. Perhaps this is a symptom of the sadism and aggression that seem to haunt cross-racial white–black imaginary identifications and that seem endemic to traditions of racial melodrama.[10] This deeply ambivalent fantasy structure may shape our "susceptibility" to the form. It certainly bears careful scrutiny, and it suggests that we need somehow to temper our susceptibility to texts that persist in forgetting or disowning—not knowing—what they know while exerting substantial and symptomatic affective appeal. As I hope to show in these analyses of the Poitier effect, racial melodrama seems condemned to repetition/reenactment rather than working through.

Melodrama's enduring appeal for the contemplation of interracial intimacy may also depend on its capacity to deploy the tropes of "Africanism" that Toni Morrison finds at the heart of white American literary tradition. "American Africanism," she writes in *Playing in the Dark: Whiteness and the Literary Imagination,* "makes it possible to say and not say, to inscribe and erase, to escape and engage, to act out and act on, to historicize and render timeless. It provides a way of contemplating chaos and civilization, desire and fear, and mechanisms for testing the problems and blessings of freedom."[11] Specifically, Morrison contends, "for American writers generally, this Africanist other . . . provided the occasion for exercises in the absence of restraint, the presence of restraint, the contemplation of freedom and aggression; permitted opportunities for the exploration of ethics and morality, for meeting the obligations of the social contract, for bearing the cross of religion and following out the ramifications of power" (47–48). But it also bears especially on the questions of history and of modernity, as the Africanist narrative permits "the construction of a history and a context for whites" that crucially depends on "positing history-lessness and context-lessness for blacks" (53). After *The Defiant Ones,* Poitier's films, as well as later cinematic representations that mine his archive, remain unconsciously committed to abstracting the black subject from history. His character always seems above the social fray; his position is already established as a fait accompli because he has no history of arriving at his present status.

As perhaps the fictional form or genre most congenial to tropes of blackness reduced to victim of—or witness to—suffering, melodrama offers another ideological resource: the figure of "black innocence" that literary critic Robert Reid-Pharr identifies in American literary and popular culture. Marked indelibly by the history of enslavement, this figure remains "innocent" of the brutal history of racial violence and oppression in the United States, as well as of the nation's imperialist drives. But to be innocent of history means to be outside it as well, as in Morrison's "Africanism." "Black innocence," in Reid-Pharr's account, remains cut off from subjectivity and agency, as if mired, and even embalmed, in the persistence of an atrocious past, one to which it is inevitably reduced. Exploring this trope's seductiveness, he suggests that it maintains at least a double address. Taking this notion much further than Williams does, he shows its ready adaptability to divergent racialized discourses and fantasies. "'Blackness' is as much a fetish object for Black Americans as it is for whites," he writes.[12] Examining the many and varied appeals of this seductive innocence, he suggests that "part of the reason for the continued reverence that many of us hold for civil rights and Black power figures . . . is that their blackness, or their performance of blackness, allowed them to articulate versions of American nationalism that were not tainted by the ugly spectacles of intolerance that typified much of twentieth-century American life" (124). "Moreover," he argues, "the heavy-handed racism that continues in American society reinforces the notion that Black American persons, as evidenced by the fact of our black bodies and the incessant racist response to them, continue to be trapped in a pre-modern state" (128). That state, of course, supports many variations and entailments, from "infantile" to "tribal," for example, but it "might also rightly be given the title 'innocent,'" he continues (124).

Reid-Pharr suggests that black nationalists may have been drawn to the figure of black innocence not only as a compromise in its appeal to "the white audiences with whom they were in dialogue but also because it allowed for the articulation of a Black American identity that was seductive and sexy because it was *in* but not *of* modernity" (129). But this innocent figure situated outside modern culture is inextricably bound to another image of unaccountability: "even when the black subject turns pathological, becomes the bad black, his antisociality, . . . once again does the important work of demonstrating that he is removed from the currents of modern society and is, therefore, nonaccountable" (131).

As the dark underside of black innocence, its bad object, this figure, too, exerts compelling cultural appeal. And Poitier's characters seem consistently, if implicitly, to be propped on his emphatic difference from his opposite number—the bad object. But they also remain cloaked in a kind of innocence. Although *The Defiant Ones* does explicitly cast him as a victim with a history—he has been sentenced to the chain gang for hitting a white man who threatened him—subsequent films leave him socially unsituated, more witness to oppression than its direct victim. Yet his black innocence suggests an ahistorical suspension in permanent proximity to enslavement. He remains, paradoxically, *of* history but not *in* history.

Mediating the Poitier Effect

Emerging from his repeated melodramatic roles as a cinematic icon for the civil rights movement in collective memory, Poitier may offer the first incarnation of what Herman Gray has called the "civil rights subject," who "embodies complex codes of behavior and propriety that make it an exemplar of citizenship and responsibility—success, mobility, hard work, sacrifice, individualism."[13] But if it was cinema that provided us this classic icon for the movement, it was television that delivered the documentary record, which generated its own iconic images, historic rather than fictional, more collective than individual. Meanwhile, Poitier's image, through its repetitions, became the iconic cinematic embodiment of wishful fictions of race relations that emphasized the individual agency of enlightened white people. Because Poitier's career so closely tracks both the civil rights movement and television's increasingly focused attention to it, we cannot easily disentangle the effect of his cinematic reappearances and the repeated television news scenes that contributed so strenuously to the historical record of the period. TV was memory in the making, and, for the most part, TV constitutes our contemporary memory of that historic moment. Not surprisingly, then, television figures centrally in this project, as we consider cinematic remembrances of the period in question.

In Linda Williams's account in *Playing the Race Card*, the appeal of racial melodrama extends into the civil rights movement itself, which, Williams argues, staged "its own melodramas of black and white in which noble black citizens suffered at the hands of villainous white supremacists" (228). She does not make clear how self-consciously she imagines this deployment of melodrama's tropes to be, nor does she examine its medium. In *Equal Time: Television and the Civil Rights Movement*, media studies scholar Aniko Bodroghkozy examines the careful construction of a consistent "script" for television news coverage of the movement. This script depends on a triangle formed by the "white moderate," the segregationist, "typically shown as 'deviant,' and 'the worthy black victim.'" "Like white moderates," she continues, "worthy black victims were thoughtful and articulate, and their representations carried signifiers of middle-classness."[14] Bodroghkozy concludes that the network news "seemed to have solidified a general script for its civil rights coverage" by 1963. That script—in part—looks like this: "search for worthy black victims of racial discrimination who could be individualized or, if in groups, largely kept silent, and have either Martin Luther King or a white reporter speak for them. Search also for representations of white Southern moderation and signs of progress and privilege that discourse. Remain suspicious and uncomfortable with instances of black people in mass movement" (60). This repeated news reporting "script" sounds suspiciously close to melodramatic staging as it plays its "victims" and moderates against the background of "deviance."

Television studies scholar Sasha Torres examines the period's media spectacles from a different perspective. She contends that "television and the civil rights movement . . . through a perhaps unlikely coincidence of interests, formed powerful allies for each other in the period." She argues that the movement "and the television industry shared the urgent desire to forge a new, and newly *national,* consensus on the meanings and functions of racial difference." The convergence of these interests happens as follows: "The southern movement's more consistent and effective gesture against segregation was to contrast the racial terrorism of the South with national ideals and democratic discourses," while "the continued expansion of the industry's profits . . . depended on its ability to exploit in programming the visuality and topicality of race across sectional borders."[15] Both television and the civil rights movement, then, invested in the project of reaching a national audience and producing a national narrative.

American studies scholar Alan Nadel makes a similar claim. He writes: "If we consider the virtual impossibility that any event will acquire 'historical' status if it escapes the scrutiny of television; if we consider, furthermore, that no other medium of communication in the second half of the twentieth century conferred the same legitimacy and that television's power to legitimize was matched only by its speed and ubiquity, we can see the great degree to which television does not report news of the public sphere but rather comprises the most significant domain that allows the possibility of news and of history." He goes on to point out that, "by many criteria, for the baby boom generation, television has been the fundamental public space and, therefore, is a necessary condition of historical possibility."[16]

As all Americans became spectators of the civil rights movement, owing to national television coverage from the late 1950s through the 1960s, members of a national audience became stunned witnesses to a collapse of the expected order of things in public life. Time after time television news showed us police reinforcing the hysterical violence of white citizens, brutally attacking African American men, women, and children engaging in peaceful protest in ordinary public spaces.

In 1963 Americans witnessed a seemingly endless series of media spectacles: police used fire hoses and dogs against demonstrators in Birmingham, Alabama, in April; the Klan bombed the Sixteenth Street Baptist Church, a Southern Christian Leadership Conference organizing center, in September, killing four teenage girls. That same year, Governor George Wallace made his famous "stand at the schoolhouse door," to block the integration of the University of Alabama, prompting President Kennedy to send federal troops to accomplish the integration. This episode echoed the previous year's events at the University of Mississippi, when Kennedy sent federal marshals and troops to protect James Meredith, the first African American to attend that school. Riots followed his entrance to the campus. On "Bloody Sunday," March 7, 1965, police and state troopers beat and bludgeoned peaceful marchers heading across the Edmund Pettus Bridge to Montgomery, Alabama. President Johnson signed the Voting Rights Act—severely compromised in 2013—into law in August of the same year.

In this period, it seemed that institutions that were meant to guarantee justice and stability, like schools and police, reacted with brutal aggression toward nonviolent efforts at integration. Hysterical white adults mobbed schoolchildren at the Little Rock Arkansas Central High School in 1957 in one of the first events to capture national television news attention. Again, the president had to pit federal troops against local authorities and the Arkansas National Guard. In 1964, the disappearance of voting rights workers James Earl Chaney, Michael Henry Schwerner, and Andrew Goodman garnered significant attention, as did the discovery of their lynched bodies some weeks later in the levee on a Klansman's farm. In the face of such sustained white violence, the law's failure to find, much less convict, perpetrators was all the more chilling. Of course, these hypervisible, highly mediatized events constituted an alibi for the less spectacular (at the time)—but systemic—articulations of racism in the North and across the rest of the country.

In *Television in Black-and-White America,* Nadel argues that in its project of constructing a national narrative and an audience for it, "late 1950s and early 1960s television attempted to reread the news coverage and, in several subtle ways, reassert the ethics of conflating the racial and the spatial" (13). Among the strategies of this not entirely conscious segregationism is the way that "prime-time programming inverted the news/drama relationship so that news coverage (and, at that, only a part of the coverage) could be seen as the anomaly, no more typifying normal American life than a tornado typified normal American weather" (119). Television's "democracy," he insists, depended on a construction of commonality. "Broadcasting," he writes, "nationalized the common person in every way that his or her values were common rather than unique . . . status quo rather than progressive" (42). In keeping with its preference for melodramatic tropes, then, broadcast television "proliferated narratives of conservative utopia, sine qua non: 'what ought to have been' in the past-perfect conditional tense—as the model for 'what ought to be'" (42).

TV managed the trauma the news delivered, then, by deploying the melodramatic strategies it shared with Poitier's films. Television scholar Lynne Joyrich explores the rapid development of television's cultural hold in relation to melodrama, arguing that it "placed itself firmly within the realm of family, domesticity, and consumerism—the very ground of melodrama."[17] She suggests that 1950s film melodrama migrates into television, "engulfing the medium as it engulfs its spectators and precluding its location as a separate category" (46). Of course, television's roots in radio already provide it with a rich melodramatic legacy. "Rather than eclipsing melodrama," Joyrich argues, "television incorporates it so as to bring the strands of passivity and domesticity associated with both melodrama and TV together in a simulated plenitude, thereby positioning all viewers as susceptible consumers," so that "television is 'occupied' by (or 'preoccupied' with) melodrama and vice versa" (45).

The compatibility and mutual attraction of form and medium allow melodrama's tropes to inflect TV across its genres, as Nadel also suggests. Broadcast television news, for instance, according to Joyrich, borrows melodramatic strategies: "By employing conventions taken from narrative television (including a focus on the family—the news 'family' and the families investigated), news programs achieve the emotional intensification and moral polarization associated with dramatic serials." "As in the explicitly fictional melodramas," she continues, "conflicts are brought to the surface and expressed through contrasts that rehearse and flatten out the issues" (49).

Our collective media memory of the civil rights period remains shaped by the melodramatic tropes that both inflected TV's news coverage and conditioned Poitier's films. As television and film worked to manage social trauma, they delivered an archive of images and icons that continue to emerge in later cinematic rewritings of the civil rights era. Just as Poitier's recurrent roles functioned by recalling his previous incarnations, later films that propose to revisit the moment that his career shared with the civil rights movement cannot seem to dispense with his iconic trace or with the scenarios that produced it. As Poitier's films developed around isolated moments of interracial recognition and reconciliation, they also worked to stabilize race, embodying it in a figure that continued to "pass through" them into a space beyond their terrain. Later films that remember the civil rights period—with a particular nostalgia, it must be said—reproduce the Poitier effect through central black characters who exercise a powerful impact on the white people whose lives they transform.

Nostalgia for What Never Was

Much of the mediatized memory of the civil rights movement takes shape in terms of the Poitier effect, which has long remained central to efforts to remember the nation's traumatic racial history under the wishful sign of that history's undoing. Poitier's films are consistently propelled by the accidents, unaccountable reversals, and epiphanies that structure melodrama. This structure permits them to function especially well as screen memories for their historical period. But similar tricks of memory shape more recent "civil rights nostalgia" films as well. The Poitier effect continues to work its magic, and it helps these cinematic fantasies mediate the sense of trauma they still associate with this history and with racial difference itself.

This book's overarching analysis explores the obsessive sameness of the characters Poitier plays, the compulsive returns of similar scenarios and conclusions, and the ideological efficacy of the routine displacement of those conclusions, as well as of history itself. Since his character is always just passing through, he continues to respond to liberal wish fulfillment, leaving situations magically transformed and white subjects reeducated.

The "civil rights nostalgia" films this book examines all long for a better past, for a past redone in the retroactive glow of the present and understood as the product of a social progress that was yet to come. In these imaginings of that past we recognize the contemporary workings of the Poitier effect. In different ways, these nostalgia films establish the progressive credentials of their contemporary cultural moment, by rehearsing the trajectory that governs most Poitier films, from a "knowing" retrospection. All proceed as if their white female protagonists, inclined as they are toward feminism, already know—without knowing—what their stories will have to teach them.

These films are all organized by scenarios of racial pedagogy. Each in its own way rewrites history to undo it in favor of a better past, one in which white people were largely innocent and well-intentioned.[18] This better past also imagines an incipient white feminism that emerges intertwined with the civil rights movement. Such a retroactive fantasy simultaneously guarantees the antiracist credentials of contemporary feminism and minimizes its debt to racial struggles. Rewritings of civil rights struggles around white feminist agency regularly rehearse the very tropes that shaped the Poitier films released in the period they depict. Those repetitions, which seem compulsive and unconscious, consistently strain the films' fantasmatic projects.

Significantly, lest we might have thought melodramas of racial pedagogy had finally run their course, *The Help* vividly proves otherwise, as it powerfully reiterates the tropes that structure these earlier civil rights nostalgia films. In its fantasy of feminism bridging the segregated worlds of Jackson, Mississippi, in 1962 through bonds among women, this film assigns Poitier's pedagogical role to the maids Aibileen (Viola Davis) and Minny (Octavia Spencer). Once they have provided the young white writer, Skeeter (Emma Stone), with their stories of the world of domestic service, these women cheer her on in her escape to New York City. The stories she has borrowed and published have catapulted her into a career in publishing. Her racial and gender politics are too progressive for this backward context—no man in this town will have her.

At the film's teary conclusion, Skeeter gets to move on. The North is where she belongs, among the enlightened white people. She passes beyond the history in which the maids remain mired—while wishing her well. Her black interlocutors remain locked in Jackson's violently enforced stasis, toiling for benighted bigots, awaiting the arrival of historical change. Much like Poitier's films, *The Help* cannot imagine them as agents of historical change. What surprises here is the reemergence of an effect whose exhaustion seemed complete. But perhaps it returns through black female figures precisely because the feminist alibi can still divert our attention from the basic melodrama of racial pedagogy. Part of the persistence/durability of racial melodrama into our contemporary moment, as demonstrated by *The Help*'s tremendous popularity with both literary and film audiences, must have to do with a continuing wishful nostalgia—that is, with white people's imaginings of a better past, a history of civil rights in which they collectively participated much more fully and unambivalently. The emphasis that the nostalgia films of the 1990s, like *The Help*, place on a feminist impulse dovetailing with antiracism promotes this fantasy of both more focused and effective white agency and some kind of white "innocence."

Because the feminism that began to arise during and immediately on the heels of the civil rights movement has been largely quite successful—for white women—collectively, we seem to imagine from the vantage point of that success a too-proximate analogy with racial equality. Popular representations, that is, may want to transfer the success of feminism to race relations. Such a displacement—along with the historical inversion that would imagine feminist impulses driving white participation in the civil rights movement, rather than acknowledge how civil rights encouraged and promoted white feminist activism—it seems to me, contributes powerfully to the popular white fantasy that we have arrived at a "postracial" moment.

But the Poitier figure does not serve only as an anchor for fantasies of a "postracial" moment. Even as he emerges centrally in popular media memory of the civil rights period, he remains a conflicted and ambivalent icon, one that can organize narratives that take some critical distance on the Poitier effect. He appears in both Kasi Lemmons's *Talk to Me* and Lee Daniels's *The Butler*, two films that seem to respond to the white-produced nostalgic retrospections of the civil rights movement. Poitier circulates through these film memories of the civil rights period, but as a complex and multivalent image.

Poitier's iconic "usefulness," however, has persisted beyond cinematic representation. Among his reappearances in the twenty-first century, of course, he emerged in the popular discourse around Barack Obama's presidential candidacy. Just a bit earlier, he had appeared at the 2002 Academy Awards ceremony to receive the Lifetime Achievement Award. Of course, this was the historic year in which Halle Berry won Best Actress for her role in *Monster's Ball* and Denzel Washington received the Best Actor Oscar for *Training Day*. Poitier's presence recalled his own Academy Award, curiously—but *usefully*—conferred upon him for the astonishingly slight *Lilies of the Field*, released in a year marked by terrible racist violence. His presence forcefully framed the awards of his colleagues, who also won for curious roles. His "usefulness," it seems, endures, in some kind of explanatory and reassuring function, to guarantee racial reconciliation, exhibited in the Academy's celebration of Berry's and Washington's abil-ity to embody "bad objects." The fantasy of "postraciality," like the fantas-matic representations that place white feminists at the heart of the civil rights movement, and like the Poitier effect, serves to reassure white cul-ture—at the price of erasing history—that we have achieved most of the change we need.

In the chapters that follow, I trace the emergence and consolidation of the Poitier character in the films of the 1950s and 1960s that made him a star, and then I track the persistence of the Poitier effect in films from the 1990s to the contemporary moment. *Love Field, The Long Walk Home, Pleas-antville, Far from Heaven,* and, most recently and strikingly, *The Help* all return with significantly pointed nostalgia to the racial melodramas of the civil rights period. Kasi Lemmons's film *Talk to Me* presents its own nos-talgic view, but from an African American perspective, in which Poitier figures as a richly ambivalent icon in the conflicted politics of black culture and style.

Finally, I consider the persistence and force of the Poitier effect as it reasserts itself in contemporary popular representations. It seems that we cannot quite do without this iconic figure, which paradoxically embodies both racial conflict and racial reconciliation. As icon, Poitier marks the site of deep ambivalences that our popular cultural representations cannot resolve, or name, or leave alone.

1

Passing Through

The Obsessive Sameness of Sidney Poitier

Implicitly tracking the vicissitudes of liberal white racial consciousness in the turbulent period of civil rights activism and violent responses to it, Poitier's films map a kind of racial unconscious. Undergirded by powerful affective charges and delivering cathartic payoffs, his films register some of the fantasmatic forces pulsing through white discourses about race in the period. As the films proliferate ironies that suggest unconscious effects, marks of repression, Poitier's own compulsive repetition as an idealized "good object" seems to signal the return of the repressed.

That "good object" must be markedly—if impossibly—distinguished from the "bad object" against which it will serve as a defense, but by which it is also menaced. We might see Poitier's roles as Hollywood's contribution to a white cultural compulsion to find—and stabilize—a reliably "good" black object, a figure that represents both reassurance and reparation. Poitier's films, then, work toward fantasmatic reparation of racial conflict, replaying essentially the same drama of reconciliation to offer idealized resolutions that must repress political and material violence around race in the real world. But even in the apparently defensive fantasies they elaborate, Poitier's films also perform the more complex and unstable function of fantasy as Jacqueline Rose describes it: "Fantasy is also a way of re-elaborating and therefore of partly recognizing the memory which is struggling, against psychic odds, to be heard."[1]

Perhaps precisely because of this instability, Poitier's circulation through a series of remarkably similar scenarios produced a split address that also appealed to African American audiences, in different, but nonetheless strongly affective, terms. Henry Louis Gates Jr. remembers *Lilies of the Field* this way: "The 1963 film that established Poitier as a significant presence in postwar cinema: noble, selfless, saintly. When I saw it, at thirteen, I was moved to tears. It was the perfect civil-rights vehicle for its moment. Its message to white America was practically telegraphed: We are a friendly and kind-hearted people, we are good citizens."[2] Gates's memory affirms the appeal of melodramatic stagings of innocence across a split address to black and white spectators.

Music and culture critic Nelson George also reports an intense affective response to Poitier, emphasizing the gravity of the actor's status as the "only one": "Being the first black man to do this or that was one of the burdens of Sidney's life. No other black actor, and few black figures, was so massive a figure in our (in this case American) psyche. No one else has meant what he did and no one else ever will."[3] Both authors, looking back to childhood, foreground Poitier's function as a civil rights vehicle himself while indicating a certain anxious tension between his most famous roles and progressive racial ideologies.

For black spectators, Poitier's appearance relieves the representational vacuum produced by a cinemascape that offers no individuated black characters who are not drawn directly from minstrel traditions. For white spectators, this appearance registers racial difference at the manageable level of a singular individual. To accomplish this fragile balance, of course, this icon must stay within a predictable and restricted orbit of consumption.[4] And Poitier himself wrestled with this contradiction. Reflecting on his Best Actor Academy Award for *Lilies of the Field*, he remarked: "Did I say to myself, 'This country is finally waking up and beginning to recognize that certain changes are inevitable'?" Bluntly, he continues, "No, I did not. I knew we hadn't 'overcome.' Because I was still the only one. My career was unique in all of Hollywood."[5]

In a cover essay for *Look* magazine in 1968, James Baldwin offers a subtle analysis of the contradictions embedded in the actor's extraordinary position. Addressing the film industry's steadfast perpetuation of the dominant "fantasy of American life," Baldwin contends that "the black face, truthfully reflected, is not only no part of this dream, it is antithetical to it." "And this," he writes, "puts the black performer in a rather grim bind. He knows, on the one hand, that if the reality of the black man's life were on the screen, it would destroy the fantasy totally." He continues, articulating the bind this way: "On the other hand, he really has no right *not* to appear, not only because he must work, but also for all those people who need to see him."[6] And both black and white audiences seemed to need to see him. With characteristically evocative economy, Baldwin establishes the representational forces that shape Poitier as icon, emphasizing the actor's imperative to appear. But his appearance will always outrun and supersede his acting—understood both as actor's performance and as character's agency.

Poitier's iconic function reaches its greatest intensity in 1967, the year in which he becomes one of the biggest box-office-drawing stars and releases three films. These three roles exemplify Herman Gray's notion of the "civil rights subject," by which he characterizes dominant media representations of "those black, largely middle-class benefactors who gained the most visibility as well as material and status rewards from the struggles and opportunities generated by the civil rights movement." Gray closely echoes Gates in describing this figure, notable for his moral uprightness and embrace of responsible citizenship. "This figure," he goes on, "is often juxtaposed against poor and disenfranchised members of the black community, where it works to reinforce and reaffirm the openness and equality of contemporary American society."[7] This formulation establishes a good object/bad object split once again—but it also represents the instability of that opposition.

In Poitier's films, disenfranchised blacks often register only as a marked absence or as an undifferentiated amalgam at the edge of the frame and the drama it encloses—a backdrop against which his extraordinariness emerges. This very extraordinariness generates unmanageable ironies and tensions. Notable among the regular strains that mark his films is this one: despite their generally accommodationist rhetoric, rarely can the films "accommodate" Poitier himself. At the level of sheer physicality and bodily performance, we find that, often, the frame has difficulty containing him. Visually this effect replicates the narrative contortions that seek to manage ideological tensions. But equally often, the film frame is strained by the sound track's pressure on its visual field. Many of the actor's films deploy musical effects at moments of intense contradiction—logical or ideological, and often both. Music haunts the image and the story, much as the actor's iconicity "ghosts" his characters. Together, these two effects trouble the cinematic frame.

If I refer to Poitier rather than his characters throughout, this is because his peculiar status as the only black male lead in Hollywood in this period meant that he was always appearing as himself alongside whatever character he was playing. This constitutes a particular version of what José Esteban Muñoz has dubbed "the burden of liveness" assigned to people of color, the obligation to perform their authenticity: "a cultural imperative within the majoritarian public sphere that denies subalterns access to larger channels of representation, while calling the minoritarian subject to the stage, performing his or her alterity as a consumable spectacle."[8]

Taking up Muñoz's term, Sasha Torres finds the "burden of liveness" crucially elaborated in television through the years of most intense civil rights activity, when TV's liberal agenda deployed "black performance in information genres" to promote progressive ends. "Television's African American spectacles," she writes, "have persistently been characterized not only by black performance as 'entertainment' but also as 'information,' to employ one of the medium's own favorite binaries."[9] In films of this period that struggle to articulate a usable integration story, Poitier seems to embody a peculiar instance of television's structuring polarity.

To the extent that both his casting and his roles depend on and reinscribe his iconicity, he is always playing himself. The actor, then, disturbs the claims of the diegesis in ways that may reassure by grounding it in his familiar singularity. This familiarity and singularity, however, also contribute to his "*burden* of liveness." As Baldwin puts it, "By the use of his own person, he must smuggle in a reality that he knows is not in the script" (56). At the same time, Poitier's person seems to import "realities" that exceed the actor's control. And these may constitute part of the appeal that at times baffles Baldwin: "He's . . . extraordinarily attractive and winning and virile, but that could just as easily have worked against him. It's something of a puzzle. Speaking now of the image and not of the man, it has to do with a quality of pain and danger and some fundamental impulse to decency that both titillates and reassures the white audience" (56).

This reading of Poitier's star appeal resonates with Richard Dyer's contention that a star's image is "related to contradictions in ideology—whether within the dominant ideology, or between it and other subordinated/revolutionary ideologies." Dyer continues: "The relation may be one of displacement . . . or of the suppression of one half of the contradiction and the foregrounding of the other . . . or else it may be that the star effects a 'magic' reconciliation of the apparently incompatible terms."[10] Both in his star image and in his characters, Poitier seems to perform magical reconciliations again and again.

But as his roles conflate the image and the man through repetitions of his familiar presence, his returns also help guarantee the exclusion of other black actors. Besides securing the authenticity of his performance and, by extension, of his films' stories and their magical resolutions, Poitier's person also stands in for an entire race even as he emerges from it as an exception. His cinematic presence, recalling a population largely absent from his films' on-screen worlds, curiously functions in a manner that parallels the work of music in a number of his films. Both mark sites of repression and displacements. But just as music gestures to offscreen spaces and realities whose social conflicts haunt his films' edges and threaten to disrupt their forced logics, so does Poitier's iconicity produce tension. A hint of "reality" insinuates itself, even as the film struggles to deflect it.

"Moving" Pictures: *The Defiant Ones*

The Defiant Ones (Stanley Kramer, 1958), the film that makes Poitier *Poitier*, is the first in which he receives top billing—shared with Tony Curtis. This role sets the stage for his later returns and inflects his characters, grounding them in a history the other films barely acknowledge but on which they depend. *The Defiant Ones* emerges in a turbulent media moment, as volatile images of racial conflict erupt not only in the news but also more broadly across white cultural production. School desegregation struggles arrive vividly on the national stage in 1957, as President Eisenhower orders federal troops to escort the black students integrating Little Rock Central High School and explains himself to the nation on TV. The popular photojournalistic magazine *Look* remembers Emmett Till's murder and the trial that set his killers free. In a January 24, 1957, article titled "What's Happened to the Emmett Till Killers," southern author William Bradford Huie writes about these still unrepentant murderers, J. W. Milam and Roy Bryant, and the boycotts and ostracism with which the black and white citizens of the town of Sumner, Mississippi, have reacted to them subsequently.[11] This shocking image of white atrocity, unpunished and unapologetic, haunts the media.

On the cultural front, contradictory constructions of racial difference play across the white imaginary. Perhaps nowhere do these contradictions of the good object/bad object split—desire and phobia, attraction and repulsion, absorption and rejection—emerge more forcefully than in the writing, and the figure, of the white hipster. Vividly represented in Jack Kerouac's *On the Road* (1957), the white hipster most ferociously asserts his relationship to blackness in Norman Mailer's essay "The White Negro," published the same year. Mailer stakes his own claim to an authenticity he sees as originating in blackness: "The Negro has the simplest of alternatives: live a life of constant humility or ever-threatening danger. In such a pass where paranoia is as vital to survival as blood, the Negro has stayed alive and begun to grow by following the need of his body where he could. . . . the Negro could rarely afford the sophisticated inhibitions of civilization, and so he kept for his survival the art of the primitive, he lived in an enormous present."[12] As desire and identification mingle in this fantasmatic image of blackness as pure embodiment and ahistoricity, Mailer remains consistent with the romantic and primitivist rhetoric of his contemporaries. Robert Reid-Pharr points out that "though for Mailer the Negro is cultureless, alienated, psychopathic, hated from within and without, he is somehow physically healthy and infinitely capable of fashioning morality, even and especially from the bottom." "Because he exists outside of culture," Reid-Pharr continues, "because he remains inscrutable, innocent, he is powerful."[13]

White identifications exhibit an unstable mix of desire and aggression, appetite and violence, in fantasies of passing into blackness. In *Black Like Me* (1962), a book project begun in 1959 with support from *Sepia* magazine, John Howard Griffin enacted a version of this fantasy of impersonating blackness by darkening his skin and seeking out real-life experience as a "black" man. This book chronicles Griffin's harrowing—and often sordid—encounters with whites, and it tracks the traumatic dislocations within his own identity.[14]

This obsession with black embodiment may remind us of Slavoj Žižek's analysis of racism. He contends that the racist imagines the "other" to possess a secret enjoyment we are denied: "We always impute to the 'other' an excessive enjoyment: he wants to steal our enjoyment (by ruining our way of life) and / or he has access to some secret, perverse enjoyment." He goes on to specify the terms in which we conceive this secret: "In short, what really bothers us about the 'other' is the peculiar way he organizes his enjoyment, precisely the surplus, the 'excess' that pertains to this way: the smell of 'their' food, 'their' noisy songs and dances, 'their' strange manners."[15] In this period's stories of "passing into" blackness, insurmountable barriers block interracial communication but enable fantasies of occupying the other to capture his "enjoyment."

Dramatizing an interracial encounter that brings about understanding through identification, *The Defiant Ones* fully inhabits this turbulent cultural landscape, partially sharing in the hipster sensibility. That it struck a chord for its moment in Hollywood is evident in the acclaim it received: nominated for eight Academy Awards, including Best Picture, Best Director, and Best Actor for its two leads, the film won Best Screenplay (Harold Jacob and Nathan Douglas, pseudonym of the blacklisted Nedrick Young), and both supporting actor categories (Theodore Bikel and Cara Williams). In this context, we may understand why Poitier's character in this film differs from any of his subsequent roles. Noah Cullen is the last of his characters to present even a rudimentary history. As a tenant farmer he has been held in abject poverty and routinely cheated by white men, including his landlord. He has landed in the chain gang for assault on that landlord, who threatened him with a gun. Asserting that he has been angry all his life, he explains how he chafed at his father's and his wife's injunctions to submit. This ambivalent figure is constructed the better to fit the film's equation: both men are angry victims of poverty. But where the white man is motivated by class resentment, committing larceny to acquire the money that will buy him showy attire, Cullen's motive is righteous outrage. In its focus on his suppressed rage and moral innocence, this film seems to accommodate the hipster sensibility.

A hint of its appeal emerges in its theatrical trailer. "Chained Fury! . . . Chained together like animals . . . At each other's throats like animals . . ." These luridly sensational titles mark the trailer's summation of the film's

highlights. Several close-ups center on the heavy chain that binds antagonists Curtis (playing John "Joker" Jackson) and Poitier together. Then a
tracking shot holds on the two men's outstretched hands as their fingers
struggle to clasp and pull apart, foregrounding the film's climactic moment:
Curtis falls behind, just seconds too late for Poitier to pull him onto the
train so that they can escape capture. The shot of two hands, suspended in
midframe and isolated against the blurred background rushing by, becomes
the film's icon, one of its most "moving" pictures. *The Defiant Ones* emphatically frames pictures that mean to "move," like the tableaux of the melodramatic stage. It thus resembles theatrical melodrama, which, Linda Williams
reminds us, "delighted in the construction of literal moving pictures and
even found a powerful emotional emphasis in the freezing of these pictures into still tableaux of the narrative's most intense moments."[16]

But this film builds melodramatic structure into its montage as well.
Parallel editing structures the chase that constitutes its narrative trajectory, as the escaped convicts flee from the sheriff and his search party. This
chase, of course, evokes imagery associated with enslavement and Reconstruction. In the baying of bloodhounds and the threat of lynching, as well
as the editing, it makes unmistakable reference to D. W. Griffith's *The Birth
of a Nation* (1915). Within these parallel structures, this film shapes its story
around dramatic alternations between movement and stasis, between pan-
oramic long shots and tight framing of confined spaces. But these structures also serve to root its drama firmly in the memory of enslavement,
dislocating it from its own historical moment.

In its concluding image of the two fugitives finally come to rest in a
stilled tableau, as Cullen cradles Jackson, this film rewrites the conventional terms of racial melodrama, replacing what Williams calls the "key
icon" of "the suffering black male body" (xiv) with the suffering, disabled
white male body to whom the stronger black man ministers. Yet the con-
flicting affective force this inversion produces presents a challenge to the
film. It must liquidate, or at least manage, the erotic tensions between
these two bodies. Freezing them in this striking bathetic pose, the film
reaches an aporia.

Poitier sings again the song with which the film has opened, W. C.
Handy's "Long Gone (from Bowling Green)," and the screen fades to black
as he utters its concluding word. His voice pulls us beyond the frame; we

hear him chuckling softly after the image has disappeared. This voice, whose body disappears from the visual field, figures an imaginary transcendence of the impasse at which we have arrived.[17] But it also circles back, closing the film in on itself, echoing its opening sequence, in which we hear Poitier singing before the uncertain image resolves upon the black screen. As a prison truck comes into view and rushes past, we continue to hear his singing for some time before his face and body come into view. He functions here as what Michel Chion calls the "acousmêtre": "the one who is not-yet-seen, but who is liable to appear at any moment" (21). Neither fully present nor completely absent from the scene, hovering between its inside and its outside, arriving in advance of the image and persisting beyond it, this voice registers as slightly uncanny and just out of reach—perhaps like the image of stable racial harmony the film wishes to establish.

Framing its story with the black voice as pure expressivity, the film elaborates a fantasy that it can magically transform its white character. Enforced proximity to the black character will reeducate, and redeem, the white racist through a pedagogy of identification, as shared circumstances force him to view the world from Cullen's perspective. To convert aversion into affection, the narrative establishes simple substitutions—knowledge for ignorance, love for hate—effected through a growing reciprocity. In its effort to prove its premise that identification may teach its characters— and its audience—a simple lesson in common humanity leading to racial equality, the film stages moments of externally imposed equivalence. But its pedagogical obsession continually falters: this exchange is anything but equal. Constructed as opaque interiority, opposed to Jackson's empty chatter, Cullen speaks only to impart practical wisdom or to challenge his interlocutor's ignorance and bigotry. While Jackson develops, Cullen remains immutable, the consistent backdrop from which this transformation emerges.

Alongside its moments of discursive pedagogy, *The Defiant Ones* elaborates a visual iconography that gives considerable weight to the chain that constitutes its literal and metaphoric anchor. This figure offers a crude icon for race relations: yoked together, black and white must cooperate out of reciprocal self-interest and necessity. But equally important, the chain keeps constantly before them the problem of their difference. The prison warden has speculated that the proximity it enforces could end in homicide: "They'll kill each other before they get five miles." In its logic of forced analogy, this film seems to posit an equilibrium of opposing forces—equal hatred on both sides of the racial divide. Even as the chain serves to render physical an equation between the two men, and a pretext for assuming identification through shared experience, it also becomes a fulcrum around which the dynamics between them shift. It literally forces them into cooperation, as in the scene when they struggle to climb out of a muddy pit in which they have taken refuge. This moment of reciprocal self-interest turns on an image that anticipates the iconic train sequence that ends the film, as their hands strain to grasp along the chain so that Jackson may pull Cullen out of the pit.

We might see this film's racial reconciliation as issuing retroactively from Jackson's imposed identification with Cullen when they are faced with lynching. This "narrow escape" resonates with the "near miss" that causes their final fall back into captivity. We may recall here the importance of timing to melodrama in the broadest sense, what Linda Williams describes in *Playing the Race Card* as melodrama's "dialectic of pathos and action—a give and take of 'too late' and 'in the nick of time'" (30). That is, the form's affective force is inevitably bound to the temporality of rescue, recognition, and reconciliation, accomplished just in time or forever lost to belatedness.

This pivotal lynching sequence informs the logic of the rest of the film, linking firmly to previous developments. Mud—with its "blackening" properties—plays a central role here. Just before they descend into a darkened hamlet in search of supplies, the two smear Jackson's face with mud, "blacking him up," so his white face will recede into the darkness. As Jackson encounters himself in the mirror of Cullen's face, he remarks, "We sure look alike." But he is not the only one to draw this conclusion: the townspeople who pursue and finally corner them at first call them "boys" and express surprise when a flashlight's scrutiny reveals Jackson's color.

Confronted with an increasingly aggressive mob, Jackson desperately asserts, "You can't lynch me. I'm a white man!" In this epiphanic moment, he finds his whiteness compromised by black proximity. White privilege disappears or fails in the very moment of its explicit assertion; if it must be spoken, it evaporates. This is perhaps the most striking of the film's pedagogical moments. Mack (Claude Akins) violently challenges his identity: "I'll tell you what kind of white man you are!" He then orders Cullen to spit on Jackson. Clearly, Mack's gesture is meant to inscribe an analysis of racism, in which fragile white working-class privilege depends on its difference from blackness. This film's logic presumes the urgency of differentiation to reach its greatest intensity among those white people whose material situations might place them in closest literal or figurative proximity to blacks. And such a logic is firmly structured by a good object/bad object split.[18]

In forcing Jackson to enact an identification with blackness, this moment will redeem him only retroactively, after he has become the object of the racism he had previously represented. When he appears in blackface, the film deposits his racism on the other white people in the mob. And this displacement of racist sentiment has happened throughout the film; it is what differentiates the enlightened sheriff (Theodore Bikel), a former lawyer, from the band of rednecks who handle the dogs that pursue the fugitives. Significantly, this moment of enforced identification between Jackson and Cullen will eventually lead to another explosion of the rage that has remained suspended between them. Once one of the townspeople, himself a former chain gang inmate (Lon Chaney Jr.), has persuaded the mob to disperse, Cullen interprets Jackson's panicked reaction as evidence that he has witnessed a lynching. Thus, this moment has radically split his identification. He finds himself in the other's place at a moment of pure trauma. It as if the other's place itself could be understood only through trauma and as trauma. So this cross-racial identification both issues from and produces trauma. *The Defiant Ones* has founded its argument on the psychology of encounter and intimacy; it posits that racism might be liquidated, as if magically, through identifications. But it is unable fully to account for trauma's role here.

Only after Cullen and Jackson have shed the chain does a voluntary alliance emerge, and one that leads Cullen to sacrifice his freedom to remain with his friend. In this film's suspenseful penultimate sequence, after several minutes of striving, the two men manage to join hands, the momentary connection highlighted since the hands appear as a still image, because the camera registers them in the middle of the gray blur of landscape rushing by. This starkly beautiful image of hands momentarily disembodied is neither sustained nor contained. It floats free to stand almost as the film's emblem. But this is an emblem of wishfulness and fantasy, abstracted as it is from the narrative texture or from any context. Cullen lets himself fall from the train, as if pulled down by the weight of his companion. His fall also allows for the formation of the film's final image, its signature tableau imported from *Home of the Brave* (1949), Kramer's earlier film about interracial male bonding during World War II: the black man cradles the white one in a *pietà* that closes the story, forcing its resolution in yet another abstraction.[19]

As they sit awaiting capture, Cullen/Poitier sings an elegiac version of "Long Gone," recalling its first assertive, resistant performance, thus looping the film back upon itself. Instead of reaching its point of no return and catching the train to freedom, then, this journey stops at the point of return. As Poitier holds his buddy, he sings in a tone of gently mocking defiance. Addressed as it is to the benign figure of the sheriff, who has just come upon them, this is a song of resignation. Concluding with this "moving," pathos-laden image, the film holds its protagonists in tight medium close-up. In the shot/reverse-shot structure it orchestrates between them and the sheriff, the camera casts them as a "picture" he "takes." Immobile under his benevolent gaze, they are the last thing we see before the film fades to black.

Lingering beyond the image, Poitier's disembodied voice chuckles softly. Transcending the characters' and the story's impasse, this voice haunts the frame as it passes beyond it. Coming to a dead end in this abstracted picture, *The Defiant Ones* offers the voice as reassurance, filling in for the conclusion it cannot reach: it cannot envision a future for this friendship, and something else, an erotic bond, is unspeakable.[20] Into this aporia flows the musical performance.

As his voice passes on beyond the image, Poitier becomes the lost object that Hollywood obsessively refinds. Future roles recycle him compulsively, dropping him as a foreign body into white territories that he leaves magically altered as he passes through.[21]

The Civil Rights Subject as Cold Warrior

In presenting him with the Academy Award for Best Actor for the 1963 *Lilies of the Field,* Hollywood was putting a "good face"—Poitier's own—on its consistent exclusion of blacks. Contemporary *New York Times* critic Bosley Crowther seems unselfconsciously to confirm this, writing: "The fact that a plurality of the Hollywood elite wished Mr. Poitier to win is strong evidence of a warm and liberal feeling."[22] In order to understand the full ideological freight this award carried, we need to look carefully at the context of the film's production. It was shot over two weeks in November 1962.[23] In October of that year, James Meredith, accompanied by federal marshals, had become the first black student to enroll at the University of Mississippi, an event that sparked intense riots, forcing President Kennedy to send federal troops to reinforce the marshals.[24] *Lilies'* complete reticence about race comes into stark relief against the staggering violence attending this landmark event in civil rights history. But October 1962 also saw the Cuban missile crisis. Can there be any doubt that the film is most interested in registering the shock of this crisis, when we consider that the nuns who motivate its plot are East German refugees?

If we consider *Lilies of the Field* in the year of its release, 1963, its distribution trajectory, along with the public appearances of its star, certainly exerts a shaping pressure on its content. In 1963 protests rocked Birmingham, beginning in April; in September, the Sixteenth Street Baptist Church was bombed. More than 250,000 participated in the March on Washington on August 28, Poitier prominently among them.

The Academy Award for *Lilies* seems to relate Poitier's "burden of liveness" to his civil rights celebrity, recognizing a curious intersection between his performance in public appearances and his on-screen role. In July, Poitier and Stanley Kramer accompanied *The Defiant Ones* to the Moscow Film Festival.[25] *Lilies of the Field* premiered at the Berlin Film festival on July 5—before its October release in the United States—and days after Kennedy's visit to the Berlin Wall. At this symbolically crucial juncture, then, *Lilies of the Field* takes on a diplomatic mission of its own, explicitly advancing a Cold War political agenda through its civil rights icon.

In the bizarre calculus that holds this film's fable together, Poitier's character, Homer Smith, an itinerant contractor, stops to fix his car at an isolated southwestern ranch inhabited by a small group of nuns. Homer, the sisters reckon, has been sent by God to help them complete the impossible task their faith has set them: to build a chapel for the local community of Mexican workers. But alongside his work as a builder, Homer also undertakes a pedagogical project. As the nuns' English is rudimentary, he volunteers to substitute himself for the recorded English lessons they listen to each evening. In the scene of their first lesson, at the dinner table, Homer begins with the objects at hand, including the vinyl language record. He soon finds that he needs to explain the concept of blackness, as his statement that "the record is black" provokes the nuns' consternation. So he shows them the stove, "The stove is black." Then, by way of reinforcing the color, he strokes his bare forearm, "My skin is black." The scene's central "joke" emerges when the nuns repeat in chorus, touching their own arms, "My skin is black." They seem to be as "innocent" of race as they are immune to sexuality.

Patiently, Homer corrects them: "*Her* skin is *white; my* skin is *black.*" For the viewer, however, the strangeness of the scene comes through emphatically as the camera holds Poitier's extended arm, waving the record, in frame. What we see is the pronounced difference between these two "blacks." One cannot help but wonder, as the lesson unfolds, why he does not avail himself of the nuns' own habits, which centrally inscribe the black/white opposition. But, somehow, nonetheless, the nuns achieve an instant epiphany of comprehension.

The nuns' apparent "color blindness" resonates through the film. Many of its tensions emerge in jokes concerning color that are rendered innocuous by the nuns' incomprehension. While Homer instructs the naive foreigners about racial difference, neither the teacher nor the pupils ever register the difference as fraught, or even meaningful. As the film works to construct an analogous innocence for itself, its project is haunted by a compulsion to "perform" race over and over. When the English lesson proceeds through a demonstration of verbs and pronouns—"I stand up. . . . We all sit down"—it culminates in Homer's producing a wildly exaggerated "dialect" for the nuns to repeat: "Ah stands up, y'all." It is as if the repression of race in relation to color returns in sound, taking the form of a "joke" whose meaning remains inaccessible to the nuns.

One good teaching moment is rewarded with more. Soon Homer is instructing the nuns in gospel music, involving them in a stirring call and response to the song "Amen," an original composition by Jester Hairston that runs through the film's sound track, starting with an instrumental version over the opening credit sequence. Standing free of the film's narrative flow, this is a scene of pure performativity, in which Homer becomes the singing star and the nuns his interactive audience. Authenticity and performance come apart, however, when we realize that Hairston's voice has been dubbed in for Poitier's here. So this central moment, coded for authenticity, shows itself to be the opposite. Indeed, this scene represents the height of film's artifice, and it highlights its unstable figuration of race. This musical moment repeats at the film's end, serving as the device by which Homer disappears. This voluntary indentured servant, having completed the willful nuns' project, brings the film to closure with his own disappearance, propelled by the vocal performance that outlasts his physical presence.

In *Lilies of the Field,* race keeps getting displaced, just as Homer is dislocated; despite the resonance of his name, he remains homeless. Innocent of history, origin, or relations, he belongs nowhere, and that seems to suit the film's purposes. A foreign body even among foreign bodies, Homer emerges as divorced from any native context. This effect registers all the more powerfully because, as the only recognizable actor in the film, Poitier's sheer visibility isolates him. Bound to no community, as the only black body in the film, standing alone between the collectivities—the nuns and the Mexican workers of the nearby town—he acts as the film's visual anchor as well as its narrative principle. By the time he makes his final exit, musical performance has transformed him from the worker, whose labor the community has consumed, into the entertainer. But in each incarnation, he is just passing through. In a story that incorporates him into and then expels him from a scene in which he finds no place, Poitier's iconicity both marks and occludes the crucial historical civil rights struggles that underlie and haunt this particular story of black labor.

In his singularity and centrality, Homer remains strangely exempt from agency, just as he is immune from development. As the 1960s progress, Poitier's films will continue to limit his agency, and his character's development, in scenarios where the eroticism that *Lilies of the Field* so successfully expunges keeps returning. As his teaching moments become more extreme, but less explicitly marked as formal pedagogy, a diffuse erotics begins to haunt the scenes he inhabits. His films seem consistently to manage this erotic pressure through scenarios of "passing through," in which he definitively departs the context he has transformed.

The Glory of Love

As the 1960s advance, Poitier's films regularly intertwine their pedagogical projects with the thematics of "love" or affection, more or less explicit, and more or less distorted. Affect, sometimes taking the form of romantic love, seems to be the ultimate instrument of pedagogy, and it obviates the need for ideological argument. Affection, and the intimate scenes of instruction it promotes, seems to require melodramatic strategies. Poitier's characters consistently sort out the good from the bad in encounters where he teaches white people—whether innocent victims or tormentedly misguided—to liberate themselves from the social or ideological prison of their contexts.

In each case, he engages in a kind of rescue, restoring "bad" actors to their authentic moral goodness. Such an emphasis on rescue and restoration is central to the "melodramatic mode," as Linda Williams has characterized it: "If emotional and moral registers are sounded, if a work invites us to feel sympathy for the virtues of beset victims, if the narrative trajectory is ultimately more concerned with a retrieval of innocence than with the psychological causes of motives and action, then the operative mode is melodrama."[26] Notably, Poitier's ability to rescue and restore seems to depend unerringly on his transcendence. Passing through white contexts, he remains above and beyond them. Himself lacking personal history or connections, he confronts characters deformed by the history in which they are mired, but to which they seem blind.

A Patch of Blue literalizes the liberal metaphor of color blindness and provides Poitier perhaps his most extreme teaching moment. This film, which came out on December 10, 1965, offers a much more anxiously repressed scenario of racial integration in the year of its release than does *Lilies of the Field*. Poitier's character, Gordon Ralfe, seems to abandon his work as a journalist in order to change the life of a blind white girl, a process that culminates in his fight for her right to equal access to education. In 1965 the civil rights struggle was centrally focused on equal access. This was the year of the Selma to Montgomery March (March 27), preceded by Bloody Sunday (March 7) and Malcolm X's assassination (February 21) soon after he visited Selma at the invitation of the Student Nonviolent Coordinating Committee (SNCC) and gave a speech supporting Martin Luther King. This year's terribly violent clashes led to the passage of the landmark Voting Rights Act on August 6.

In this context, *A Patch of Blue* winds together most of white liberal ideology's key tropes, offering a dizzying series of displacements and condensations organized by the central metaphor of color blindness. As the liberal dream is embodied in literal blindness, race is concomitantly thrown into analogy with disability. Gordon Ralfe, an earnest liberal journalist, vigorously intervenes in the life of Selina D'Arcey (Elizabeth Hartman), whose family keeps her homebound as a kind of indentured domestic servant. Kept out of school, Selina is confined to the isolated world of her white working-class tenement. Her stunted intellectual development correlates to her disability, both results of her mother's agency: Rose-Ann (Shelley Winters) has accidentally blinded her. Rose-Ann works as a cleaner and entertains "clients" on the side; her father, Selina's grandfather, Ole Pa (Wallace Ford), a spectacular alcoholic, barely holds a job. In their marginal lifestyle and vicious racism and child abuse, the family is figured as an exaggerated version of the "white trash" to whom liberal discourse attributes anti-integrationist fury. But the family also figures a kind of white version of the dysfunctional inner-city black family envisioned by the Moynihan Report (*The Negro Family: The Case for National Action*), published in the same year.

In this universe of delirious condensations, perverse equations emerge. Gordon embarks on a single-minded quest to provide Selina with access to education, and the film ends with him making sure she gets onto the bus that will take her to her new life at a vocational school for the blind. On the brink of their separation, and still convinced that Selina remains ignorant of his race, Gordon explains that they cannot contemplate marriage instead of or along with school: "We're from different worlds." "Is it because I'm blind?" Selina asks. "Because of where I come from?" Within the film's heavy-handed strategy of ironic inversion, this moment also implicitly equates race with disability and ignorance.

When Gordon insists that he wants to tell her something about himself, and we understand he means to produce the revelation of racial difference that he thinks will shock her, Selina responds: "I know you're good and kind. I know you're colored, and I think you're beautiful." Gordon is indeed the "good object"; he promotes Selina's independence, providing a prop to her autonomy. She is convinced of his beauty, of course, because she knows what he is like "inside." In this dream of color blindness, one bypasses the surface to find sameness—and goodness—in the inner depth.[27] But in advancing this proposition, the film asks us to bypass precisely Selina's own key characteristics. Would not her youth, her class position, and her lack of any education constitute obstacles to Gordon's desire for her as a wife? Yet, in keeping with its perversely twisted equations, the film reinforces his apparent conviction that only his own race renders the union impossible.

Curiously, music helps, once again, to manage and contain some of the film's most volatile thematics. When Selina visits Gordon's apartment, under the disapproving eye of his brother Mark, a "race man" played by Ivan Dixon, lately of *Nothing but a Man* (Michael Roemer, 1964),[28] she discovers a music box. This box plays a pastoral folk song about a shepherd. We know this because Gordon sings the lyrics. The words, in standard French, are not translated; thus they inflect Gordon with a certain foreignness. But the box comes with a story that, in turn, draws a story from Selina. Its owner, Gordon's grandmother, Pearl, had the same name as Selina's only childhood friend. Like Gordon, that Pearl, too, Selina says, used to "teach me things." But Rose-Ann drove her away because she was "colored."

"Ironies" abound as Selina presses for details about the grandmother, who received the music box from a man. Asked why he never married her, Gordon explains, "The man was from a different world. He was very rich and important." The phrase "a different world," of course, will echo in the film's last scene, which reinforces its evocation of racial difference. When Selina asks knowingly and suggestively if they were lovers, Gordon confirms this, but teases her about her own experience. This episode brings her to reveal that she has been raped by one of Rose-Ann's clients. Lurid flashback images interrupt Selina's coyly suggestive speculations and the seductive path they open. Abruptly the box snaps shut, bringing the grandmother's story, which suggests interracial romance in a context that the French language establishes as foreign and displaced (probably Caribbean), into safe containment. This containment, however, remains troubled by Gordon's giving the box to Selina, as the token of another impossible love.

Resonating as it does with Selina's declaration of her love for Gordon, this scene also establishes the dominance in Selina's world of the *heard* but not *seen*, foregrounding again the central trope of color blindness. As this moment emphasizes the separation of visual and auditory, it might remind us of the power of the black voice in U.S. musical culture, a presence heard but not seen. But it also again links color blindness to literal blindness, as the film relies on Selina's blindness to preempt an erotic consummation. She is in love with Gordon's voice, not his body. His intimate proximity operates predominantly through the voice, like popular music, which enters private spaces through the mediation of recording or radio. And Gordon helps the film to maintain the erotic partition it grounds in Selina's blindness by refusing her touch, her tactile vision. In the strange imaginary space the film creates for spectators watching this blind girl fall in love with a voice, whose source they can see, Poitier is both there and not there. He is central but just out of frame for Selina, like the analyst for the analysand, or like the mechanically reproduced voices that penetrate our most private interior spaces.

This music box returns at the film's end to mark its conclusion. After Selina has boarded the bus that will take her away to school, Gordon notices that she has left behind the music box, the gift she has treated as a talisman. Arriving melodramatically seconds too late to restore the box to her, he can only watch the departing bus. Here again is the image of a bus—and often a bus pursued—so significant to desegregation, that disappears, leaving Gordon with the talismanic box that so effectively collects and contains unruly impulses.

1967: "The Useful Negro"

Despite appearing in two of the films nominated for the Best Picture Oscar in 1967, Poitier received no nomination.[29] Although his character was the primary catalyst and organizing principle of the dramas that unfolded in both *In the Heat of the Night* and *Guess Who's Coming to Dinner,* Best Actor nominations went to his costars, Rod Steiger and Spencer Tracy, respectively. When *In the Heat of the Night* was named Best Picture, and Rod Steiger and Katharine Hepburn won for Best Actor and Actress, respectively, how do we understand Poitier's erasure from the nominations bestowed on two films whose central concerns are racism and cross-racial negotiation?[30] Perhaps the explanation is that neither of these films is about Poitier's character. As both confine him to the role of catalyst and mentor, he registers as an effigy through his fundamentally immobile characters, neither of which is allowed to develop.

In the socially and politically turbulent climate of 1967, it is striking that Poitier's roles in *To Sir, with Love, In the Heat of the Night,* and *Guess Who's Coming to Dinner* all require him briefly to display rage, but then masterfully contain that outburst. Even before the release of *Guess Who's Coming to Dinner, Variety* (July 26) dubbed him "the useful Negro" in an article that declared, "Poitier on the screen is the only Negro which [*sic*] myriads of Americans feel they know and understand."[31] This revealing assertion inscribes the definitive exclusion of "Negro" from "American." And this segregation clearly contributes to Poitier's "usefulness" in this politically agitated year.

In his comforting returns, he remains the same from role to role, just as his characters remain unchanged despite the dramas that develop around them. As Hollywood seems obsessed with recycling him, we may speculate that the very reliability of his return and his familiar consistency reassure "the myriads" of white Americans to whom *Variety* refers. Goudsouzian notes that this article deemed the end of *In the Heat of the Night* "at least a comforting sight for eyes sore from watching the television tube recently out of Newark and Detroit" (271). No doubt Poitier's unchanging immobility provided a comforting image of repose in the face of upheaval. But contemporary cultural trauma continues to hover at the edge of the melodramatic frame, breaking through in its visual strategies.

The year of the "Summer of Love" also saw intense race riots spreading across Detroit, Newark, Memphis, and Boston, among many other urban centers. According to Richard M. Nixon's rather strident disquisition in *Reader's Digest:* "The nationwide deterioration of respect for authority, the law, and civil order reached its peak this past summer when mobs in 100 cities burned and looted and killed in a senseless attack upon their society, its agents and its law." Nixon drew a close connection between civil rights agitation and antiwar protests, declaring that the "permissiveness" of cultural and political authorities had produced "not only a growing tolerance of lawlessness but an increasing public acceptance of civil disobedience."[32] And as unrest increased in African American communities, the antiwar movement was galvanizing toward the October March on the Pentagon.

Also in 1967, the same year that Thurgood Marshall became the Supreme Court's first black justice, Muhammad Ali was sentenced to prison for draft resistance, and Martin Luther King came out against the war in a speech on April 4 that analyzed the connections between that war and continued racial and social oppression domestically, William Styron's *The Confessions of Nat Turner* was published.[33] It immediately became a Book-of-the-Month Club selection, and it earned Styron the Pulitzer Prize in 1968. This deliberately controversial first-person fictional account of Nat Turner's rebellion deservedly provoked more controversy than its author and publisher had bargained for.[34] Styron's appropriation of Nat Turner's voice in a narrative that obstinately focused on his sexuality sparked a significant interracial struggle over the right to representation: of history, of racial dynamics, of voice. At the same time, this year was marked by rather remarkable productivity among black writers and public figures: Stokely Carmichael and Charles V. Hamilton's *Black Power: The Politics of Liberation in America* appeared, as did Martin Luther King Jr.'s *Where Do We Go from Here: Chaos or Consent?* Eldridge Cleaver published *Soul on Ice,* which resonates perversely with Styron's Nat Turner fantasy.[35] And the Black Arts Movement was arguably reaching its apogee.

As black voices were making themselves heard in a variety of venues, television news proliferated spectacles of race. TV divided its focus between the singular public faces of diverse leadership—celebrated, reviled, or feared—and the public sphere of the crowd, the struggle as a mass movement, or the chaos of rioting mobs. Poitier's films, by contrast, emphasize privatized individual encounters, ideal for pedagogical moments. His characters emerge as isolated, dislocated figures, unmoored from solidarities. Staged as strangely immobile tableaux, which reach an extreme in *Guess Who's Coming to Dinner,* his films reassuringly reduce the politics of racial conflict and debate to matters of personal appeal to affect and persuasion.

Reducing conflicts to manageable interpersonal dramas, these melodramatic scenarios require Poitier to embody a version of historical memory that offers an alibi for forgetfulness about their contemporary context. And if he is embodying history, he cannot be its agent.[36] Around this figure his films build melodramatic strategies that suggest what E. Ann Kaplan has called, in *Trauma Culture,* "displaced" knowledge, which remains unavailable to the text that displays it. "This is not because the events are literally unable to be recalled," she writes, "but because, for political or social reasons . . . it is too dangerous for the culture . . . to acknowledge or recall, just as the 'forgotten' contents in the individual consciousness are too dangerous to remember."[37] Poitier's films, like their characters, cannot afford to know what they know, and so they produce stray details and throwaway moments that point to meanings that elude them.

In the Heat of the Night restricts Poitier to the role of mentor and catalyst—even though he is the detective who solves the murder that is ostensibly central to its plot. In the film's complicated tangle of missteps and strained convolutions, it maintains a central, if skewed, focus on the racism from which it aims to rehabilitate Police Chief Bill Gillespie (Rod Steiger). To accomplish this, it keeps Poitier's Virgil Tibbs consistently off balance and in danger, so that he provokes Gillespie's better instincts, becoming the agent of his conversion. And this process turns out to be easily achieved in a world where nothing is what it first appears to be.

From its beginning, this film concerns itself with sight, obliging us to consider how it channels our view, especially as it calls our anxious attention to the space out of frame. As gorgeous, blurred spots of red and blue light against darkness resolve into images of a train and the theme song concludes, we see a man's legs stepping off the train. As he crosses the platform to the station, we see only two-thirds of his body. His head withheld from view, Poitier remains a mystery. A cut brings into frame an enormously magnified fly alighting on a wall calendar. As an elastic band strikes the fly, a reverse shot produces a close-up of the diner's counterman, Ralph Henshaw (Anthony James), who, we will learn at the end, has committed the murder that is discovered just as Tibbs arrives.

In the tightly structured opening sequences, we follow Officer Sam Wood (Warren Oates) to discover Tibbs at the train station, but only after he makes a habitual stop, cruising past the home of Delores Purdy (Quentin Dean), who regularly exhibits her naked torso before a window. This exhibitionistic girl, to whom the film will brutally return, becomes the catalyst for the murder of Mr. Colbert, a wealthy Chicago investor who has been building a factory in town. After an interlude watching Delores, Sam finds the body, and he soon shows up at the train station. Only now does the camera reveal Tibbs to our view. His enforced elusiveness turns out to be crucial to his cinematic construction here. For, while he becomes engrossed in the crime's investigation, the film's central interest lodges in Chief Gillespie's own interest in Virgil. And this is where it builds its most strained and strange equations.

If we read the plot's convolutions against this film's striking visual strategies, like the frequent zooms in and out, we may better understand the precise shape of its confusions. The zooms in, or the use of a telephoto lens to bring something under intense scrutiny, produce the feel of surveillance, and they visually replicate the series of false arrests that structure this investigation. Tibbs, of course, is in a position to be drawn into the story because he is falsely arrested. Significantly, however, his involvement in the investigation is overdetermined. Gillespie attempts to bring it to an abrupt end by dispatching him to the train station after arresting a suspect whose obvious innocence Tibbs can demonstrate. But the widow (Lee Grant) of the northern factory owner insists that Tibbs continue investigating, threatening to withdraw her husband's investment if he does not. She, then, drives the investigation, and the plot. Tibbs becomes her agent—the agent of northern liberalism embodied in this professional woman.

In the Heat of the Night's preposterous and fragile pretexts mark its wrestling with the repressed history that keeps returning to haunt it, and of which its visual environment is symptomatic. Set in contemporary Sparta, Mississippi, the film immediately registers the memory of recent events around civil rights: upon hearing that Tibbs is from Philadelphia, Gillespie inquires, "Mississippi?" Philadelphia, we remember, is the town where the bodies of voting rights workers Chaney, Schwerner, and Goodman were found in August 1964—a fresh reference for contemporary audiences. And Poitier's northern homicide expert clearly recalls that federal law enforcement professionals were sent to Mississippi to investigate those murders. While the drama opens with Tibbs wrongly detained for the murder, circumstances quickly evolve to demand his participation in the investigation, because, unlike the local police, who come across as lazy, demoralized, and ignorant, he is a professional, and an expert in forensics.

Tibbs initially suspects that the Chicago businessman has been murdered because of his integrationist ambitions: he had intended to hire blacks as 50 percent of his workforce. Thus, Tibbs soon runs afoul of cotton tycoon Eric Endicott (Larry Gates), who controls the town economically and whose explicit racism suggests a strong motive. In a pivotal moment, which arrives at the film's temporal midpoint, Tibbs is questioning Endicott, who has peppered the encounter with racist references. Suddenly, the white man slaps him. When Tibbs slaps him back, Endicott demands that Gillespie take action, and the police chief's resistance here marks the beginning of his alliance with the other policeman, however uneven its course.

When Endicott threatens Tibbs obliquely, the film has laid the groundwork for an inversion: the detective finds himself stalked. As Jared Sexton reads this development, "the subversive force of this dramatic reversal of racial violence—an image of black counterattack, a trace of black self-defense during a historical moment when the question is paramount in the political field—is overwhelmed in the film by a diegetic milieu of helplessness."[38] "We find this black male agent of the state," Sexton reminds us, "nonetheless *unauthorized*, subjected entirely to the caprice of whites," as well as *"unarmed*: a cop, alas, with no gun, no badge, and no jurisdiction" (43).

This film structures our interest and attention, as well as most of its suspense, around explicit references to racist violence. Like Tibbs, the spectator consistently returns to a paranoid position of suspicion and anxiety. Visual strategies reinforce our interest in Gillespie's shifting positions while aligning us in an oblique way with Tibbs himself. But his point of view remains unstable. It tends to dissolve, fragment, or dislocate. Even as Haskell Wexler's virtuoso camera performs the attention to detail that grounds Tibbs's expertise, it refuses to coincide fully with his point of view. Indeed, its meticulous scrutiny seems consistently to exceed Tibbs's purview.

Not least of the factors contributing to this effect is the extreme close-up, which does not code for a realistic human gaze. Such a close-up lingers on the black lawn jockey at Endicott's house. We see it twice, as Tibbs and Gillespie enter and exit the house. Pausing to amplify this grotesque object, the camera invites us to contemplate the intensity of its impact for Tibbs, but without aligning itself with him. To lift the image out of its surroundings this way, magnifying its impact while keeping it untethered from Tibbs, is to suggest an implicit appeal to a white gaze. Indeed, the camera seems to operate as an independent commentator, registering shocks through objects. Can it be that the camera does not quite believe the film's logic/story? It seems unable to allow Tibbs a point of view; instead, it mediates or relays his view through an anonymous agency.

At other moments, the "establishing shot" that disorients, rather than specifies locale, produces a similar effect. It installs us in a paranoid attentiveness to the "space off." We assume we are accompanying Tibbs, but the camera withholds his presence. As a result, we become aligned with an anonymous surveying look. Given that Tibbs is endangered by gangs of white men, this camera effect splits our position between his point of view and that of these menacing thugs. Moreover, because we know that Gillespie is also shadowing Tibbs and trying to protect him, we can associate these unattributed views with the chief as well. Overall, the dislocation of the camera's surveying gaze enhances our anxiety because we cannot stabilize ourselves as either menaced or menacing. And I would argue that this is the means by which the film invites us to invest in Gillespie's "redemption"—because it may be our own as well. By driving us to inhabit Gillespie's tormented position, to occupy his ambivalent observation of Tibbs, and then forcing us into an uncomfortable alignment with the racist thugs, the film reinforces its corollary project: it aims to distinguish Gillespie sharply from the rednecks and to rescue him from his context and, indeed, from himself.

But another offscreen expanse haunts the film; it appears in the form of visual "digressions" interrupting the narrative thrust in two driving sequences that bracket the pivotal scene at Endicott's. The first of these comes after a characteristically dramatic cut. Tibbs has expressed his intention to go "up there" to Endicott's house on the hill, and the next shot brings an extreme close-up of a cotton plant. As Gillespie and Tibbs drive, the camera tracks and pans the view from the car window, capturing in long shot the bodies of the black people laboring in the fields, their faces communicating nothing. Gillespie watches Tibbs observing the field hands, and he remarks, "None of that for you, huh, Virgil?"

Thus does the film remind us—as Gillespie reminds Tibbs—of Tibbs's difference from this population. At the same time, this documentary digression exhibits workers and conditions that appear nowhere else in the film. If this sequence visually jars us and interrupts the fictional plot for a moment, it makes special claims on our attention not only for its sustained duration but also because its sound track presents the only reprise of the title song that opens the film: Ray Charles's "In the Heat of the Night." Thus pulling us temporarily outside the diegetic frame, the song registers the social world and the history that haunt the film's edges as ghostly effects.

After the visit to Endicott, Gillespie clearly grasps the threat to Tibbs. A striking cut then gives way to an image magnified in a car's side-view mirror. It frames a red Thunderbird speeding up from behind. This car belongs to the "redneck" gang that Endicott has set upon Tibbs. Through close-ups in the mirror and regular zooms, the camera focuses on the Confederate flag on the car's bumper and the American eagle painted on its hood. As the camera tracks with the cars, it zooms in on the bumper that repeatedly rams Tibbs's car. Intercut with the tracking shots that emphasize the deserted countryside are views from the interior, looking back at the pursuing car's hood. Zooms magnify the detail and suggest the terror this car invokes. A chilling recollection of very recent history, this sequence relies on one of the most enduring images in the collective imaginary of murderous assaults on voting rights workers.

But as the cars careen into town, an apparent visual "digression" takes over momentarily. When they pass through a dump, the camera abruptly drops the chase to focus on a battered and filthy doll lying in the dirt. It proceeds to track and pan across the surreal juxtaposition of broken discarded objects, debris, and garbage. Diverting our attention into close examination of refuse, the film seems visually to offer a heavy-handed pun. This is the underside of the town: it is populated by "trash." And the concept of "white trash" is absolutely crucial to this film's flimsy equations. But, in its literally "gritty" realism, its encoding as cinéma vérité, this sequence directly echoes the drive past the cotton fields. Both stand starkly apart from the narrative progress, which does nothing to recuperate them. Indeed, at this point, we recognize that the camera strays from the film's explicit logic.

Visually, this film emphatically brings to our notice its strategies of indirection; repeatedly, it draws our attention to shadows and reflections. Its visual maneuvers are symptomatic: the film has difficulty looking at things straight on. An extended pun is emerging: we remember that Tibbs has been looking at the wrong things in his investigation. Just as the white cops make decisions at first sight, casting suspicion on him, Tibbs himself gets thrown off by appearances. As he tells Gillespie, once he has realized that the motive for the crime might have been simple robbery rather than racism, "If Delores Purdy hadn't come into your office I would never have seen the truth. I was too hung up trying to get Gillespie for personal reasons." In a weird conflation, Tibbs's obsession with the racist rich man has become a personal issue, and one that has blinded him to what lies in "plain sight"—or, rather, to what the film has placed right up front for the spectator to contemplate before the plot has unfolded. That is the first face we have seen, and one that returns again and again as the cops repeatedly visit the diner: Ralph's face.

Significantly, a musical cue marks Gillespie's recognition of Tibbs's self-criticism. At an earlier moment, discerning that Tibbs's rage has reinforced his obsession with indicting Endicott, Gillespie gleefully announces, "Ooh, boy. Man, you're just like the rest of us, ain't you?" Another musical cue indicates that Tibbs has taken this in and registered its truth. These pronounced cues construct an equivalence between the characters, marking their pivotal insights with an identical note.

At this point, we are asked to connect Tibbs's judgments "on appearances" to those of the white police. Likewise, we are invited to equate his "personal" political animus toward the explicitly provocative racist Endicott to the prejudices of the bumbling but likable cops, Gillespie and Wood. This shakily balanced equation surely helps to accomplish the effects that media studies scholar Allison Graham attributes to the film in her book *Framing the South.* She contends that it redeems southern political authority: "Literally overnight, the enforcer of illegitimate law—states' rights and Jim Crow—metamorphosed into the protector and defender of legitimate law" (181–82). "In the process," she argues, the film "redeemed whiteness itself by projecting the criminality of the race onto its lowest member" (182).

But in examining the shaky racial equation organized around looking and sight, and supported by these musical punctuations, we should recall the film's repeated evocation of a haunting space offscreen. Parallel to the space associated with menacing white surveillance and pursuit of Tibbs lies another space, steadfastly coded as beyond looking. While the plantation sequence brackets this space as digression and marks it as black, another scene indicates a different inaccessibility. In a sequence notable for its bizarre camera angles, we meet the only other named black man in the film, Jess, the auto mechanic, from whom Gillespie commissions a car for Tibbs. The scene's obscure establishing shot focuses on the hood of the car and a body beneath it. In a shot/reverse-shot pattern, we see Tibbs and Gillespie from the dizzyingly—and destabilizingly—low angle of a man lying on his back. Coming right into the middle of things, the camera leaves us underoriented; it deprives this location of context or of relation to the rest of the town. Perhaps not surprisingly, after Jess laughs off

Tibbs's suggestion that he will get a hotel room, announcing to his wife that they will be having a guest, we never see his house, or him, again. With characteristic vagueness, the film seems to suggest that Tibbs would need to seek lodging in an African American home. But it cannot seem to see its way to *seeing* that home, or that neighborhood. Nor, apparently, can it figure Tibbs in a black context.

So, even as the film de-racializes the murder, and in the process reprimands Tibbs for viewing the crime through a racial lens, it continues to keep racial issues and conflicts before us. In the tormented conclusion of the mystery and the film, race is both reinscribed and displaced. First, as Delores Purdy's pregnancy provides the motive for Ralph's bungled robbery—he had meant merely to club the man unconscious—her sexuality eclipses race. She has been cast as perverse from the beginning, but when her brother brings her to the police station to accuse Sam Wood of rape, she comes across as completely sordid. Writhing suggestively, speaking in a breathlessly seductive voice, she seems both mentally ill and cognitively challenged. Ultimately, the compulsively seductive white woman, coded exaggeratedly as "white trash," emerges as the source of violence.

Curiously, even as it de-racializes its central crime, the film sets about re-racializing its context. Tibbs announces on his last night in town that he's going "someplace where 'Whitey' ain't allowed." But in a stark contradiction, all the people we see there are white except for Mama Caleba, played by Beah Richards, cast in jarring contrast to her role as John Prentice's saintly mother in *Guess Who's Coming to Dinner*. Her primary function seems to be to provide a racial inflection to the white girl's illicit lust and the criminal solution to the pregnancy that results. And as the film wavers, endlessly prevaricating about the force and the weight of race and racism, it continually falls back on its uneasy identification of Gillespie with Tibbs, the reliably, unquestionably "good object," through which it differentiates the police chief from the "bad objects" it condemns.

Finally, we are asked to imagine—if only momentarily—that Tibbs can learn from Gillespie as Gillespie learns from him. We remember here that, when Tibbs's chief back in Philadelphia assigns him to remain on the case in Sparta, Tibbs is heard to protest, "No. I'm not prejudiced." Early on, then, the film hints at symmetrical prejudices: Tibbs's view of small-town southern law enforcement is set up as "northern prejudice" that balances the racism of the townspeople. But, ultimately, that's a dead end. Tibbs has nothing to learn here. And not just because he is surrounded by people who are ignorant, or at best naive, but because the film needs him to be constitutionally incapable of development or change, since he must serve to *cause* change.

This film is not about him at all, really, except as the object of Gillespie's growing fascination. As spectators, then, we register Gillespie's interiority through his responses to Tibbs. And our visual apprehension of Tibbs increasingly props itself on Gillespie's fascinated gaze. In a world shaped by a diffuse—and rather sordid—eroticism, the chief's gaze becomes slightly tinged with the erotic as well. This effect is of course consonant with the film's convoluted transfers of investment from race to sexuality. No doubt, Baldwin has something like this in mind when he refers to the parting scene at the train station with which the film concludes as "the obligatory, fade-out kiss." "The obligatory, fade-out kiss," he writes, "in the classic American cinema did not really speak of love, still less, of sex: it spoke of reconciliation, of all things now becoming possible."[39]

Whether erotic or melancholy or both, the affective charge here attends an image of reconciliation, but with no future. And this effect leaves Tibbs suspended. Because Gillespie's fascination provides our only access to him, he remains an effigy. Thus, the iconic actor emerges once again from the film's fictional texture, which cannot stabilize him as a character among the others. Consequently, he must disappear, he must continue the thematics of passing through that are so crucial to his films of the period.

Shaping Acoustics

Nowhere are Poitier's passage through a white context and his burden of liveness more pronounced than in *Guess Who's Coming to Dinner,* the central drama of which turns on an utterly implausible premise: his John Prentice, a world-renowned thirty-nine-year-old physician, wishes to marry twenty-two-year-old Joey Drayton (Katharine Houghton), but he will not marry her unless her parents agree to endorse the match. In a classic family melodrama structure, the film confines itself primarily to their home. Temporally it allows them twenty-four hours to make this decision before Prentice must depart to take up a new post somewhere in Africa. The film elaborates the psychic journey of the good liberals Christina and Matt Drayton—

Spencer Tracy and Katharine Hepburn—as they seek to uphold their own espoused liberalism. Quite simply, the entire story articulates a pedagogical project that aims to remind Matt Drayton of what he really believes in.

Poitier's icon reaches its most contradictory intensity in his last widely popular big-budget film. *Guess Who's Coming to Dinner* treats explicitly—if still with considerable indirection—the eroticism that lines, and perhaps structures, racial and racist fantasies. It strives to bind together the many contradictory impulses that circulate around his figure, contradictions that appear most often as traces marking sites of repression in his previous films. In this iteration, Poitier's character seems meant to inoculate against intense anxieties about eroticism in racial relations. And the film registers, without ever mentioning it, the landmark Supreme Court decision in *Loving v. Virginia,* which struck down race-based legal restrictions on interracial marriage in the United States. Susan Courtney observes that, through *Guess Who's Coming to Dinner,* Hollywood was joining the Court in "renounc[ing] codes against miscegenation."[40]

In its inversion of the real-life interracial pairing (Mildred Loving was black; her husband, Richard Perry Loving, was white), the film tackles the more intensely unstable and fearful white fantasy. Eroticism and "miscegenation" come here packaged in a consumable form: there is no lust, no dominance and submission within this couple. This version of the Poitier icon has gained perhaps the most enduring traction within the collective cultural psyche and has helped to perpetuate in popular culture many of the contradictions the film displays.

Structurally, this film turns around a vacuum in the middle ground. Its poles—Poitier on one side and the Tracy–Hepburn couple on the other—communicate from their isolation across a vast space whose emptiness is filled by music. This rigidly partitioned architecture relates to the central actors' iconicity, which continually troubles the boundaries between diegetic and extradiegetic space. This iconicity, we learn from Poitier's own account, also troubled the scene of production, since he could not always perform in his costars' presence: "It wasn't easy for me to work opposite them. I wasn't able to get this out of my head: I am here playing a scene with Tracy and Hepburn! It was so overwhelming. . . . I played the scene against two empty chairs as the dialogue coach read Mr. Tracy's and Miss Hepburn's lines from off camera."[41]

Notably, the scene that introduces Matt Drayton to John Prentice is the only one that takes pains to establish that all four main figures are physically present at the same time. Once Matt has finally realized the nature of his daughter's relationship with John, he joins the family at the table on the terrace, tie askew, plopping down with resignation. The camera captures his look of consternation in medium close-up, and it registers the reactions of the others. Then it carefully centers Joey and John, framed between the heads of Tracy and Hepburn. An odd sort of "family portrait," this image resonates with the younger couple's persistent inscription as a "picture" for the other characters. This pictorialization becomes one of the film's dominant motifs, echoing its overarching trope: its liberal project invites a white audience to "picture this," safely contained within the melodramatic movie screen.

Equally important, as the camera begins to pan across the scene, it brings the back of Tracy's head into the middle of the screen, where the huge dark blur completely obscures our view of Joey as she speaks. Tracy obstructs our view just as he obstructs the couple's plans. At the same time, however, this camera move resolutely asserts that all the actors are present together, whereas in much of the film's development editing consistently separates them.

But this sequence dramatically establishes something else: it identifies the camera with Tracy/Matt's consciousness. Before he joins the others on the terrace to learn of the intended marriage, Matt meets the family maid, Tillie (Isabel Sanford), in the hallway. Squaring off, he and Tillie occupy the whole screen as she tells him that "all hell" has broken loose. After a brief peremptory conversation in which he is introduced to the doctor, Matt takes his leave to go play golf. The camera follows him through the doorway and holds him in full shot as he pauses, wavers, and turns around again. Visually, the film registers the traumatic shock of his recognition that Prentice is his daughter's lover, since the handheld camera matches its motion to his, wavering as he hesitates. Physically miming Tracy's movements through the intimate touch of the handheld technique, this camera "acts" just like its object, aligning both itself and the spectator with him. This slight trick, then, establishes Tracy as the film's center of identification by visually inviting us to imagine an almost physical access to his interior.

Presiding over the drama of white parental consent to an interracial marriage, Tracy and Hepburn, revered icons of the screwball comedy, promise the fulfillment of their signature genre in a successful negotiation.[42] But together, Poitier, Tracy, and Hepburn consistently ruin the frame, since they appear as themselves. Poitier is straitjacketed in his iconicity, while Tracy and Hepburn seem embalmed in theirs. They appear here for the last time as a couple, since Tracy was to die within weeks following the film's shooting. Thus, the pathos evinced by Hepburn's tears in the film's climactic resolution bodies forth from its melodramatic diegesis. Against the collective extradiegetic pressure generated by actors continually eclipsing the characters they mean to embody, the film pits its obtrusive musical sound track.

Though it begins from a foregone conclusion, the film proceeds as if the convoluted, agonized series of heart-to-heart talks among its characters amounts to an argument for interracial coupling. Instead of argument, however, it proceeds by epiphany. In this project, it relies relentlessly on its sound track, which endlessly repeats various arrangements of "The Glory of Love" to propel both story and characters and to reduce our sense of glaring contradiction. In the film's hermetic universe, all the principals float in the same acoustic bath as the song returns to punctuate its unfolding, to signal shifts and transitions. As the film struggles to establish a coherence and logic to its wish fulfillment, its camera's overstated subjectivity works with the sound track, straining to plaster over the contradictions that threaten to shatter it into fragments.

Emphatically dependent on one of melodrama's oldest and most obtrusive tropes, this film propels its drama through music from the start. In a space saturated by "The Glory of Love," John and Joey virtually dance through the San Francisco airport as if in a musical. They seem borne across space by the music that separates them from the other figures on-screen, as they glide around the other human traffic in this public space. While their speech is withheld from us, music shapes the couple as it wraps them in an aural envelope, veiling the contentless domain of their relationship. As sound "sculpts" and interprets the image for us, this sequence exemplifies Michel Chion's concept of "added value" in the cinematic image: "the expressive and informative value with which a sound enriches a given image so as to create the definite impression, in the immediate or remembered experience one has of it, that this information or expression 'naturally' comes from what is seen, and is already contained in the image itself."[43]

Firmly established as the couple's theme from the beginning, this tune returns with tenacious frequency to shape the narrative. This musical signature sets them in striking contrast to the articulate and steady dialogue that characterizes the Tracy and Hepburn couple. But it also calls attention to the problem of surface and depth with which the film struggles. We see them speaking, but instead of this conversation, we hear only the chorus of singing voices. Completely filling the acoustic space, the music emphasizes distance. Rather than providing a conventional illusion of depth, the sound track only emphasizes the superficiality of the image.[44]

Visually and aurally, the lovers inhabit "their own little world." For this reason, the film's opening sequence stands as an example of the "utopian excess" that Caryl Flinn finds so commonly associated with music in classical Hollywood film.[45] Only when they steal a kiss in the cab's backseat does their idyll risk invasion. And, notably, the kiss comes after the song that has propelled them out of the airport and onto the highway has ended. Retroactively, this musical punctuation encodes the previous moment as a "refuge from the diegetic present," in Flinn's terms (109). We see the forbidden kiss across the cab driver's (John Hudkins) sight line as he glances into his rearview mirror, which frames it. Accessible only in a highly mediated form, isolated as a small insert at the top of the screen, this kiss acts as an emblem of the relationship. It is something seen from a distance and on the relay of another's gaze, held in frame, part of a pattern that presents the couple as miniaturized and pictorialized in square frames that often remind us of the television set.

Besides serving as the sign of this couple's interiority, however, "The Glory of Love" (copyright 1936 by Billy Hill and first recorded by Benny Goodman) suggests a comfortable anachronism, gesturing nostalgically out of the field of contemporary popular music toward the era of classic romantic film comedy (and the early years of Spencer Tracy's career).[46] Thus it layers the contemporary drama and the love relationship it impedes with a regressive pull toward an idealized past.[47]

Significantly, the sound track's most sustained concession to contemporary musical developments comes in a freestanding vignette in which Dorothy (Barbara Randolph), the maid's part-time assistant, dances with a white delivery boy (Skip Martin) to the music on his car radio. Diegetic music creates a distinct "integration" scene, where contemporary popular music obtrudes into the Draytons' world; it obtrudes, that is, in a way that the social and historical context of 1967 San Francisco almost never does. This moment saw aggressive "urban renewal" projects displacing tens of thousands from stable, historically black neighborhoods, as well as the Black Panther Party's founding. This moment of utopian excess, then, really exhibits the film's wish fulfillment. It can imagine a scene of interracial coupling only as a staged performance, provoked and supported by the contingency of broadcast music.

This apparent "throwaway," however, is structurally crucial. Falling almost exactly one-third of the way into the film's duration, it marks a pivotal moment. And it also resonates with a parallel sequence at the film's midpoint when the Draytons go to a drive-in for ice cream. Loud contemporary popular music from the radio at the concession stand penetrates the sealed bubble of the car, to the agitation of its passengers, just before the car collides with a sports car driven by a young black man.[48]

Equally striking, however, is the interracial dance sequence's framing. It ends with a cut to Tillie at her post in the kitchen, taking in the sight of John and Matt talking on the terrace, framed in extreme long shot through the square pane of the window. Turning away to look obliquely offscreen, she comments with irritation, in an aside meant for us, "Civil rights is one thing. But this here is *something else!*" Repeatedly establishing her as a commentator, the film makes Tillie into the voice of what is "unspoken," or of what must remain "unspeakable," for its principals. It is as if Tillie smuggles in what the film wants to neutralize: the voice of popular white anxieties about integration. Voicing the crudest criticisms, she guarantees its white characters immunity from bald-faced racism. Tillie's use of contemporary "black" and youth vernacular throughout seems meant to secure her authenticity as a "black" spokeswoman, and she prefigures the curious "balance" the film wishes to posit between whites' and blacks' opposition to interracial marriage.

Tillie's view—her look and her judgment—provides our only access to Mr. Drayton and Dr. Prentice "talking." And this reminds us of the ways music marks this film interpretively, filling in for speech when character interactions emerge as sharply framed and distant pictures. Something similar happens in the sequence that precedes Dorothy's dance with the delivery boy. Arguably the strongest image of unproblematic interracial communication the film has to offer, this freestanding dance number seems to respond directly to what comes just before it. After establishing John and Joey playfully chatting on the terrace, the film abruptly zooms out to cast them in extreme long shot and to reframe them from Christina's point of view as she describes how happy her daughter looks. While the film frames the couple as a picture, Christina must *tell* us how to read what it shows.

As if to emphasize the tension between what it can show and what it must tell, the film cuts directly from Tillie's commentary on the men talking to Joey's interpretation of the same scene. Interrupting an intimate chat with her mother, Joey goes to the window; the camera presents the men framed from her point of view, captured again in extreme long shot. Once again, the wooden frame of a windowpane obtrudes emphatically; placing the men under glass, it bisects the scene, isolating each of them in a little square. Such squares may remind us of the TV screen that brought black people as pictures into white living rooms. At this distance, and mediated by the glass, the men's speech is inaccessible. Joey interprets the duration of the conversation as a good sign but wonders what they could be talking about: "They're *still* talking. Wouldn't you think they'd have said everything by now?"

Here some of the film's unmanageable stress breaks through in its clear admission that it itself cannot imagine what these two men could possibly have to say to each other. Indeed, when the film does supplement our view by granting us access to this exchange, we may have trouble believing our ears. This pedagogical moment reaches a stereotypical extreme. Framing the men in two-shot, the film catches them in the middle of things. "Are you saying they don't have any special sense of rhythm?" Matt is inquiring. Laughing, John responds amiably, "That's right." "But, hell, you can see it," Matt continues undaunted. "You can't turn on the television set anywhere without seeing those kids dancing. And I say the colored kids are better than the white kids." Television delivers the spectacle of integrated dancing that confirms Matt's assumptions, in the process "integrating" his living room with the ubiquity of black youth. But John concludes by offering an even more definitive essentialist reading: "But there's an explanation for that. It's our dancing and it's our music. We brought it here. I mean, you can *do* the watusi, but we *are* the watusi, you know what I mean?" Once again, the picture gives way to music, but this time as rhetorical figure, which conflates it with identity.

We are reminded of Dorothy, who has no lines, appearing only as a figure of native rhythm, such as those dancers Matt has watched on TV. Silent though she is, she performs significant ideological work here. Her youth and beauty catch John Prentice's eye in ways that the film notices emphatically, as it highlights Joey's look registering his interest. Dorothy thus operates to secure Poitier's healthy black male sexuality: his erotic tastes do not run to a general fetish for white women.

But Dorothy also links firmly with Tillie. Together, these black women evoke the social context that the film consistently edges out of frame. Significantly, Tillie is the only character who shares Matt Drayton's ability to affect the film's visual field. Maintaining a special relationship to the camera, Tillie also relates to the frame in distinctive ways. Each time she appears with Poitier, her glare presses him to the opposite edge of the frame, as if her look itself shapes the space.

Performance and Epiphany

In a key scene, never accounted for in the narrative, Tillie confronts Prentice as he changes his shirt. Structurally, she grants us access to his body as erotic spectacle, and she calls attention to the repressed sexual side of things by suggesting that his motives are illicit. When Tillie bustles into the bedroom, Prentice defensively veils his torso with his shirt. As she leans in toward him—literally getting up in his face—the frame cants to accommodate the arc of her assault, and it positions Poitier tilted backward as she presses him to the right edge of the frame. Framed in tight medium close-up, this shot creates a densely claustrophobic space whose pressure is not relieved by the dully flat comic effects for which this scene strives. "Let me tell you," she snarls. "You may think you're fooling Miss Joey and her parents, but you ain't fooling me for a minute." She gets to specifics: "You *think* I don't see what you are? You're one of those smooth-talkin', smart ass niggers out for all you can get with your Black Power and all that other troubling nonsense!" And she finishes off with a threat: "Boy, you bring any trouble in here and you're just likely to find out what Black Power *really* means."

Among the most heavy-handed of this scene's ironies is that Tillie produces the film's only references to black power. She seems to serve an inoculating function here. Her allusion points to crucial developments in racial politics of the moment: the Black Panther Party was founded in 1966, in Oakland, just off the film's map, and the Panthers marched on the California State House displaying arms in the summer of 1967. Her contemptuous condemnation of black power and her suggestion that Prentice is a charlatan effectively ventriloquize popular white anxieties of the time while comfortably containing them by assigning them to a comically exaggerated avenging black matriarch.

Reducing Prentice to silence as a body on display, the sequence assigns to Tillie the film's most forceful "black" verbal performance to this point. But this scene also emphasizes the film's rigid division of labor between body and speech, spectacle and discourse, appearing and acting. We notice that mostly it is the Draytons and the priest who actively engage in conversations—but only with each other. Otherwise, characters seem confined to soliloquy. Effectively, Tracy / Matt, the only character to evolve in a measurable way, acts as the film's discursive center. He is the one to whom all persuasion must be directed, and he gives the film's summation; all others become the audience for his transformation. When it exhibits Poitier's torso in this segregated space, the film marks its steadfast erotic nullity. Staging him momentarily as erotic spectacle, the film then voids the sexual threat through Tillie's explosive performance.

Casting this scene as a comic parenthesis, the film hints at history and politics without subjecting these to analysis or interrogation, and without their disrupting its continuous substitution of crude assertion for argument. This performance of black female reprimand—in defense of the white family—bursts forth from the narrative progress.[49] But the scene's parenthetical structure also aligns neatly with the film's rigid compartmentalization. Tillie, "a member of this family," again evokes the film's social context while also erasing it in her very isolation from any family or home of her own.

Tillie's performance here suggests the particular complexity of her character's relationship to discourse in this film, since both Christina and Matt "borrow" her voice. Just before John Prentice's parents arrive for dinner, Tillie blurts out, "I don't understand nothing no more!" As she bustles away, Christina turns to face the camera and ventriloquizes Tillie in a

grotesque cliché of "black speech": "*Nobody* understands nothing no more."
Matt appropriates Tillie's voice in the speech with which he resolves the
film's central conflicts, as he begins his account of the "extraordinary day"
by citing his encounter with Tillie through an exaggerated imitation. Christina and Matt appropriate a black female voice to produce comic asides
that pointedly signal their own helpless incomprehension. Clearly, the film
itself can no more do without Tillie than can the Drayton family. Yet,
while it borrows her voice to utter reassuring clichés, it ends by emphasizing her central marginality. After concluding his final summation, Matt
brings the drama to an end when he orders her to serve dinner. Having
dragged her into the tight circle of family his speech has constructed, he
abruptly ejects her back into her servant's role.

This borrowed black woman's voice resides in uneasy counterpoint to
that of Mrs. Prentice (Beah Richards), to which the film grants significant
rhetorical force, since Mrs. Prentice delivers the crucial pedagogical speech
that brings Matt back to his liberal senses. This persuasive force emerges
in a drama of choreographed "confessions" that bring these characters
together in a series of one-on-one encounters. Establishing a set of equiv-
alencies and displacements, these scenes orchestrate Matt's final epiphany
and the film's "resolution."

Once the Prentices have arrived for dinner, the fathers quickly declare
their common resistance to the marriage. This exchange prompts Mrs.
Drayton to invite Mrs. Prentice for a private conversation on the terrace,
where they admit to sharing support for the children. It is the women's
complicity that seems to catalyze the rest of the sequence, since the sight
of the wives talking triggers Matt's private encounter with Mr. Prentice
(Roy E. Glenn Sr.). The women are on John's side. The problem, it turns
out, is patriarchal authority. And the closing sequence will partially over-
turn that authority, but only partially—and perversely—by brutally dis-
mantling the black father's claims and asymmetrically nudging Matt toward
a gentler articulation of his.

The force of Mrs. Prentice's key speech depends not only on its content
but also on its context, its particular place in the excruciating series of ever
more tormented logics of persuasion that emerge in the film's last segment.[50] Her speech unfolds in a parallel sequence that moves between two
scenes of instruction: her appeal to Mr. Drayton and her son's encounter

with his father. And the "lessons" delivered in these parallel soliloquies express the racial problem as generational.

As it displaces racial struggle onto intergenerational, intraracial conflict, in the process veering into ever more implausible and incoherent scenarios, the film creates an echo between John's encounter with Tillie and that with his own father. Both these scenes seem to provide the film with a safety valve for the release of what it so energetically represses: black anger. As Tillie castigates and threatens John, so, in turn, does he berate and condemn his father, finally reducing him to silence. Perhaps strangest of this film's convoluted strategies is its perverse displacement of John's outrage from its proper target in Matt Drayton, containing it instead within the framework of familial and oedipal conflict.

Mrs. Prentice's persuasive speech comes intercut with the final argument between the father and son. In the father's appeal to his son, strangely enough, this scene presents black paternal authority evoking that of the law, as he reminds John that his marriage would be "illegal in 16 or 17 states," in the film's only reference to *Loving v. Virginia*. Their dialogue, calibrated to a vernacular register the film wants to code as somehow authentic, breaks off when John tells his father to shut up, and the father erupts: "You know I worked my ass off to buy you all the chances you had. You know how far I carried that bag in thirty years? Seventy-five thousand miles!" As Mr. Prentice concludes, noting his wife's sacrifices, the film cuts back to her and Mr. Drayton. Strikingly, the two sets of figures are positioned almost identically in the frame. Compositionally, each of the recalcitrant fathers fills up and seals off the far right side of the frame, constituting a blockage or impasse in the other character's field of view.

As she enjoins Matt to remember his own youthful passion with his wife, Mrs. Prentice is slowly pushed to the edge of the frame, receding into a soft dark shadow in the front of the picture plane, blending into the frame that highlights Matt's stark visual illumination. Flattening the space between them as rack focus renders one distinct and the other blurred, the film visually inscribes the distance between them as unstable and unmeasurable.

Significantly, the visual rhymes that link the parallel instruction scenes supplement their shared thematics of blindness and (in)sight. Ironically, we might read them as performing the film's own ideological struggle: the central insights that it urgently and relentlessly advances depend on its recalcitrant blind spots. Mrs. Prentice begins her speech by asserting, "I believe those two young people need each other, like the air they breathe in. Anybody can see that by just looking at them. But you and my husband, you might as well be blind. You can only see that they have a problem." This virtual blindness, in her account, relates to forgetfulness—a problem they share with the film itself, which stubbornly forgets its own context. Having forgotten their own youthful erotic passion, she argues, the two fathers remain blind to what appears to anyone else "just looking at them." Just looking at the couple, of course, is pretty much all the film can do, and what it invites us to do: they are an image without content. As Mrs. Prentice concludes, she appeals pedagogically to memory, to the restoration of something Matt already knows, "true passion": "You knew once, but that was a long time ago." In *Hollywood Fantasies of Miscegenation,* Susan Courtney remarks tersely, "The power of this speech is registered in part by Matt's profound silence and by the fact that he will require several more scenes of contemplative gazing before he can muster a response" (286).

Another graphic match brings us back to the Prentice men again. We note that their positions in the frame have reversed, and that visually John and Mr. Drayton have been aligned. John begins by insisting that his father cannot tell him "what rights I've got and haven't got." We feel the film's rhetorical strain in this line, which anticipates its final mapping of civil rights onto family obligations. "I owe you *nothing,*" he continues. "If you carried that bag a million miles, you did what you were supposed to do, because you brought me into this world. And from that day you owed me. . . . But you don't own me." In this chaotic hodgepodge of references, it is nonetheless difficult to miss the sharply dismissive reference to bus boycotts, to the actual cost and value of walking miles in order to work. But here John's speech veers off into the broader social context, rewriting the civil rights movement as a generational struggle: "You will never understand. You and your whole *lousy* generation believe the way it was for you is the way it's *got* to be. And not until your whole generation has lain down and died will the dead weight of you be off our backs. You have got to get off my back!"

Throughout this savage reprimand, the father remains mute. He is pressed to the left side of the frame, most often shot from behind, so we do not see his reaction. When the camera does bring his face into view, it presents a static, silent mask. And silent he will remain, while John adopts a conciliatory tone. Strains of "The Glory of Love" come up on the sound track again, and the music marks a shift in John's affect, as he approaches his father more gently, explaining, "You think of yourself as a *colored* man. I think of myself as a *man*." As the son chides the older generation for its fixation on color, he opposes that to his own modern "color blindness." Simultaneously, his speech casts his father's disapproval as a form of racial separatism and then makes the leap to construct the parent generation of African Americans as the primary obstacle to integration.

Here Poitier embodies a fantasy of the modern civil rights subject crushing and symbolically killing off his father and, in the process, completely displacing the historical generation that produced the movement itself. Having handed the black voice over to Tillie for much of its progress, the film restores it to John Prentice so that he may silence his father before descending into muteness himself. Because this scene violently renders the senior Prentice a mute effigy, who remains silent for the rest of the film, while Matt Drayton discourses for some ten minutes uninterrupted, we might conclude that the white father's final speech comes at the direct cost of the black father's voice and the effective cancellation of his authority. In this violent repudiation of genealogy, as well as of his father's history, context, and identity, John asserts his own transcendence in his claim on the universal: he thinks of himself as "a man," unmarked. He thus casts himself as innocent of and beyond history, both past and contemporary, just as he passes beyond community and beyond embodiment.

Strikingly, the film's structure at this point casts John Prentice and Matt Drayton as doubles, each alone contemplating his decision. Left alone to his silent contemplation, Matt circles and paces on the terrace, isolated in frame and propelled by the theme song the film has definitively transferred to him. As he paces to a slow-tempo version of "The Glory of Love," the camera follows him and picks up the images of Mr. Prentice and John. Father and son are in separate rooms, isolated in illuminated windows, tightly framed and out of focus. As ghostly images haunting the edges of Matt's wanderings, these characters are reduced to distant pictures, framed to the measure of a television flickering in another room.

As Matt ponders his decision, circling on the terrace in search of his awakening, music encircles him, filling in for discourse and producing our sense of "overhearing" his deliberations. While Matt walks slowly through the harsh illuminations and inky shadows on the terrace, Mrs. Prentice silences her husband again in the living room, just before the film cuts back to Matt's epiphany. Sound cues indicate a shift in his thoughts, as we see him in close-up, his brightly lit head standing out from the dark background. His psychic illumination is striking, because music functions here as interiority, representing his epiphanic return to his authentic liberal conscience.

As the camera zooms in on his face a second time, a chorus of female voices joins in the strains of "The Glory of Love," and Matt pronounces, "Well, I'll be a son of a bitch." We are invited to share in his realization as music and camera produce a literal shift in perspective. This scene envisions the epiphany as a kind of inverted trauma: it figures a temporal dissolve superimposing two moments—"before" and "after." A dramatic change registers that has not passed through experience; it cannot be worked through. This unearned epiphany might be described as a moment of "filled affects," which Flinn characterizes, following Ernst Bloch, as a "faux utopia" whose aim is "restorative and idealized," such that "future fulfillment involves simply the preservation of the present, changing it by redressing a few present-day lacks, adding objects as they are desired and so forth" (106).

Matt proceeds to narrate the events leading to his epiphanic conversion, in the process putting all the other characters "in their places" as support-ing players in the central drama that he organizes. His extended disquisi-tion echoes the structural balance of his theme song's lyrics: "You've got to give a little, take a little." In replicating its "on one hand, on the other hand" alternation, the film itself levels all the participants in the scene into equality. Camera and editing collaborate to structure the space around Matt as its central pillar, steadily rounding the room, plastically pulling all the others into solidarity as audience. Commenting on Tracy's perfor-mance in his autobiography *This Life,* Poitier identifies a certain force of "liveness" here: "We, his fellow actors in the scene, began falling under his spell until he had succeeded in converting all of us, one by one, into a single captivated audience" (286). Effects of liveness that have accompanied Poitier himself through the film transfer powerfully and pivotally to Tracy, whose dramatically failing health ensures that Hepburn's tears index the reality beyond the screen. And what more compelling instantiation of liveness could we imagine than the one produced by what we know to be a final performance? But this scene also constructs Prentice/Poitier as a mute spectator, who, we remember, will depart that very evening for an unspecified African destination.

After finally giving his blessing, Matt brings the drama to closure by putting Tillie in her place: "Tillie, when the hell are we gonna get some dinner?" As they file into the dining room, "The Glory of Love" comes up on the sound track, obliterating all dialogue. Most pointedly, we can only watch the two fathers chatting as they bring up the rear. What could they possibly be saying? In our last view of them, the group is framed by the doorway on one side and heavy drapes on other, obtrusively figuring the scene as theater. As the credits begin to roll over the static scene of a "family portrait," we hear these lyrics: "As long as there's the two of us, we've got the world and all its charms / And when the world is through with us, we've got each other's arms." The song pointedly emphasizes the film's definitive expulsion of the couple from its world and into empty abstraction, sending them "back" to a fantasmatic Africa.

The more Poitier has embodied the "sign" of real racial difference, it seems, the more displaced and de-realized he has become, and the more he has displaced the reality his presence is meant introduce into his films. Representing blackness through his own exceptional embodiment of it, his presence displaces and disavows—in the technical sense of positing by denying—the reality it marks absent. Prentice's forceful verbal performance with his father has literally enacted the recriminatory repudiation with which a subject incorporates—and buries—its lost object. In his definitive appearance as the civil rights subject who has violently erased the movement that produced him, Poitier emerges as pure effigy frozen in its reassuring iterability. Once more, the dominant culture has refound the "good" lost object in order to send it safely on its way, retaining only its static portrait.[51]

Surely, the theatrical stasis of the final family portrait registers an inertia, or an exhaustion of the tropes deployed not only in this film but also in Poitier's other films of the 1960s. Indeed, *Guess Who's Coming to Dinner* seems to mark an impasse in racial representation. In this moment of representational crisis, Poitier himself becomes displaced. As a Hollywood in ruinous decline from the classical period that Tracy and Hepburn repre-sent struggles to reorient and resuscitate itself, blaxploitation emerges. In some ways the most powerful statement within this form is writer-director Melvin Van Peebles's extremely low-budget independent film *Sweet Sweet-back's Baadasssss Song* (released on April 23, 1971, in New York City and May 12 in San Francisco, just before Gordon Parks Sr.'s *Shaft* opened on June 25). These films, along with *Superfly* (Gordon Parks Jr., 1972), seem to respond pointedly to the sustained Poitier effect on which *Guess Who's Coming to Dinner* depends.

Van Peebles's exuberant and extreme critical challenge to Hollywood's representations of black masculinity, as centrally embodied by Poitier in the 1960s, depends crucially on the body of his eponymous protagonist. Since Van Peebles plays Sweetback, he underscores his character's assertive embodiment with his own.[52] Staging his own sexual potency as his pri-mary weapon in the struggle against white violence and legal and cultural authority, Sweetback radically inverts the Poitier figure, resolutely assert-ing his opposite number, the "badass," to mobilize precisely the powerful eroticized racial fantasies whose repression gives rise to those previous representations even as they mark them with their traces.

Strange though it may seem, however, Van Peebles's character may have more in common with the Poitier icon than is obvious at first glance. What these figures share is the historical "innocence" for whose represen-tational centrality Robert Reid-Pharr makes such a powerful argument in *Once You Go Black*. Analyzing Sweetback alongside Mailer's white Negro, Reid-Pharr contends that "Sweetback exists outside history, whether one names this history 'white' *or* 'black'" (160). "Van Peebles's great error," he argues, "is that he has set about announcing a black character without subjectivity," a "vacant blackness" (160). Insisting that Sweetback adum-brates the asociality and primitivism that emerge in Mailer's fantasies, he suggests that "Sweetback represents such a pure fantasy of blackness (the outraged, running Negro who exists wholly outside the social) that he becomes less a man than a specter, a dream, a ghost" (160). So this power-ful "bad" object may remain deeply implicated in and intertwined with the figure it means to repudiate and to banish, instead remembering it in its own opposing form. Interestingly, the extended chase structure that organizes this film propels Sweetback from his Los Angeles neighborhood into the desert across the Mexican border; like Poitier's characters, Sweet-back too is passing through.

If Poitier exits center stage on the big screen to reemerge, "under-ground" as it were, inverted in the figure of Sweetback, his image also per-sists, as we will see, in a different kind of revenant, a ghostly icon deployed by later films that explore or seek to recapture the civil rights period. He reappears in the good objects that the culture cannot seem to do without. If popular movie culture cannot relinquish this figure, it seems most par-ticularly inclined to recall its incarnation as John Prentice in the melodra-matic world of *Guess Who's Coming to Dinner.* That film provides recurrent tropes for interracial love, desire, bonding, and "family." The persistence of its tropes may be explained as follows. *Guess Who's Coming to Dinner*'s fore-gone conclusions represent an extreme instance of the melodramatic pref-erence for effects over causes. Its overwhelming preponderance of effects—often figured as reactions—works to foreclose even any consideration of cause. This foreclosure marks the film's own enunciation as thoroughly as it does the world the characters inhabit. Such effects prove strikingly per-sistent, emerging as they do in films of the 1990s that remember the civil rights period through the framework of "maternal" melodrama.

2

Feminism as Alibi

When White Women Encounter Color

Images and Icons

Poitier's characters seem inevitably enmeshed—usually on the side of women—in melodramatic scenarios, which they also seem to conjure; but those scenarios also shape his figure to their measure. If melodrama seems to be the figure's natural habitat, this may be because of melodrama's particular aptitude for managing social conflicts obliquely and assigning meanings to them. It should not surprise that popular cinema may remember the civil rights era melodramatically, highlighting the Poitier effect that catalyzes white enlightenment. Nor, perhaps, should it surprise that this cinematic "memory" retrospectively imagines its white characters as readily susceptible to melodramatic transformations that place them on the right side of the historical struggle for equality.

If we needed confirmation of this effect's persistence, 2011 brought Tate Taylor's *The Help* (with the tagline "Change begins with a whisper"), which provides us with a stunning contemporary iteration. Set in Jackson, Mississippi, in 1963—the year of Medgar Evers's assassination—this film rehearses a pedagogical scenario in which an alienated protofeminist, Eugenia "Skeeter" Phelan (Emma Stone), learns a progressive analysis of race relations from the black maids she interviews about their work experiences. She launches her literary career by appropriating/ventriloquizing the maids' voices as they construct an ethnography of their white employers. In this film's account, while the maids encourage Skeeter on her feminist and antiracist trajectory, she promotes their resistance. Equally important, Skeeter's ethnographic project originates in a family melodrama: the maid who raised her, Constantine (Cicely Tyson) has disappeared from her parents' employ under mysterious circumstances.

Like *The Help,* the three films under consideration here—*The Long Walk Home* (Richard Pearce, 1990), *Love Field* (Jonathan Kaplan, 1992), and *Pleasantville* (Gary Ross, 1998)—revisit and revise the civil rights period in melodramas that seek to position white women protagonists in the midst of the movement's progress. In each of these peculiar films a "shared" oppression mediates cross-racial encounters, highlighting gender and featuring a protagonist who is retroactively inflected as feminist. They share a central interest in a misfit, an alienated wife/mother figure, whose confrontation with racial conflict propels her into a taking a political stance.[1] And while the first two of these films are decidedly "smaller," their organizing tropes are centrally embedded in popular white retrospection on the civil rights period. *The Help* depends crucially on their archive of the Poitier effect. The runaway success of its contemporary repetition—uncanny as it seems—demonstrates the tenacity of this effect and the particular form of racial melodrama it sustains. Clearly, we need to be attentive to its enduring appeal in some popular imaginings of the history of race relations.

Each of the 1990s nostalgia films foregrounds its feminist figure through the relay of a child witness, whose confusion and trauma color the narrative. Their emphasis on child spectators suggests that all of these films elaborate their directors' memories of this period. These white filmmakers are all of a generation in which childhoods were somehow marked, in ways that may have remained ill defined, by the civil rights movement, whose dramatic effects they would have seen on TV.[2] This period seems to remain a kind of historical primal scene for the postwar generation: a crisis they witnessed without being fully able to process it experientially or representationally. That history unfolded, for the children of this generation, in an "elsewhere" of unstable distance. But these films also figure this period as a primal scene for feminism, which serves as a kind of fantasmatic bridge back to the civil rights movement.[3] Marked by mass-mediated iconic memory, these representations figure history, it seems, through the lens of family romance, as feminist melodrama, in which private cross-racial exchange becomes the terrain for exploring and managing social conflict and cultural upheaval. But melodramatizing historical memory involves substantial reimaginings of the record.

Linda Williams has argued for a link between "melodrama and the melodramatic form of contemporary discourses of race and gender in American culture." Such a connection depends on the particular form "race" takes as a central cultural category in the United States. For Williams, "race has precisely become an 'occulted' moral category about which we are not supposed to speak, yet which, far from disappearing, has remained as central to popular thought and feeling as it was in the mid-nineteenth century."[4] Our contemporary media memory of the civil rights movement continues to borrow affect and energy from the conventions of melodrama. But we may want to ask if it is not the melodramatic imagination that creates race as an occulted moral category, or as a metaphor for morality itself, especially within the moral consciousness of white American women and men.

In Williams's view, the American civil rights movement won racial equality "before the law," "through stagings of its own melodramas of black and white in which noble black citizens suffered at the hands of villainous white supremacists at voting booths, public schools, and lunch counters" (228). If we imagine civil rights struggles as self-consciously mounting melodramatic tableaux, we must also consider their audience. For Williams, civil rights "stagings" of melodramatic scenes constitute an embrace of the form on the part of both the black authors and the spectators of those scenes. But we need to ask to what degree civil rights activists themselves deployed melodramatic spectacles as strategic appeals to white spectators whose political sympathies they understood to be historically shaped by those forms. In other words, while Williams's argument seems to hold effectively for white cultural producers and consumers, I am not convinced the form exercises the same thorough appeal evenly across the social field.

But certainly dominant white cultural memories of the civil rights period continue to stage themselves in melodramatic form. In arguing that melodrama provides a form for processing traumatic cultural memory, film scholar E. Ann Kaplan contends that it "repeat[s] in fictional form a suppressed cultural trauma to do with the overthrow of prior authority." She goes on to argue specifically that "Hollywood melodramas are arguably impelled to repeat the rent in the dominant fiction occasioned by historical trauma while at the same time seeking unconsciously to repair and reveal that rent." Speaking of postwar melodramas, she suggests that the trauma they do not address directly, and that the culture has chosen to "forget," lies "so close to the surface that a whole series of displacements have to be instituted in order to keep that split-off part in its place."[5] Perhaps the ambivalence at the core of this form accounts for its persistence, and for its persistent association with white-produced imaginings of interracial negotiations. Melodrama continues to displace social conflict and cultural crisis into symptomatic and symptomatizing narratives that repeat the Poitier effect in new configurations, in which white characters undergo a broadening and humanizing education through their encounters with black struggle.

Among the primary symptomatic effects structuring melodramas that explore the civil rights period we find a striking mix of memory and forgetfulness. Forceful images and icons recall a national narrative in the making, but they often stand free of historical context; they emerge fully formed, their development—their construction—forgotten. Film scholar Steve Neale's account of melodramatic form foregrounds its "unmotivated (or undermotivated)" events and developments.[6] In a world of "undermotivation," unexplained coincidences and accidents hold sway over the characters' agency. History appears as chance events that cannot be fully accounted for; it happens to us but eludes analysis, much less intervention. For Neale, part of the form's affective appeal, its ability to move us to tears, issues from the sense of helplessness the spectator may share with the characters. "What is impossible is not change as such," he writes, "but the spectator's ability to intervene and make the change. The spectator is powerless not so much before each situation, the state of affairs at any one point in a film, but rather in relation to the course the narrative will take, whether the state of things changes or not" (11).

An extreme cinematic rewriting of civil rights history in white-centered melodrama is furnished by *Forrest Gump,* which, with its oddly feminized and cognitively limited white male protagonist, shares the impulses—and even crystallizes the paradigm—of the historically minded films under consideration here. Robert Zemeckis's wildly popular 1994 production struck a deep chord in the popular historical imagination, as demonstrated by its Academy Awards sweep—Best Actor, Best Director, Best Picture, and Best Visual Effects. This last is, of course, crucial, since the film's digital retro-engineering constitutes its foundational effect, implanting its simpleton hero into history as mass-mediated memory. Forrest (Tom Hanks), that is, keeps popping up in our iconic media memories of the period the film traverses. More important, he returns in mediatized memory as, precisely, an innocent white witness, one whose magical interventions in historical moments continually escape his agency, and even his notice. Vivian Sobchack trenchantly describes *Forrest Gump*'s project: "Since history can't happen without us, the film seems to say through its putative hero, we've played our part simply by 'being there.'"[7]

An innocent passive agent, Forrest retains a permanently infantilized perspective that the film invites us to occupy. Securing his innocence of perspective throughout is the maternal voice, as Forrest recurs to his mother's (Sally Field) repertoire of vapid aphorisms, even as he begins to produce his own vacuous clichés—smiley face, "shit happens"—that range broadly across popular discourse to persist in collective memory. Strikingly, in relation to the films considered in this chapter, Forrest's picaresque trajectory anchors itself to melodramatic tropes. His only childhood friend, Jenny (Robin Wright), becomes the love of his life as he repeatedly loses and finds her across turbulent U.S. history from the 1950s to the 1980s. A sexual abuse survivor who becomes a free-spirited hippie, passing through a radical period under the tutelage of a quintessentially misogynist leftist boyfriend, Jenny finally ends her peripatetic wanderings by returning to Forrest—too late. Melodrama exerts its full gravity once she, Forrest, and their son are reunited in his dead mother's home, as Jenny quickly succumbs to an unnamed AIDS-like affliction. Into the bargain, as it follows the accidental crossings of their paths, permitting Forrest repeated opportunities to try to rescue Jenny, the film inscribes him as feminist.

But the Jenny plot does not exhaust the melodramatic forces at work in this film. Another figure shadows Jenny. Forrest's army buddy Bubba (Mykelti Williamson), who will die in Vietnam, bears considerable resemblance to her. Like Jenny, he breaks through collective hostility toward our innocent misfit hero, and helps to "integrate" him, by offering him the seat next to him on the bus. In his gentle compassion for this slow outcast, shunned by black and white servicemen alike, Bubba evokes the specter of

Poitier. Bubba's innocence, like his tragic death, works to underscore Forrest's own racial innocence. And this compelling portrait of innocence bears considerable ideological weight. As Sobchack contends: *"Forrest Gump* tells us with great sincerity not to worry: one can be in history, can make history, without paying attention and without understanding." That is, we can remain innocent of history. "Thus," she continues, "reflection and reflexivity are a waste . . . : there is no point to comprehending the overwhelming complexity of motives and acts and material causes that make up history since, in the long run, history will comprehend and confer meaning on even the most simple-minded of us" (2).

This film's drama of historical innocence unfolds through digital effects that inscribe its hero as contemporary subject within our shared media record of events, as if retrofitting those collective memories around his uncomprehending gaze. As Robert Burgoyne puts it, the film "employs digital technology to 'master' the past by 'remastering' archival material, grafting the figure of the main character into historical film and television footage."[8] But the archival "record" of Forrest's innocence hardly remains innocent itself. As the hero describes his namesake, a Civil War general, sepia-toned footage of Hanks in period costume digitally merges with a famous clip of charging Klansmen from Griffith's *The Birth of a Nation*.

Our naïf characterizes the Ku Klux Klan as a "club" given to silly practices, "acting like a bunch of ghosts, or spooks." Forrest reports his mother's reduction of history: his name constitutes a simple reminder that "sometimes we all do things that, well, just don't make no sense." *The Birth of a Nation* becomes part of a family archive of regrettable eccentricity. One of the most powerful of American racist fictions becomes documentary evidence of an unpleasant moment in "family" history. Thus does Forrest Gump displace Griffith's epic melodrama into the privatized and manageable frame of family history.

A later sequence literally implants Forrest into news footage of the 1963 integration of the University of Alabama, where he appears as Governor George Wallace faces off with federal troops. But here he does more than just show up. He enters the frame again, picking up and returning a notebook dropped by the black woman student who proceeds past Wallace to register. Just as digital effects fictionalize this documentary footage, so this film's whole progress merges the archive of cinematic fiction with the news archive in a sustained mash-up. Burgoyne points out that *Forrest Gump* dramatizes the Vietnam War through the "iconography" drawn from cinematic memory, from iconic Hollywood fictions, "revisions of sequences from *Apocalypse Now, Platoon, Born on the Fourth of July,* and *Full Metal Jacket.*" "Parasitizing these films in a way that empties them of their original context," he contends, *"Forrest Gump* in a sense 'samples' the Vietnam genre and converts it to a different message" (110). In its exhilarating mix of archives, in the back-and-forth flow of fiction to documentary, history becomes a special sort of screen for our fantasies. Primary among these, it seems, is that we get credit—and progressive political credentials—for just showing up, or for putting ourselves in the picture, and for lending a hand that retroactively places us on the right side of history.

Public Images and Private Fantasy

Love Field and *The Long Walk Home* both plot dramatic upheavals and transformations of white racial consciousness at traumatic moments in history: the 1955 Montgomery bus boycott and the assassination of President Kennedy. At key moments they introduce fragments of audiovisual memory excerpted from television's archive. These iconic documentary records, of course, link spectators' private recollections with collective mediatized memory of the civil rights period. In the process, they pull us into the historical picture. But these films pointedly deploy actual footage from the television news archive in narratives that vigorously mine the archive Poitier's films produced. In both cases, white transformation emerges in a melodramatic structure organized by intimate personal encounters with "black" experience and the inequality it makes visible. *Pleasantville,* in contrast, consistently allegorizes the period of the civil rights movement through the emergence of color television. But it also reworks the 1950s sitcom as maternal melodrama. Its protagonist remains nostalgically obsessed with the archive of television shows that formed his mother's media landscape. And through him, the film elaborates the fantasy of entering into TV's fictional world, or literally getting into its picture.

In all three films under consideration here, we can see cinema attempting to reclaim a distanced past through the lens of intimacy that television introduced in the very period they revisit. Not surprisingly, this reclamation elaborates itself through iconic imagery from the televisual archive of a national narrative in the making. But it also overwrites that narrative, writing white protagonists into central roles in this mediated memory. And this rewriting seems to require the melodramatic tropes that underwrite the Poitier effect.

It is the complexity of these operations in each film—by contrast to *Forrest Gump*—that makes them worthy of our attention, despite their more restricted audiences. Their vexed, and even contradictory, approaches to historical and media memory reveal some persistent collective fantasies about that national narrative, which should have garnered them more attention. Even while these films seek to remind us of the historically uneven and intermittent, complex, and conflictual relations between feminism and civil rights, they also repeat or continue some of the history of representation they mean to critique, as they often seem to conflate these movements. But in their uneasy treatment of civil rights, these films somehow split the Poitier effect, refracting it across and among characters, and even the media itself, in complicated ways. Some part of the Poitier role transfers to television in particular, which seems to emerge both as screen memory for the culture and as Hollywood's repressed, since movies at the time kept out of frame much of the complexity that TV was registering.

Both *The Long Walk Home* and *Love Field* are centrally concerned with the relationship of media images and icons, beginning with the bus as a site of contentious racial interaction and struggle. And certainly the bus has remained iconic of the civil rights movement for generations; many memories of the movement were shaped by struggles for and on the bus during the boycotts, and later by busing as the primary force in school desegregation. Historian Robin D. G. Kelly accounts for the status of the bus as both concrete site and icon: "In some ways, the design and function of busses and streetcars rendered them unique sites of contestation. An especially apt metaphor for understanding the character of domination and resistance on public transportation might be to view the interior spaces as 'moving theaters.'" Kelly elaborates: "The design of streetcars and busses themselves— enclosed spaces with seats facing forward or toward the center aisle—lent a dramaturgical quality to everyday discursive and physical confrontations."[9]

As if to break open *Guess Who's Coming to Dinner*'s hermetic terms, *Love Field* organizes its melodramatic narrative around the irreversible detour the lives of its protagonists, Lurene Hallett (Michelle Pfieffer) and Paul Cater

(Dennis Haysbert), take when their chance meeting leads to a complex involvement. Through its pairing of a startlingly naive white Dallas hairdresser with an African American professional from the Northeast, this film seems organized by the Poitier effect. But it seeks to undo that effect by exploring the missed encounters and misrecognitions that shape the actual discursive relationship that develops between these obviously mismatched partners. What, in other words, might Joey and John have said had they been allowed to talk to each other in *Guess Who's Coming to Dinner?*

Traumatized by John F. Kennedy's assassination, Lurene determines to travel by bus to his funeral. En route she meets Paul, accompanied by his daughter, Jonell (Stephanie McFadden), whom he has rescued from an orphanage after her mother's unexpected death. Like Mr. Tibbs, he is heading home to Philadelphia when his journey derails, and his contact with Lurene precipitates a momentous run-in with the law, echoing Tibbs's own fate. Like Poitier's characters, Paul is unaccountably kind and sympathetic to his white interlocutor. And as with a Poitier character, his interest in her remains insufficiently motivated. A series of misunderstandings and missteps on Lurene's part force the three to leave the bus in flight from the police. The greater part of the journey, then, passes in the public privacy of a stolen car, rather than in the iconic space that the bus presents for our memories of the period.

Centrally concerned with the status of icons and images, *Love Field* explores the work of public images in private imaginings as it tracks the shifting perspective of its protofeminist heroine when she leaves her domestic orbit and takes to the road. Beginning in the moment "just before" the trauma that precipitates Lurene's journey, the film's credit sequence emphasizes her obsession with Jacqueline Kennedy, aligning us with her as she contemplates her collection of "Camelot" images. A montage of glossy photographs drawn from magazines reproduces the media staging of the First Family's "daily" life. As a screen for Lurene's projected fantasies, these photographs suggest the White House as the stage for a family melodrama. Her identificatory obsession has intensified over the loss of a baby. Matching her trauma to Kennedy's, she processes her mourning through the First Lady's widely publicized miscarriage. But the photographs also already memorialize mourning itself, both private and public, as we remember the collective trauma of the assassination.

Significantly, however, early on the film constructs Lurene as a relay for our identifications through television. Like us, despite her proximity to this event, she experiences it *televisually. Love Field* successfully captures the unprecedented televisuality of the Kennedy assassination as national trauma. Familiar and much-circulated contemporary TV footage breaks into its plot: Walter Cronkite's emotional announcement of Kennedy's death, Mrs. Kennedy and Caroline at the casket, the assassination of Lee Harvey Oswald. These central moments in collective memory also emphasize television's liveness, as we remember the traumatic events breaking through its flow in their unfolding. Crucially, each televisual intervention into the narrative and visual flow is marked by the complete coincidence of the cinematic frame with that of the television; we experience the TV here as its own point of view, since the film gives itself over to the television screen dilated to monumental proportions. This overlay of frames becomes all the more disruptive because it produces a stark textual contrast—from color to black and white, from film to video. Historical distance is literally embedded in the images and sound track; yet, television's effects of liveness produce a sense of the traumatic breaking through of the real. Our position itself splits in an overlay of temporalities, as we are pulled into a dizzying proximity with contemporary viewers whose collective point of view we directly share, even as we remember our previous viewings of these images.

At Dallas's Love Field, where Lurene has gone to join the throngs greeting the presidential plane for the fateful November 22, 1963, visit, we first see the scene at the airfield on the monitors television news production crews are watching. When the camera pans to focus on the TV cameramen shooting the event, the film emphatically foregrounds television's liveness as Lurene moves into the field of live televisual coverage. Even as she tries to enter the terrain of the news, a diversion causes her to lose her place at the front of the crowd; she misses the chance to glimpse her idol in person. Paradoxically, then, she would have gotten a better view on television.

TV literally interrupts her trajectory home from the airfield. As she drives back through town, an agitated crowd gathering around a television playing in an appliance store window arrests her progress. Her gaze follows theirs to the live newscast, and the camera registers her stricken reaction, framed in close-up through the car's windshield. Slow motion and the silent sound track figure Lurene's trauma, and television sutures her into the national audience, as she joins a group of distraught spectators.

But the public scene of grief before the television gives way to a domestic drama, as the film cuts from Walter Cronkite's tearful announcement of Kennedy's death to a match on full-screen television images showing the president's casket arriving in Washington. This temporal ellipsis brings us into Lurene's home, where she begins to plan her private pilgrimage to the funeral. Her decision provokes direct conflict with her insensitive husband, Ray (Brian Kerwin). He attempts a definitive exercise of patriarchal authority in forbidding her to take this trip, suggesting that she can watch the funeral on TV and "get a better view." Highlighting the gender politics here, the film continues to suggest Lurene's protofeminist tendencies. She will later make an explicit connection between her defiance of his patriarchal privilege, her defiance of the law, and Kennedy's assassination: "They killed the president; now I'm lying to the police, and my husband's about to divorce me." With the annihilation of her image of benign, enlightened presidential authority (a better spouse?), she radically questions the law she finds incarnated in both the police and her husband.

In a sequence that pivots around the ambivalent figure of the TV, Lurene is propelled by the historical trauma that it delivers to leave a domestic environment shaped by television fictions and women's magazines. A telling image substantiates Lurene's utter incompatibility with her husband: on the night of the assassination, Ray lies passed out on the couch in front of the TV as Lurene slips out to go to the bus station. Later, she observes to Paul, "He thinks he's found the center of the universe on the living room couch"   that is, in front of the TV. By contrast, she has fallen out of the framework of privileged ignorance that he comfortably inhabits.

Through an elaborate complex of images and identifications, Lurene explains her alienation this way: "I don't get ordinary life."[10] What she doesn't get, the film will show her discovering, relates quite precisely to the circumscriptions imposed on "ordinary life" by gender and race, and to the place of images in constructing those categories. But she will need to develop a much more subtle way of seeing. Thus, this film tracks the transformation of Lurene's relationship to images as she takes on a voice and a critical position through her discursive contact—and conflict—with

Paul and with white culture's responses to him. As a figure provoking hostile, and even violent, white reaction, this couple suggests what *Guess Who's Coming to Dinner* might have encountered had it followed John and Joey beyond her parents' home.

Loquacious Lurene pays homage to her iconic idol at the level of image by imitating her physical appearance, copying Jackie's signature suits and hats. Confronting the breach between herself and "ordinary" life, she plasters it over with the mediating image, relying on the force of her identification to shape her life into meaningful events. Of course, her Marilyn Monroe hairstyle, platinum blonde and slightly disheveled, functions as a telling false detail. A decidedly anti-Jackie element, it recalls the president's putative mistress as well. To this failed image, the film adds Lurene's propensity for chatter, a compulsive sound track running over a fantasy life organized by the silent images she collects. As much as Lurene's story is about the use and the meanings of images, it is also about the meanings of everyday speech. Talk though she must, Lurene learns only with difficulty to say anything, to tell any story.

Paul's initial assessment of her consciousness registers when, interrupting the stream of her chatter, he offers her a magazine, "one with lots of pictures," *Look*. She recognizes this sign of dismissal; not a shrewd reader of texts, she must confine herself to the world of glossy images. But the magazine's title also comes across as an injunction: "Look!" Reaction shots capture black and white passengers' disapproval of this exchange and map the divided space of the bus. Lurene has apparently failed to notice the color line across which she converses with Paul. In the first of several such moments, the camera figuratively aligns us with his active gaze: watchful, interpretive, analytic.

As if to confirm Lurene's defective gaze on the world around her, the film next cuts to her point of view as she takes in, apparently for the first time, the poverty that marks the landscape outside the window. "Look!" becomes the implicit injunction that Lurene's story obeys. Her failures of sight—to see or to interpret correctly what she sees, or to realize how she looks in connection with Paul—drive the plot's development, which forces Lurene to see through a different frame, one that includes but also exceeds identification. She pursues an apprenticeship elaborated through looking, which leads her to an awareness of the ambient white gaze that surveys and partitions the social field, aggressively impinging on her private relationship.

This apprenticeship develops through the relay of Jonell, with whom Lurene sustains regular look exchanges of the sort she has not established with Paul. But she also allows the child's gaze to lead her own in framing a view. She first encounters Jonell when, seeing the girl's distress at the "out of order" sign blocking the entrance to the "colored" washroom, she volunteers to take her to the unmarked "women's" room. Once again, she seems not to have observed the segregated demarcations of public space. Of course, historically, her obliviousness appears all the more striking given the intense television coverage of the Birmingham protests that began in April 1963, and that explicitly aimed to desegregate public facilities.

This encounter is fraught with misreading, as Lurene speculates on the basis of what she thinks she sees. Physically timid and verbally reticent, Jonell fails to recognize her father unambiguously. When Lurene discovers some welts and bruises on Jonell's body, she immediately concludes that Paul has kidnapped the girl and calls the FBI to report him. When Paul produces evidence of his paternity, through photographs of himself with Jonell's dead mother, and indicates that she has been abused at a county home from which he has abducted her, Lurene joins them in flight from the police pursuit she has unleashed.

Just as Lurene's profound misreading launches their definitive flight, so do her misapprehensions continue to propel and shape the journey and the narrative. But as she continues to fail to see and to understand, the child witness, Jonell, mutely registers her own close observation and her confusion and fear about adult encounters she only partially comprehends. Her naïveté at times seems to parallel Lurene's. But, more powerfully, it provides a relay for an adult spectator's gaze, split between our contemporary moment and retrospection on this historical period through childhood witnessing.

Love in the Field of Vision

Working through contentious intersections of looks and speech, *Love Field* maps a plot that develops through conflict, misunderstanding, and interpretation rather than resolutions. Will Lurene's blindness give way to insight before something terrible happens? Its extent becomes clear, for instance, in her exchanges with African Americans about Kennedy's racial politics. Stopped in a small black town, they engage a mechanic (Johnny Ray McGhee) to repair their stolen car, whose engine cannot propel them faster than forty miles per hour. (What a metaphor for the "deliberate speed" of integration!) Lurene speculates that many of the town's residents will be attending the Kennedy funeral. Met with the mechanic's resistant questioning about why they would do that, she ventures, "He did a lot for your people." "Look around, ma'am," he replies, matter-of-factly, "look like he done much *here*?"

Lurene cannot register that what she sees around her gives the lie to her assertions that Kennedy "did a lot for the Negroes." Through Lurene's fantasmatic obsession with the president and his family as images, the film implicitly reminds us that, after all, Kennedy's progressive racial politics was largely a televisual effect. As television crossed geographic distances and bridged segregated spaces at the local level, political struggle raged in and around its news coverage. In June 1963, in the wake of a partial political victory over integration at the University of Alabama, the president went to television to make a definitive statement, one for which civil rights leaders had long been agitating, in a twelve-minute live-telecast speech on civil rights as a pressing national moral issue. As television scholar Mary Ann Watson recounts, "The President made an uncharacteristically sudden decision to go on television. At 6 P.M., the White House asked the television networks for a fifteen-minute block of time beginning at 8 P.M."[11]

Just as Kennedy had shown a certain genius for working within the television format in his campaign and throughout his time in office, his decision to appear on short notice with little preparation suggests that he was well aware that a spontaneous appearance would help to highlight the state of crisis and his response to it in a performative manner. Rhetorically, the impromptu feel of his speech might read as the spontaneous expression of a more personal, and hence authentic, conviction. But equally important, according to Watson's account of the events, he must have been responding to a recent televisual event, an interview with Martin Luther King on David Susskind's talk show, *Open End*. Sharply critical of Kennedy's "inadequate" responses on civil rights issues, King "called on the President to revive fireside chats and explain civil rights to the nation on television. He asked the President to speak not in purely political terms, but in moral terms" (104). Kennedy may have risen to this occasion, but, of course, he rose to it on a tide created by the struggle of civil rights activists. From Lurene's point of view, however, the president's televisual image is that of someone "doing a lot for the Negro," while all that African Americans were doing for themselves recedes into the background.

Her captivation by Kennedy's image blinds her to its context, and this limitation remains consistent with her apprehension of the world: she makes sense of things by identification and resemblance. Thus, her view maintains a gap between effects and causes. Paul, by contrast, is a vigilant reader of differences and of contexts. Where for Lurene the meanings of things are fixed, if incomprehensible, for Paul they are situational and demand analysis. As readers of the visual field and their place within it, Paul and Lurene remain similarly mismatched. Significantly, the mechanic's injunction to "look around" reverberates through the car repair sequence, which marks the film's precise temporal center. Lurene has retreated to join Jonell on a swing. Her newly alerted gaze will let her see herself through the black men's eyes. Joking uneasily about Paul's "bad luck" in his traveling companion and about the very real dangers of his being seen with a white woman, the mechanic suggests that she should be riding in the backseat to mitigate their dangerously provocative appearance. Paul jokes that he would really like to put her in the backseat because of the way she "runs her mouth."

This is a moment of truth for Lurene. And the film emphasizes it by showing the men's conversation from a point aligned with her view, yet closer to them than she actually is, while the amplified sound track lets us hear clearly their distant voices. These displacements into implausibility— what appears to be Lurene's point of view allows for closer sight and clearer hearing than she could possibly achieve—highlight the intensity of her effort to penetrate the meanings of the men's exchange, even as that exchange emphasizes the distance that separates them. More important, however, these displacements inscribe a developing realignment of Lurene's view in general.

As their journey continues, Lurene eventually returns to the front seat from the back, and she discusses her failing marriage in terms of gendered opposition. During this conversation, we see that Lurene has fully crossed the color line, though she remains unconscious of it. Dining on sandwiches she prepares as they drive, and stopping by the roadside to relieve themselves, the party is bound by the limitations segregated facilities pose for black travelers in the contemporary South. Still, this seems lost on Lurene, who demonstrates in the next sequence that she remains unconscious of the color lines drawn around them. In a curious coincidence, Lurene seems to arrive at an explicit critique of the gender ideologies that govern her life and her marriage while remaining steadfastly oblivious to the effects of racist ideology. Unmindful of how she looks with Paul in a visual field dominated by the white gaze's surveying authority, she will place him at serious risk.

As the car peters out once again, billowing steam, the film cuts abruptly to a long shot of another car approaching on the deserted dirt road. It stops at Lurene's hailing, and a reverse shot reveals the hostile faces of the two white men inside. To Lurene's request for a lift, one of the men demands, "What's your business with him?" Lurene's naive reply, "He gave me a ride," prompts the hostile eruption, "Where you *from*, lady?" During this exchange, Paul has remained by the car and has given his frightened daughter a protectively vigilant look. Striking here is the contrast between Lurene's apparent ignorance of the danger facing them and the child's confused anxiety. After the men roar away, in an effort to ward off further trouble, Paul instructs the still uncomprehending Lurene to walk up the road to flag someone down. As he crouches with his daughter behind the car, Lurene easily secures a ride with the next passing driver.

Duly alarmed, Paul prepares to disappear entirely, departing with his confused daughter before Lurene can return to pick them up. But we soon discover the white men's car returning. Instructed by her father to lie in the car's backseat and "not to look up, no matter what," the terrified child disobeys. In the first sustained point-of-view shots the film grants her, we observe Paul's confrontation with three angry white men in extreme long shot. Shot/reverse-shot structure captures his struggle and beating and Jonell's traumatic reactions as a witness. Alternating between long shots of the men and increasingly close views of Jonell, the film aligns us with the traumatized child observer. Finally, the sequence concludes with an extreme close-up of her face, framed through the car's windshield; the camera shakes rhythmically, as if she were physically registering the blows through her own body. This moment of visual trauma sutures the adult viewer to the helpless child witness, and its framing through the screen of the windshield echoes the televisual images of police beating civil right protesters that the spectator (like the film's director) might have watched as a child.

This terrifying sequence—catalyzed by Lurene's blindness—ends in cutaway to her arrival at the home of the Enrights, relatives of a friend, to whom she appeals for help. Telephoning Ray, she initiates what will become their definitive break, defying his injunctions that she separate from Paul and return home immediately. And this episode's development will reinforce the connection between her defiance of her husband and her resistance to misguided—and racist—police. Subsequent sequences at the Enrights' home reveal definitive breaks with the past in general, as Lurene's angle of view shifts.

These sequences are compellingly marked by the television. As the travelers follow Mrs. Enright (Louise Latham) into the bedroom in search of a first aid kit, the television broadcasts in the background. Coverage of Kennedy's body lying in state is interrupted by the famous footage of Lee Harvey Oswald's assassination taking place before network news cameras. The characters' collective stupefaction at witnessing Oswald's assassination on TV continues across a temporal ellipsis until images of Mrs. Kennedy at the casket emerge. Since the TV screen coincides exactly with the film's, we share their rapt attention. No one in this group seems to have noticed Paul's incongruous presence in the bedroom of this white couple to whom he is a complete stranger. That trance is broken, however, when he reaches for Lurene's hand as images of Mrs. Kennedy and Caroline touching the casket pass across the screen. This first intimate gesture acknowledges his sensitivity to Lurene's identification with the First Lady, but it also produces a shocking effect, as the camera catches Mrs. Enright's sharply disturbed look. Television has mediated a moment of intimacy whose consequence is the couple's exposure to the phobic scrutiny of a white gaze. Their host's look echoes that of the men on the road; once Paul and Lurene are framed as a couple, they are abjected.

Mrs. Enright's hostile scrutiny of the couple before the television ends with her sharply taking a moral distance from Lurene, in a moment that marks her definitive crossing of the border of racial taboo. This moment of interracial intimacy, framed by the disapproving white gaze, coincides with Lurene's relinquishing her imaginary identification with Jackie Kennedy.

Private fantasy gives way to a more critical interest in difference and the social world around her. Rather than functioning as a screen for fantasy, and for guaranteeing the stable sameness of the domestic sphere, the TV functions to highlight difference in the public sphere, recalling its capacity to bridge cultural as well as geographic distance, an effect that *The Help* will echo.

Lurene's shifting relationship to identification and difference, and to articulations of private fantasy with public historical events, emerges sharply in the next sequence, as Paul demands that she acknowledge the violent social effects of difference. In the most brutally excruciating of their exchanges, Paul insists that they separate. Apparently remaining blind to their hypervisibility for the police, Lurene speculates that he wants to go on without her because she has manipulated racist language in deflecting the policeman who has come to the house looking for him. And now she struggles to manage the contradictions that her ready access to the language of racism has revealed. She disavows her use of the policeman's racist discourse: "I said it, but I didn't mean it."

This claim precipitates an explosive confrontation. Paul attacks her for her consistent incomprehension and for her failure to recognize the dangerous consequences of their visibility together for the white gaze. "Thank you for not *meaning* nigger. Thank you for calling the FBI," he shouts. "And, baby, thank you for sticking out that thumb and bringing those crackers down on me." When she expresses concern for Jonell, he responds that when she has a child of her own she can judge him, thus deploying her grief against her. "Until then," he continues, "you can sit tight in your little clean world where the First Lady *gives* a fuck about you." In the face of this hammering on her fantasies and symptoms, Lurene ventures, "I thought we understood each other. We're both running. We're both wanting something different . . ."

Paul interrupts to attack the subtext of identification that underlies her sense of understanding. "Being bored and being black are different. . . . I want my child to be free . . . to grow up as bored and stupid and useless as any white woman. We are *not* the same." But paradoxically, even as he denies that they understand each other, Paul has shown a developed knowledge of her interior landscape, even if only to use it against her. In this deeply gendered framework, he simultaneously makes Lurene stand in for white women in general and, in turn, makes white women a symptom of whiteness itself. Yet his position provides a glimpse of another reading. It is precisely the alienation Lurene experiences in her domestic situation—which may manifest itself as boredom—that allows her, in whatever uneven and clumsy ways, to meet him at all.

Even as Paul has kept Lurene off balance, cinematographically this scene itself stays a bit off-kilter. As the characters argue, the camera captures each in medium close-up, though it gradually moves closer to Lurene while maintaining a more constant distance from Paul. Our perspective inhabits a point slightly behind her, but at her eye level. The effect is curious: we seem to be physically aligned with Lurene, almost in her place, but buffered by her body. Not quite the addressee of Paul's critique, the spectator remains visually implicated in a scene that inscribes the characters' difference as it maps them differently into its space.

This painful scene establishes difference as the ground for any productive identification, displacing the more primitive imaginary formulations that annihilate both difference and the other. Their difference acknowledged, Paul and Lurene finally reach erotic intimacy. Refusing metaphors of "seeing through the other's eyes," this film instead emphasizes that Lurene goes on to find herself beside Paul in the visual field, framed by a surveying white gaze. In this field, their encounter is never entirely private; rather, it is also irrevocably public. In recognition of this fact, the next day Lurene finally agrees to let Paul and Jonell go on without her. But, in an image that anticipates the film's conclusion, we watch Paul drive away and then circle back, as if drawn gravitationally, to collect her. Inevitably, once they complete the journey to Washington, they will be caught when her husband alerts the police. And they will be caught precisely because of their radical visibility.

The three are arrested and definitively separated after they become stuck in the Washington, D.C., traffic jams caused by the funeral Lurene has just missed. That missed encounter anticipates another. Just after she has exchanged a last look with Jonell, who gazes in despair out the window of the police cruiser that is taking her away, Lurene spies a shadowy Jacqueline Kennedy passing in a limousine. In this visual crossing, Lurene symbolically exchanges Jackie for Jonell, trading her fantasy icon for a reciprocated gaze.

She materializes this exchange a year later when she visits Jonell at her foster home as the girl awaits her father's release from prison. Lurene arrives with identical lockets, which contain photos of the two of them taken at the bus station, to memorialize the relationship they have developed in Paul's absence. Having achieved a form of identification that acknowledges the difference it crosses, Lurene has also refashioned her own look. Now divorced, she is clad in slacks and flat shoes, her hair cut in a straight bob. She has definitively left her celebrity model behind.

In this last sequence, Jonell's gaze accomplishes the fantasy of reuniting her symbolic parents. We watch from her point of view out the window as Lurene drives away, and Paul replaces her in the room. Lingering on the view through the window, the camera aligns us with Jonell's look at the space Lurene has vacated. As the camera holds on the window, Lurene's car circles back, as if called by this insistent gaze. But this melodramatic development ends suspended on the image of the car outside. Watching Jonell look out the window in anticipation, we can no more imagine the future of this potential interracial family than we could that of Joey Drayton and John Prentice from *Guess Who's Coming to Dinner*, or, for that matter, of any of the Poitier characters, once they have passed through the white contexts they visit. This unfinished interracial love story becomes displaced from father to daughter, just as our gaze now remains suspended in the relay of the girl's look toward her potential white "mother." Among the effects this displacement of the gaze accomplishes is the mediation of contemporary white spectators' memory of historical trauma across the black child contemplating a reconstituted family.

Much has gone missing: only an ellipsis produces this final picture, for which no causal development accounts. Such effects of undermotivation link this film to *The Long Walk Home*, a bigger film anchored by the star power of Whoopi Goldberg and Sissy Spacek, and one whose striking lacunae *Love Field* seems to want to fill in. Goldberg brings to the film a history of roles reminiscent of the Poitier effect. In *Clara's Heart* (Robert Mulligan, 1988), she plays Clara Mayfield, a Jamaican who moves to Baltimore to work as a maid and nanny for a troubled white family. Her close therapeutic/pedagogical relationship with the distressed son helps to transform these lives marked by tragedy. In 1990's *Ghost* (Jerry Zucker), released just six months before *The Long Walk Home*, her role as Oda Mae

Brown won her the Academy Award for Best Supporting Actress. In a spectacular incarnation of the "magical Negro," she establishes communication between the murdered Sam Wheat (Patrick Swayze) and his widow, Molly Jensen (Demi Moore). Her work as a medium allows them to catch his killer, which in turn allows the ghost to reach eternal rest. In the film's climactic and most magical scene, Oda Mae becomes a literal medium, her body enabling the couple's last sexual encounter when she lends it to Sam.

The Face of Integration

The Long Walk Home's drama of white racial consciousness plays out across the triangle formed by two mothers, white and black, and the relay of the white daughter who witnesses it. This relay helps to conflate white ignorance with innocence in a cinematic "memory" that consistently overlays its fantasies on the history it seeks to recall. Framed as a maternal melodrama in which a middle-class white housewife, Miriam Thompson (Sissy Spacek), comes to a political awakening during the Montgomery bus boycott, this film emphasizes its protagonist's defiance of male authority. A sharp gender divide cuts across the white side of this segregated world. Aligning Miriam with her maid, Odessa (Whoopi Goldberg), in the fiction-fantasy that she abets the boycott by transporting her employee to work, the film ties her evolving racial consciousness to an incipient feminism. Strikingly, *The Help* plays on precisely the same field: Skeeter's boyfriend—who had seemed to appreciate her intelligence and independence—leaves her abruptly upon learning that she is "Anonymous," the author of the book that reveals the maids' testimonies about their white employers.

Odessa, the film's moral anchor, embodies the stoic dignity and resistance to oppression, the extraordinary ordinariness, and the black innocence that marks Poitier's characters. Guaranteeing Odessa's moral authority is Martin Luther King Jr., who "appears" in this film only as news headlines and as recorded voice. The force of his voice registers in the expressive reaction of his black listeners. This moment, of course, reinforces his absence from the scene in which he persists only as a recording. Odessa emerges as a delegate for King's remembered, mediatized authority.

Miriam's alliance with Odessa develops as maternal melodrama, in which Miriam's now adult daughter's memories frame her evolving political views and their impact on the family scene. Its perspective split between the child's view and the adult's, at the level of the narrating voice-over and of the diegesis itself, *The Long Walk Home* functions like a screen memory as the adult pictures her childhood self in the third person. It provides us an "innocent" access through the evolving comprehension of the child, Mary Catherine (Lexi Faith Randall), while it assigns explanatory power to her adult voice (Mary Steenburgen). Curiously, *The Help* seems haunted by this film. Sissy Spacek appears in *The Help* as the feisty and eccentric mother of Hilly Holbrook (Bryce Dallas Howard), the film's most odious racist, and she supports the black maid, Minny, against her daughter. Steenburgen, the voice of the feminist future, plays the New York Jewish editor, Elaine Stein, who takes a chance on Skeeter's "topical" book—for she fears the civil rights moment will quickly pass.

Introducing Odessa in *The Long Walk Home*'s opening sequence, Steenburgen's adult voice tells us: "As far as anyone knows, this was the first woman to rock me to sleep. There wasn't anything extraordinary about her. I guess there's always something extraordinary about somebody who changes and then changes those around them." Understood at the level of privatized individual consciousness, this statement makes little sense, but it demonstrates the film's fundamental contradiction: that of trying to explain a mass movement and its consequences as a melodrama, a private familial drama of change. Most compelling among the film's oversights is that it fails to see that Odessa herself has not needed to change. She has needed to engage in active resistance and agitation to change not the Thompsons' minds but, rather, concrete social practices and institutions. And while the film effectively remembers that political change involves affective as well as analytical or intellectual channels, it also promotes melodrama's premise that the deep structure of feeling is primary.

Significantly, the film figures its preoccupation with the relation of public to private through its own framing of images. A powerful resonance between the opening and final sequences of *The Long Walk Home* gathers around the shifting shapes of images themselves. Opening on a black screen, the film presents an initial image that appears to be a still, a black-and-white negative. Gradually, both color and motion animate this image of an empty street. Slowly filling with color, from black-and-white to sepia tones, to a full palette, the image resolves into focus on the motion of a bus pulling into the frame. After observing several black women paying their fares at the front of the bus and then boarding through the rear door, the camera isolates Odessa. An eye-line match shows the empty seats beyond the color line that she contemplates while standing in her crowded section.[12] As Mary Catherine begins her narration, the camera slowly zooms in on Odessa's face, producing what could be a still portrait, captured in medium close-up.

Striking in effect, the sequence gives the impression of reanimating for us a past that had been immobilized, frozen. In so doing, it seems to promise to bring the past back to us, in a move that may be analogous to the distance-bridging function of the TV image (as footage familiar from popular memory appears in its original context). But it also produces another dramatic effect, as a cut brings us, along with Odessa, into the Thompson family kitchen. "That's me." Like an adult displaying a family album and identifying her childish self, Mary Catherine establishes a displacement in memory. Subsequent developments uphold the structure of screen memories, framing sequences that lead to the beginning of the Montgomery bus boycott through the adult voice but visually remaining anchored to the child's point of view.[13]

When Miriam leaves Odessa to watch Mary Catherine and her friends in a park, we view the incident that ensues through two dramatically distinct perspectives, owing to the focus pulling that regularly characterizes this film's handling of space. As a policeman berates Odessa, ordering her out of the park, we observe from Mary Catherine's point of view. Even as the presence of a child witness amplifies the brutality of the cop's verbal abuse, this sequence also sets up a complicity between mother and daughter around Odessa, as a kind of structural pivot within the family. An ellipsis returns us to Miriam, telephoning Police Commissioner Clyde Sellers (an actual historical figure) to inform him that one of his officers has thrown her daughter out of Oak Park. The previous scene, then, has served as a pretext to establish Miriam's willingness to act on her knowledge of "what's right."

A subsequent sequence reinforces this alignment as we observe a cocktail party from the child's vantage point. She receives a tray of hors d'oeuvres from Odessa, and she walks directly toward the camera, which is placed at the height of her own head. As the party progresses, the camera intermittently returns to the child's-eye point of view, moving through a forest of headless adult bodies. Like a child ignored by the animated partiers, the spectator eavesdrops on the adults. Significantly, overhearing the racist jokes people are making, the child structurally links us to the servants who are obliged to overhear them as well. And this effect will recur.

In the meantime, Mary Catherine's voice returns, bridging a radical spatial break into the next sequence. "Back then my world was a bubble. A war coulda been going on outside our door, and I woulda been all but happy," she muses. Continuing across the cut, she concludes, "In a way, a war was about to start in Montgomery . . . a war of wills." As she speaks, the camera introduces two black boys; we learn that they are Odessa's sons when they run into their house. Here the camera splits off from the voice; Mary Catherine would never have seen these children or this house. This effect replicates the splits that shape the film: this narrator's curiously naive commentary seems marked by the temporal and spatial splittings that structure trauma.

Moving Images/Still Images

As in *Love Field,* in *The Long Walk Home* the TV produces a doubled temporal structure. Television footage that has become iconic in collective memory and the national narrative appears in all its liveness, contemporary to the period these fictions represent. We watch in two times, aligned with characters watching collective, public conflict and trauma unfold through the medium's mediation in their private interiors. At the Christmas holidays the television offers both the comforting sanctuary of fantasy and the uneasy intrusion of the world into the domestic interior. Seen across the family dining table, a droning background to the family dialogue, the television inhabits the space of its margins, much like the domestic servants, always present but largely to be ignored. TV interrupts the family banter with a mock news report signaling that an "unidentified flying object" has been spotted over the "North Pole."

In the very next segment, a news report on the day's events in the boycott briefly intrudes into this domestic scene, prompting the family to extinguish the set abruptly. But as the news penetrates the private interior, we see the way that television presents a newly intimate history in the form of current events taking place in proximate but noncommunicating spaces. This is an effect Norman Thompson (Dwight Schultz), Miriam's husband, resists; he grumbles angrily that such media attention only enhances the boycott's effectiveness. (This seems an enduring iconic moment, since Charlotte Phelan—Skeeter's mother—makes the same insistent appeal in *The Help.*) History shows their concern to be valid. Sasha Torres reports that "throughout the boycott, local television played a crucial and unusual role by breaking the local newspapers' monopoly on information," since Frank McGee, news director of the new NBC affiliate, WSFA-TV, "understood that he had a very good story on his hands, and covered it assiduously," where the newspapers "covered the movement only reluctantly and disparagingly." This unusual exposure had important consequences. "Bridging local and national audiences," Torres writes, "McGee's coverage allowed protesters to see themselves represented as social agents, both within Montgomery and within much larger struggles for human rights in the U.S. and internationally."[14]

Television scholar J. Fred MacDonald also notes the power of television in the period, writing that "images of chanting demonstrators being sprayed by fire hoses and attacked by dogs, freedom riders being abused, sit-in participants being taunted or beaten, and small black children needing military escorts to enter public schools—these pictures made television a powerful propaganda tool for those wanting progressive change."[15] These remain the indelible images associated with the civil rights movement for those who witnessed the original coverage as well as for those who gain access to the period through later film and television reframings of this archive. Such television images emerge as self-consciously fashioned icons in a civil rights media field that Linda Williams has characterized as itself melodramatic. This "was the moment when African Americans began to fashion their own role according to a self-conscious awareness of the power of the public spectacle of racialized suffering," she writes (298).

Norman's theory that to publicize the boycott as newsworthy is to advance black resistance perfectly epitomizes his sense of his world and everyone's place in it. We can situate his position in the context of racial issues that emerged in and around television in the 1950s and 1960s. On one hand, many whites, like him, actively blamed television for promoting civil rights and inciting demonstrations.[16] On the other hand, even as network executives and sponsors worried about losing white, especially regional, audiences, others within and around the industry actively sought to promote ideological and material change through representation.

MacDonald observes that while roles for blacks in television fiction decreased in this period, TV paid increasing, if ambivalent, attention to civil rights, expanding from the news to current events programming on magazine and talk shows.[17] In this televisual landscape, blacks are mostly appearing as transient figures, and primarily as "themselves," in the ad hoc performances of entertainers or athletes, or of distinguished political leaders in interviews.[18] Otherwise, they appear as part of massified blackness, in demonstrations. As social agents, then, with the exception of political leaders like Martin Luther King or Malcolm X, if blacks are rarely seen they are even less often heard, and mostly they are heard as the singing voice, the entertainer or the mass voice raised in church or in protest.

In a world where, for the white people, blacks are "news" or nothing, invisible unless they make the news, the shift in Miriam's consciousness at first registers as an ability to bring Odessa not so much into perspective as into view. But once Miriam begins to see her, Odessa has a new job: that of the native informant. Just as the domestics in this film are always shown to be working overtime, caring for two homes and families, and just as the white people insist on making most of their labor disappear while always expanding their tasks, Miriam thinks nothing of enlisting Odessa as her civil rights "instructor," in a distinct echo of the white interlocutors Poitier's characters enlighten.

Another key sequence in the evolving drama that dismantles and rebuilds white racial consciousness through images involves Miriam's family album. Norman has just decided to join the White Citizens' Council, and his decision seems to be precipitated by the televised evening news: "40,000 local Negroes walk and carpool, while buses run empty on day 49." Shortly thereafter, Martin Luther King's home is firebombed. A long tracking shot takes us past the King house from the point of view of an unseen driver. When a cut establishes the next scene in the Thompson house we retroactively identify the driver as Miriam. As is characteristic of these domestic views, we watch the maids, Odessa and Claudia (Cherene Snow), in medium long shot, squeezed into the frame of the window between kitchen and dining room. Zooming out slowly, the camera reveals Miriam to be the subject of this contemplative vision of the distant and silent maids arranged in tableau, as they so often are in this domestic space. A temporal lapse figures Miriam's prolonged effort to establish the connection between the King house and her own domestics.

What happens next is striking: Miriam begins to pore over her family album. A sightline match focuses on a picture of herself. As a little girl in a white dress, Miriam stands before her house, holding the hand of a black nurse, the top of whose head is cut off by the upper frame of the photo. A fragmented body, she is emphatically *not* its subject. In a picture on the album's next page, little Miriam holds a black hand whose body is cropped by the left edge of the frame.

Through these images the film invites us to believe we are observing Miriam discovering herself propped on the maid. And thus it aims melodramatically to account for her emerging political consciousness, an effect whose cause remains otherwise obscure. Miriam's identity, like her childhood, and like her self-image, has always been, as it is now, propped on that of black women, just as her household is sustained by their labor. Equally important, this propping must remain invisible. Likewise, the maid has remained invisible in memory, requiring this indexical trace of her presence to restore her to Miriam's history. In the film's structural logic, this recourse to indexical document allows Miriam to place herself in the historical context of racial difference and to understand herself as having a stake in the public struggle that goes on around her household. Significantly, the photographs' function for Miriam seems analogous to the way television anchors the film's fiction to the real of its own indexicality, guaranteeing that the memory it restores is authentic. Paradoxically, while this film emphasizes the maid's restoration to the picture in the family album, its overarching narrative drive will eventually—and distortingly—install Miriam within the historical "picture" of black resistance.

Captivated, like Miriam herself, by the power of visual impressions—images from the past—the film seems unable to overcome its own drive to construct Odessa as a permanent and fixed image across which it can elaborate its own project of recording day-to-day resistance. Like its white female protagonist, whose gaze contemplates the black women, the film compulsively frames them as pictures or shoves them to the edge of the screen. In the rigidly coded topography of this interior, whites alternate between prolonged contemplation of the mute surface of the black face and near oblivious glances. These glances catch the black body as a shadow at the edge of the frame or see it in instrumental fragments, hands washing dishes or polishing silver, for example, or arms extending a tray.

In this defensively self-enclosed world, whites freely examine mute blacks, who studiously appear oblivious to the discourse they are overhearing. This is the tension played out in the Christmas dinner scene, where Norman's mother (Gleaves Azar)—the bad Mrs. Thompson against whom the daughter-in-law emerges as heroic—makes a speech about the domino effect of civil rights protest: "Next year you wouldn't even be able to have this Christmas dinner, without having the maids sitting here at the table with you." This scene calls attention to the perverse intimacy and the privileges of ignorance that hold this interior together, since the two maids are right at hand, serving food all around this table.

The Thompsons' changing world registers, on one hand, in TV's moving images of a mass movement and, on the other, in the family photo album. By contrast to the TV, photos are still, silent, private memorials that may serve as fetishes as well as repositories of private interpretations of the past. But the film also makes a visual metaphor out of movement and motion, political action and its image in pictures. In this connection, the full visual significance of the film's closing sequence comes to light. We leave Odessa, again in medium close-up, lined up with the mass of singing women who have just faced down a white mob at the carpool garage. So we return to the still, individualized image and to a mass black voice on the sound track. Odessa's act of resistance is reframed as *the image* of resistance. Through her, the film has put a face on resistance, to be sure. But that face is a picture in a metaphoric family album organized around Miriam; this scene also commemorates the moment when she leaves her husband's side—literally and figuratively—and emerges from the white mob to join Odessa and the other black women, in a kind of conflation of feminist and antiracist impulses. By putting Miriam in the picture, this moment offers the film's most fantasmatic revision of history.

Historian Jennifer Fuller has noted that Rosa Parks, whom the film's producers had invited to its premiere, indicated that "'to my knowledge there were no white women who actually drove in the carpools.'" According to Fuller, the film's production company, New Visions Pictures, responded by asserting that Miriam was meant to represent "an amalgam of white men and women who took various actions in support of the boy-cott. . . . If white women didn't drive, then we have documented evidence that white men did." Fuller concludes that the film "avoided considerable challenges to its credibility by depending on the idea that women are more capable of interracial cooperation than men, and by shifting the story from docudrama to drama, from public space to domestic space."[19] It thus seems emphatically connected to the lure of a "feminist alibi." Stunningly, we see the same alibi effect perpetuated in *The Help,* which radically distinguishes Skeeter from her racist white friends, who are decidedly not feminist.

Marked as it is by the focus pulling through which *The Long Walk Home* has persistently dramatized the notion of the field of vision, of perspective itself, the film's last sequence alternates between individualizing and collectivizing, or "massifying," visual gestures. So, its conclusion offers us a final and monumental image to commemorate its own, and Miriam's, visual apprenticeship. She, the film, and, by extension, the spectator have learned to distinguish one black face from the mass and to reorient our visual field around it as representative.

As this last sequence concludes, the film zooms in on Odessa. Her stoic, tear-streaked face fills the frame, and she is effectively isolated from the line of black women around her. A cut brings her into view from the side, and the next shot reveals that it is from Miriam's point of view that we study Odessa's face. Miriam directs our gaze to Odessa and symbolically allows all the other women to fade away, clearing the way for a direct exchange of looks between the two women. The adult Mary Catherine observes in voice-over, speaking of the moment when her mother "stepped over the line," the color line, putting herself in their picture: "It would be years before I understood what standing in that line meant. To my mother, and, as I grew older, to me." This concluding—and conclusive—voice-over emphasizes that the film's, and our own, access to Miriam and Odessa's relationship, opaque though it may be, comes through the mediation of this curiously doubled child narrator.

If the incident becomes fully intelligible to the daughter only after years, we must imagine it as stored, as an image she revisits the way her mother revisits the family album. It is almost as if the film believes the same to be true of white interpretations of civil rights: this is to be understood through private retrospection. Thus, the film shares a historical perspective that television scholar Mimi White uncovers in the 1990s television repre-sentations of postwar social change through family dramas. The "tacit explanatory frameworks" they provide for subsequent gains on the fronts of civil rights and of feminism, she contends, are "based in the temporal structures of historical narrativity. These are in turn embedded in more particularized story trajectories which displace and reconstrue these inter-ests in relation to individual, fictional characters."[20] Mediatized memories, then, function melodramatically through retrospective recognition and understanding of moments that have remained unanalyzed.

The Long Walk Home's perspective on change is unwaveringly particular-ized in its attachment to its white female characters, from whose individ-ual points of view it aims to construct a generalized, collective—but still white—gaze. And the voice-over reinforces the steadfastness of the film's emphasis on the particular: "50,000 people boycotted the buses. I knew one." Mary Catherine and her mother, like the film itself, come to "know" about the African Americans who carried out this boycott and the sub-sequent struggles it propelled by a process of subtraction—isolating one representative.

This last sequence produces a near-perfect reversal of the process through which Miriam has moved from the photographic record of private history into solidarity with collective action in the public sphere of history. Odessa comes to stand as a synecdoche for a population and a movement, cut to the measure of private subjective memory, almost as a fetish. The film concludes by offering us Odessa's frozen image before it fades to black under a sound track of voices singing "Marching Off to Zion" and Martin Luther King making a speech. Reduced to pure voice, the black masses become music, organized around the representative cadences of Dr. King. Almost reverentially, the film consigns Odessa back to the image, evanescing her back into the mass black voice, which appears here as the sound track to white enlightenment.

Like *Love Field, The Long Walk Home* elaborates shifts in white conscious-ness through accidents, unforeseen circumstances that establish connec-tions that usher in solidarity. Such encounters seem to be governed entirely by chance, and the relationships they establish develop through the tropes of melodrama: coincidences, failed communication, missed opportunities, sudden revelations, conversions, and undermotivated insights.

Both these cinematic accounts anchor their interracial melodramas in feminine and feminist sensibilities. In "stepping over the line," Miriam and her daughter literally cross a gender line as well as a racial one. As the boycott intensifies, the public and private domains polarize along gender lines, since Miriam acts in direct opposition to her husband. Narratively, the film articulates the gender and racial conflicts together, as it projects a screen memory across this history. Like Miriam, Lurene develops a relationship that challenges and finally undermines the authority of her sexist and racist husband. We need to ask what representational work these complex and contradictory white women, figured as protofeminists, perform, particularly since this scenario has proven so durable and persistent, as *The Help* emphatically demonstrates. Strikingly, each film seems obliged to repeat the scenarios that produce the Poitier effect: the white protagonist gets credit for a change catalyzed through encounters with blackness.

These are melodramas of sight. Miriam's epiphany emerges structurally from her examination of a photograph of herself. Contemplating it, she retrospectively constructs the whole picture, restoring to memory the forgotten—because invisible—other in the frame. Lurene, likewise, comes to see racial oppression once she finds herself the object of the white gaze. With Paul she constitutes a phobic image in the visual field of the dominant gaze. In each case, then, the heroine learns to see the broader picture by putting herself, as it were, in the picture. While these films' melodramatic strategies enable them to raise certain questions, they also foreclose others: How do relationships elaborate themselves historically and in social—rather than private and isolated—contexts? How do private affective dramas intersect with social struggles?

White women get deployed both as symptomatic of white consciousness and as emissaries toward blackness. Without wanting to diminish the agency of white women in the 1950s and 1960s, we might want to ask what 1990s—and contemporary—gender politics and ideologies must forget in order to produce confident assertions of feminism's "natural" alliance with civil rights activism and with progressive racial politics. In their emphasis on feminist awakening, these films imagine the white woman entering history as the subject of social change, as *The Help* does, in a quite unreconstructed manner, in 2011. These feminists serve as a forceful alibi for their race, rewriting its history as redemptive screen memory.

Fantasmatic Ethnography

In the fantasmatic ethnography that *The Help*—like the book at its center—constructs, black domestics become native informants on white middle-class life. Its framing voice-over from Aibileen Clark (Viola Davis) means to secure our sense of this black knowledge. However, because the film so quickly slips from this frame into a sharp focus on its white protagonist, Skeeter Phelan (Emma Stone), we never really get a full sense of the maids' knowledge, much less of the texture of the lives they live beyond white spectatorship. As in the 1990s films it echoes, *The Help*'s central story is a pedagogical one: Skeeter has to learn how to navigate in Jim Crow culture so that she can make private contact with black maids and collect their testimony for a book that will offer their perspective on domestic service in white homes. She has to carry out this project without endangering her subjects, and then she has to learn to depart from Jackson, Mississippi, leaving the maids who have enlightened her behind. But it is not as if Skeeter's coming to grasp the "rules" of Jim Crow, which allows her to complete the book, makes those rules go away.

The Help mostly replicates its white protagonist's untroubled assumption that she can capture the voices of the domestics and that she can transparently translate black women's authentic experiences for white audiences. This film seems unable to maintain its distance from its "feminist" heroine, as it folds its own project over on the fictional book project at its center, in its fantasy of rewriting history so that feminism bridges the segregated worlds of Jackson, Mississippi, in 1963—the year of Medgar Evers's assassination—through bonds among women.

Like the best-selling Kathryn Stockett novel (2009) of the same title on which it is based, this film imagines that Skeeter's budding feminism both depends on and guarantees her antiracism. Installing Skeeter squarely on the side of the civil rights movement, it casts her against her racist white girlfriends, all of whom, apparently, like her, have attended the University of Mississippi (Ole Miss), but none of whom share her protofeminist attitude. Strikingly, given the film's setting in 1963, it is hard to imagine that it can forget that at least some of them—and certainly Skeeter—might have been on campus for the riots that ensued when James Meredith integrated that school in 1962! Except for Skeeter, these women went to college to find husbands, and they quit to get married. They do not love or care for their children; and they especially harm their daughters, damaging their self-esteem and inhibiting their autonomy. Their resolute sexism and racism remain not only inextricably bound together but also mutually explanatory.

The insufficiency of a melodramatic framework that strictly aligns the "good" with feminism and progressive racial politics and the "bad" with sexism and racism reemerges powerfully in the *The Help*. As Patricia A. Turner argues in an op-ed column that appeared in the *New York Times*, this structure remains very problematic: "The housewives of Jackson treat each other, their parents and their husbands with total callousness. In short, they are bad people, and therefore they are racists." "There's a problem, though, with that message" she continues. "Jim Crow segregation survived long into the 20th century because it was kept alive by white Southerners with value systems and personalities we would applaud. It's the fallacy of *To Kill a Mockingbird*."[21]

But to see how seamlessly this film deploys the strategy of immunizing Skeeter from racism through its depiction of the antifeminist and racist positions of her milieu, we need to examine its central tropes of metonymy—or its uneasy proximities. Two sites of racial intersection that *The Help* highlights are toilets and television. White Jackson culture is unsettled by the way TV coverage threatens Jim Crow, in a powerful echo of *The Long Walk Home*. But this film also highlights its obsession with separate bathrooms, a phobia arising from the intimate proximity domestic service installs at the heart of Jim Crow. This obsession most especially grips Hilly Holbrook (Bryce Dallas Howard), the film's most demonized foil for Skeeter's liberalism. Hilly's primary project is to make sure that *they* "take their business outside," and she drafts an initiative that the White Citizens' Council endorses, which enjoins white home owners to build "separate but equal" outdoor facilities for domestics. Significantly, when we first see this character she is sitting on her toilet marking the toilet paper roll with a pencil, so that she can determine whether her maid Minny Jackson (Octavia Spencer, who received the Academy Award for Best Supporting Actress for the role) has used her bathroom.

This film's pseudoethnographic account, beginning with Aibileen introducing its principal characters, brings the toilet to the fore from the start. She announces that among her primary tasks as maid is "taking care of white babies," "getting them to the toilet before their Mama's even outta bed." Among the first scenes with her charge, Mae Mobley, is a toilet training moment—a success the child's mother fails to acknowledge. But a key plot point overlays the maids' domestic knowledge and white bathroom phobias. At a bridge party, Hilly—obviously needing the bathroom she refuses to use—loudly encourages her host, Elizabeth Leefolt (Ahna O'Reilly), to improve the value of her house by making an outdoor bathroom for Aibileen.

Not long after this moment, Hilly fires Minny for using the indoor bathroom during a dangerous storm. Aibileen's voice-over returns to give a full account of the tornado that emerged from the storm—"18 people died that day." A cut establishes a parallel that highlights this indictment of Hilly's callous brutality toward Minny: we see Aibileen hunkered down in a closet protecting Mae Mobley in a scene from which, not incidentally, the child's mother is absent. In the very next sequence, however, we confront the uncomfortable image of Aibileen's legs as she sits on the toilet in the freestanding, shack-like bathroom her employers have just constructed for her. As the toddler hovers outside, making ready to burst in on her, we are impressed by the failure of something like "black privacy" in this film. But we are also uneasily aware that the film and the novel are framed by a child's curiosity about Jim Crow as a kind of primal scene. This is perhaps not surprising, since both the director and the author were both born in Jackson in 1969, a "post–civil rights" moment in which Jim Crow practices persisted.

In a cringe-inducing 2009 article for the *Daily Mail,* Kathryn Stockett outlines the autobiographical impetus that propels her story, very much as the loss of the family maid, Constantine, drives Skeeter's project: "In 1970s Mississippi I didn't have a single black friend or black neighbor. Yet one of the closest people to me was Demetrie, our family's maid." She goes on to evoke the image from which the film's bathroom scene originates: "When our family took holidays at the coast . . . We'd stay in our cousin's tiny one-bedroom house and Demetrie had a special cot and a toilet outside."[22] Obviously, to the white child's perspective that shapes this film, like the novel before it, the toilet is central—as are issues of intimacy, privacy, and boundaries.

The phobia that the film identifies as structuring these Jim Crow obsessions seems to have much to do with fear of the intimate proximity on which domestic service is founded. Public/private boundaries, too, seem always at risk. This is where the maids' uniforms come in. In the private home, as in the public space of the grocery store, for example, the uniform functions as a boundary: it makes the maid both invisible and unthreatening because it metonymically signifies white sponsorship.[23] Stockett underlines that "that white uniform was her 'pass' to get into white places with us—the grocery store, the state fair, the movies."

Evoking paranoid white anxieties surrounding intimate proximity—dirt, exposure, and shame—*The Help* remains obsessed with the toilet. It returns with considerable force as a structuring trope when Minny, the film's most boisterously—and satisfyingly—aggressive character, revisits her former employer to offer one of her signature chocolate pies. Encountering her friend Aibileen and another maid, Yule Mae Davis (Aunjanue Ellis), Minny asserts that she has some "business" to take care of. This business, the film will later reveal, bears a central significance, disclosing as it does a crucial and unstable metonymy—that of ingestion and excretion. Minny, whom Hilly has always prized for her culinary skills—for which other white housewives have envied her employer—has added a "special" ingredient to the conciliatory pie: her own shit. Thus, she has literalized the vulgarity "Eat shit!" But whose fantasy is this? Especially striking in this image is the self-abjection required for Minny to abject Hilly. *The Help* will keep this question in view.

Perhaps the most interesting feature of this film is the way that the tropes it deploys depend centrally on metonymies—both visual and discursive—that structure the segregated intimacy of its characters' world. Particular attention to these metonymic structures that both collapse and maintain interracial distance may allow us some insight into the film's drive, following the fictional book project at its center, to gain access to the black domestics' "situated knowledge" of white privacy and secrecy. In its own peculiar way, *The Help* seems alert to what may be a structuring anxiety of this white domestic sphere: the intimate knowledge the maids possess and fear of its exposure.

But if white privacy remains perpetually at risk, black privacy eludes this film altogether. It cannot imagine black privacy except as invaded or exposed. While Skeeter does enter Aibileen's home space, almost never does anyone else appear there. Nor do we get much sense of its surrounding context. Skeeter's encounters with Aibileen in her home are ethnographic, but with a specific twist: the maid is a native informant about white women bosses and their children. Perfectly replicating the prevailing attitude of the white women employers, never does Skeeter ask about any aspect of black life apart from domestic service. Like the diegetic book that Skeeter is "writing"—or transcribing, or editing—the film concerns the question of how white women look to the black women who take care of their children and their dirt. Only once do we gain entry into a black home without Skeeter's sponsorship: this is when Aibileen takes refuge with Minny on the night of Medgar Evers's assassination.

Significantly, this film's points of greatest visual interest—and these are few—involve curious montage effects, striking and strange metonymies. These effects establish uneasy and unstable proximities that echo the anxieties its white characters, like its producer, struggle to manage. Close to the film's midpoint, an especially dense nexus begins to form through montage. At a pool party, Elizabeth callously remarks about her daughter's endless appetite, prompting Skeeter to remind her that the little girl is overhearing this—directly referencing the position of "the help" in relation to their employers' conversation about "separate but equal" toilets. This scene leads in to Skeeter's prank: she announces Hilly's *coat* drive in the Junior League newsletter as a *commode* drive, leading to the deposit of numerous toilets on her friend's lawn. This moment neatly condenses the film's metonymic threads around the fragile public/private divide, as the toddler Mae Mobley mounts a commode and proudly exhibits her toilet training. Her mortified mother, Elizabeth, swoops in to spank her violently, and Aibileen follows up to compensate the child with her mantra: "You is kind, you is smart, you is important." Here again the film reminds us of the metonymic alignment of the white female child and the black maid, and it invites us to share this regressive point of view.

At this point, sound bridges across the cut from Elizabeth's disapproving glance at her maid and child to a TV image. Medgar Evers's voice enjoins black consumers not to shop on Capitol Street. As the cut reveals the TV image, the console fitting to the edges of the frame, we are aware of watching along with diegetic spectators: Skeeter and the family servants, Jameso (Henry Carpenter) and Pascagoula (Roslyn Ruff), who are standing on either side of the armchair she occupies. As the camera brings them into view, Skeeter's mother, Charlotte (Allison Janney), appears, descending the stairs to cross the room and extinguish the TV, saying, "Don't encourage them like that!" (Of course, we remember Mr. Thompson's identical attitude in *The Long Walk Home*.) As the servants quietly flee, Skeeter insists, "That is *national* news!"

The split between mother and daughter—like that between Skeeter and her friends—maps onto the divide between the national perspective that TV upholds, and that the civil rights movement solicits and promotes, and the regional angle the backward whites embrace. Significantly, though the film "remembers" Evers through this televisual moment and through its focus on the night of his murder, June 11–12, 1963, it "forgets" that President Kennedy gave a landmark speech at 8:00 P.M. that evening in which he responded to Governor George Wallace's attempt to prevent the integration of the University of Alabama. So, we find a symptomatic splitting in this film's memory of the very specific period it represents; this kind of splitting, I would suggest, marks all the films under consideration here.

In the very next sequence, Evers's assassination has just occurred. Aibileen runs to Minny's house, where the radio news describes the killing. In this, the film's only moment of black domestic privacy not sponsored by Skeeter's agency, Minny declares, "We're livin' in hell. Trapped. Our kids trapped." But they also worry about their connection to Skeeter's project: "We aren't doing civil rights. We're just telling stories, like they happened." A cut metonymically aligns Skeeter with Minny and Aibileen as we find her perusing print accounts—in *Life* magazine and in newspapers—of the assassination and its aftermath while she delays handing in her housekeeping tips column at her own newspaper employer.

The turning point of *The Help*'s plot—that is, when Skeeter acquires enough informants to complete her book—comes shortly after Evers's assassination and just after the arrest for theft of Yule Mae, Minny's replacement at Hilly's. Significantly, this sequence opens at the lunch counter, with Skeeter remaining separated from her friends who sit at a table. Henry advises her to visit Aibileen's immediately. Once there, she finds a congregation of maids willing to contribute to her volume—collectively motivated not by Evers's assassination, it seems, so much as by Yule Mae's very public, very brutal arrest. History still haunts the edges of this pseudo-ethnographic exchange. We remember that Minny is propelled into the book project when she barges in on Skeeter and Aibileen to announce that "they" have thrown a firebomb at Medgar Evers's carport. But history, once evoked, folds back in to the domestic melodramas.

In a striking montage, we move from the moment of the maids' testimonies to find Celia Foote (Jessica Chastain)—perpetually excluded from the Junior League circle—being refused entrance to Elizabeth's home on yet another bridge day to which she has not been invited. Adding to the strain of the moment, while she waits outside as if to be sent to the service entrance, she waves a chocolate pie made by Minny, who has recently become her maid. Thus, the scene establishes a striking metonymy between Minny and her new employer, the only woman in town who is so far from Hilly's circuit that she is oblivious to her bad references. (Hilly will assume Minny has shared her awful secret with Celia, forging an interracial alliance against her.) And this moment of exclusion leads to a scene of instruction in which Minny enlightens Celia about her position in the hierarchy of these Junior Leaguers: she is an outcast because she has married Hilly's ex-boyfriend, Johnny, and because she is "white trash." Minny's privileged insider knowledge of this white society allows Celia finally to understand her position and, eventually, to challenge it. In this same scene, Celia rewards Minny's revelations by urging her to fight back against her abusive husband. Again, *The Help* asserts a link between feminism and interracial solidarity.

From this moment, the film cuts to aerial shots, as if to establish some broad commonality across Jackson, and the voice-over of a TV news anchor narrates a moment in the Kennedy funeral—in a striking resonance with *Love Field*. History becomes sutured into private family life as we again see the TV console in the Phelan living room. Above the family gathered around the set, the servants Pascagoula and Jameso watch from the stairs; this time their copresence goes unchallenged.

A weird montage takes us from this scene of racial proximity around national tragedy to a shot of Aibileen's wall: now it is revealed that a picture of John F. Kennedy hangs beside the photo of her son and the image of Jesus that we have seen before. Again, pure metonymy—visual sleight of hand—means to establish the political solidarity here. As the camera reveals Aibileen, Minny, and Skeeter talking nervously about how "it's all gone crazy," Minny finally discloses the secret of the "awful, terrible" that she has done to Hilly. This scene cements their solidarity in the shared secret that will prevent Hilly from unmasking them as the "authors" of this book.

In the end, once Aibileen and Minny have furnished the feminist white writer with their stories of the world of domestic service, these women cheer her on in her escape to New York City. The stories she has borrowed and published have catapulted her into a career in publishing among the enlightened white people of the North—where she clearly belongs, in the film's fantasy. Her racial and gender politics are too progressive for this backward context—no man in this town will have her. At the film's teary conclusion, Skeeter gets to move on. She passes beyond the history in which the maids remain mired—while wishing her well. Her black interlocutors remain locked in Jackson's violently enforced stasis, awaiting the arrival of historical change. Significantly, *The Help* can no more see beyond Skeeter's departure than it could imagine the private lives of its black domestics.

What's a Mother to Do?

Pleasantville differs from the three films discussed above in that it traces a different trajectory of exchange between history and fiction as it explores TV's version of the 1950s. Moving us from the world of the news to the "refuge" of a family sitcom, since its protagonists literally put themselves in the picture television delivers, the film emphasizes questions of agency within its fictional world. Through its narrative progress, sitcom becomes melodrama, and it highlights the elements of fantasy and sexuality that *The Long Walk Home* rigorously excludes and that *Love Field* and *The Help* manage through their familial frameworks.

Set against the other films that foreground television's role in the recording of history in the making, *Pleasantville* playfully exhibits television's fascination with itself as an archive of itself. Indeed, it opens with an "establishing shot" that delivers us not a physical location but a television screen. Surfing channels, the film finally settles on the one that announces, "You're watching TV Time, the only network playing lots of old stuff in nothing but black and white." Title sequences of real sitcoms pass before us, concluding with *Pleasantville.* Director Gary Ross describes the channel-surfing sequence as "our version of Nick at Nite."[24] Immersing us in "TV

Time," the sequence emphasizes that this televisual history endlessly replays a loop that overlays, collapses, and mingles "then-ness" and "now-ness." In its permanent contemporaneity, TV constantly reproduces itself as inter-generational memory.[25] In the Nick at Nite world, where we can all share a common TV childhood, a son may go back and rewrite the period of his mother's youth by manipulating its iconic television tropes.

In an early sequence, *Pleasantville*'s adolescent protagonist, David (Tobey Maguire), watches his favorite 1950s sitcom while his mother (Jane Kaczmarek) argues with her ex-husband about custody arrangements for the coming weekend. As the film confines her in the cramped kitchen's doorway beside the TV David is watching, she becomes an image as dis-tant as the one on the screen. Subsequently, a series of shot/reverse shots captures David speaking lines along with his *Pleasantville* family, George (William H. Macy) and Betty (Joan Allen) Parker and their kids, Bud and Mary Sue, in a dialogue that runs parallel to his mother's one-sided conver-sation. This sequence concludes as Betty Parker utters a question familiar to anyone who watched TV in the 1960s: "What's a mother to do?"

That line ironically establishes a parallel between the fantasmatic mother and the real one, and it foregrounds the radical difference in their worlds. David's mother's problems would be unthinkable in the world of *Pleasant-ville*. But Betty's maternal question will subtend some major developments in the sitcom onto which David has been projecting his nostalgic yearnings. *Pleasantville*'s fantasy plays out the "family romance," which, in Freud's account, emerges once the social begins to figure the outside of the house-hold and the child can imagine wishing to trade his parents for better ones, "grander ones."[26] As David magically enters the sitcom world of 1958, the year of his mother's birth (we learn that she is forty when he returns to the film's contemporary moment), his fantasy takes on another inflection; his journey into the sitcom also entails a variant on the "primal scene," in which he places himself in the moment just before her birth, rather than his own, to master and change it. As David discovers trauma within *Pleas-antville*'s world, the film rewrites the sitcom as melodrama, where gender and chromatics provide an unstable allegory of racial difference.

This film takes as its subject a kind of "prosthetic memory." Cultural historian Alison Landsberg uses this term to define our "mass-mediated experience of a traumatic event of the past." "Prosthetic memories," she argues, "are neither purely individual nor entirely collective," but are instead "privately felt public memories that develop after an encounter with a mass cultural representation of the past, when new images and ideas come into contact with a person's own archive of experience."[27] *Pleasantville*, we might say, performs, at the level of both form and content, the work of prosthetic memory that formally—if largely unconsciously—shapes *Love Field* and *The Long Walk Home*.

Deploying the fantasy of an interactive relationship with the television medium, *Pleasantville* deposits 1990s teenagers directly into the world of a 1950s family sitcom. Its development emphasizes the central importance of race relations and racism to sitcoms of the period, precisely by highlighting how thoroughly their world was sanitized of all racial reference. This is why the struggle the film stages between the black-and-white characters and the "colored" ones resonates so effectively as it pointedly recalls what the shows themselves had so successfully banished. Television historian David Marc reminds us that "blacks virtually disappeared from television comedy during the developing years of the medium," from the cancellation of *Beulah* (ABC, 1950–53) in 1953 to the premiere of *Julia* (NBC, 1968–71).[28] Thus the heyday of the white suburban family sitcom roughly coincides with the height of the civil rights period—and of Poitier's career—as the run of *Father Knows Best* (CBS, 1954–55, 1958–60; NBC, 1955–58) indicates.[29] Marc describes these shows as follows: "Drugless and anti-erotic (though never asexual, for explicit courtship instructions abound), this suburb of dreams is devoid of dangerous strangers, public transportation, economic fluctuation, and other anxiety-producing phenomena associated with the urban experience" (52). The tension between TV's commitment to "liveness" and its commitment to serial repetition echoes in the stark contrast between violent upheavals and conflicts in the news and the reliably static sameness in its sitcom series.

David's sitcom becomes a habitable world to which he and his sister, Jennifer (Reese Witherspoon), are transported just after they have broken their television's remote control in a squabble. A TV repairman magically appears before their television set and offers them a "special" remote. As he departs, we notice that his truck displays a luridly colored image of a family of four crowded around the eerie light of a TV set, above a logo that hints at a sinister underside to the 1950s sitcom universe: "We'll fix you for good!" Of course, the repairman "fixes" David and Jennifer, and they in turn become the agents who "fix" Pleasantville for good. This is a world that can change only through the accident of external agents entering it.

Significantly, the agent of transformation here is himself recycled from 1960s TV. As the repairman, Don Knotts immediately conjures his iconic role as Barney Fife on *The Andy Griffith Show,* which ran from 1960 to 1965 in black and white, and then in color until 1968. Thus, it underwent the same shift to color on the air as does the world of Pleasantville in the film's course. Equally significant, *The Andy Griffith Show* echoes the fictional *Pleasantville* in its long-running syndication and its idealized isolation from social conflict; Mayberry remains undisturbed by racial difference. Curiously, and pointedly, in the context of this film, it even lacks teenagers to cause trouble.

Before David literally enters the picture, *Pleasantville*'s televisual world has constituted his fantasmatic refuge from his contemporary environment. A dizzying montage sequence of zoom shots on his high school administrators and teachers presents their litany of future disasters facing today's youth: diminishing economic opportunity, global warming, the chances of contracting AIDS. All of these dangers are emphatically unimaginable in the Pleasantville to which David retreats at home. In its world, just as there is no weather, there is no economic change or deprivation, no sex, and no toilets.

Pleasantville offers a retreat into borrowed media nostalgia, returning to the previous generation's youth. Jennifer and David enter its world in 1958, the year of their mother's birth. In the academic year 1957–58 the Little Rock Nine integrated Little Rock Central High School. Once they had completed their difficult first year, the city's school board closed all three of its high schools for the coming academic year, thus entirely foreclosing integration. Historical record strikes a sharp contrast with the relative speed and facility of Pleasantville's fictional "integration."

Just as it highlights cable television's landscape of pure contemporaneity, *Pleasantville* also plays with figures of pure ideology. Permanently contemporary, the town of Pleasantville (*Present*ville) harbors no memories and consequently admits no history and no future. Its memory, in effect, remains external, produced by fans like David. And Pleasantville's immobile temporality matches its spatial fixity. There is no outside. Jennifer discovers the perfectly ideologized nature of this world in geography class, when she inquires what is at the end of Main Street. The question baffles her teacher. "The end of it is just the beginning again," she finally replies with smug knowingness.

This is a world without chance or change, as represented by its conventional sitcom episode introductions, which move from the exterior of the family home to the interior front hallway, where George is hanging up his hat and calling out, "Honey, I'm home." Lynn Spigel analyzes this powerful convention in a discussion of *Father Knows Best*: "The exterior shot and dramatic music made the viewer aware that the Anderson home was more than just a private haven, more than just a world of interiors and family relations." "Instead," Spigel continues, "the family home was represented as if it were a public spectacle, a monument commemorating the values of an ideal American town."[30] This is the fantasmatic public/private picture that David and Jennifer will disrupt.

"Colorizing" America

The change over which David symbolically presides, the shift from black and white to color on television, consistently allegorizes integration. Thus, *Pleasantville* links changing gender relations to desegregation through the medium of TV. Against its framework of changelessness recalled, *Pleasantville* plays on the melodramatic idea of accidental, inadvertent transformation. But it also mobilizes and explores the optimistic belief that if we could just change things on TV, we could change them in the world, a theory widely shared in the 1960s—from the NAACP to white critics.[31] Such optimism about television coexists with much darker fantasies about its power; these underlie continually renewed calls for the regulation of television imagery as dangerously invasive of household, family, and children's minds. Some of these anxieties relate to television's capacity for introducing the distant into the intimate domestic sphere, so the protection of the child becomes a stand-in, then as now, for the protection of social privilege and partitioned, or segregated, spaces.[32]

Significantly, we can track the incipient changes in Pleasantville through appearances of color, which are initially linked to unprecedented suggestions of sexuality. Women and girls become the—initially—passive agents, the medium, of these appearances. TV Time has promised that *Pleasantville* offers "a marathon of pure 'family values,' proper nutrition, and safe sex." An image of twin beds, which are ubiquitous in Pleasantville, directly figures this last claim. Double beds will supplant them, toward the film's climax, as wives begin to request them, just as the color TV set emerges to signal the end of black-and-white television culture. When women and eroticism begin to dominate this televisual world, advancing a disturbing tendency toward "colorization," the film cleverly recalls Philip Wylie's overwrought alignment of women and TV in a cultural conspiracy against masculine vigor and authority.[33]

Mary Sue/Jennifer first introduces sex and color to Pleasantville when, on her first date with Skip Martin (Paul Walker), she "pins" him sexually in response to his promise to pin her symbolically (as in going steady) and he panics at the erection that ensues. Skip arrives home stupefied, and he sees a single red rose in the bush outside his house. Once the ball is rolling, color begins to crop up along both metaphoric and metonymic lines. A girl's mother brings her to a doctor for an examination of her bright pink tongue. Later, bright-pink bubble gum appears in a girl's mouth, and Mary Sue lasciviously consumes a bright-red cherry. These images provide a consistently suggestive equation of female sexuality with orality as women and girls begin inadvertently to promote change. A pivotal moment at the film's temporal center definitively figures women and female sexuality as the driving force behind colorization. In a hilarious parody of parental discourse, Mary Sue has just explained the facts of life to Betty. As Betty tests her newfound knowledge in the bathtub, her ecstatic moans seem to bring out color—pink in the bathroom wallpaper, the pastels of soaps and lotions. A cut to an exterior shot of the house permits us to see a tree bursting into flames coinciding with her climax on the sound track.

Until this point Bud has struggled to remain noninterventionist, telling his sister, "You can't alter their universe; they're happy like this." But she insists, "Nobody's happy in a poodle skirt and a sweater set." Through the course of events, Mary Sue develops a retroactive feminist critique, and her assertiveness shifts from the erotic to the analytical and intellectual plane. But when the town's first fire erupts at Betty's sexual awakening, Bud does intervene to teach the firemen how to use their equipment, which they had previously applied only to rescuing treed cats. Thus emerges a perfect primal fantasy: that of getting back to a time before you were born and making a difference.

This incident unleashes a chain reaction, as the progress of events produces "news." Its previous absence is evoked by the image of the paperboy who keeps falling off his bike in the face of any new development. Rather than delivering newspapers, he witnesses and reacts to the "new." In another print-related development, the teens at the soda shop inquire about the content of their books, all of which have to this point remained blank. As soon as Bud summarizes its story, text fills in a copy of *Huckleberry Finn*, notoriously controversial in the 1950s, and sometimes banned, for its offensive racial language.[34] In this scene, the film recalls the competing cultural forms that challenged the 1950s sitcom world.[35] Miles Davis's "So What?" comes through on the jukebox, replacing Dave Brubeck's "Take Five," and thus the scene crosses a musical line in what Krin Gabbard describes as the film's "invisible color coding."[36] Linking books, music, sex, and color as the ground of cultural struggle, *Pleasantville* figures anxiety about change as a fascistic fear of knowledge. This fear culminates in a book burning, an event that also issues in a gendered conflict. Mary Sue, who has sublimated her sluttiness into scholarly impulses through reading D. H. Lawrence, an activity she prefers to going on a date with Skip, rescues a volume of Lawrence, tearing it from her boyfriend's hands.

Strictly speaking, the fire introduces the possibility of an event into the sitcom world, which is based on episodic repetition within the closed domestic arena. Subsequent events, which appear as its direct consequences, will unravel the sitcom world to show the social struggle from which the form works to seal itself off. *Pleasantville*'s critical melodramatization of the sitcom operates through images that continually relate civil rights references to women's desire and agency. As conflict escalates, the film tracks change and its consequences in a strictly gendered framework.

George joins the ominously named Citizens' Council. On the night of the town's first rainstorm, he returns home to find his wife gone. He wanders through the dark empty house, demanding his dinner. But the sitcom plot has ground to a halt. George retreats to the company of other middle-aged men gathered at the bowling alley. Led by Citizens' Council chair Big Bob (J. T. Walsh), they escalate their ongoing discourse about change, identifying a variety of its symptoms, all generated by women: George's missed dinner and Roy's shirt, burned by his wife in the ironing. At this point the sitcom form has spun out of the tight control of its repetitive episodic structure, which consistently restores paternal authority. In response, the men agree to unite and take action through a general meeting for "true citizens" of Pleasantville.

Mother Knows Best?

Betty's refusal to attend this meeting, or to obey any of her husband's demands, demonstrates her developing alienation and resistance, since she has discovered she is "colored" on the night George joins the Citizens' Council. In this pivotal sequence, her failure to respond to his call for refreshments alarms Bud. We follow his hesitant approach to Betty, distraught at the kitchen sink. When he protectively puts his hand on her shoulder, she turns to show her face and hair in full color. "What am I going to do?" she asks plaintively, echoing the sitcom question she has asked over and over in characteristic mock resignation.

Her helpless collapse in anguished tears definitively shatters the sitcom frame as, visually, the space of the kitchen, that center of domestic interiority, seems to split apart. Held in two-shot, her head and Bud's seem to occupy dramatically different planes; hers stands in relief against the grays of the background, while Bud's flattens into the surroundings. Sitcom turns into melodrama, and its transformation is governed by color. In a long, mute sequence, shot in extreme close-up, Bud applies concealing "gray" makeup to her face and arms. While this makeup successfully "normalizes" her look, much exceeds this scene's resolution. The remarkable sensuality of the makeup's application anticipates the sensual delight the soda shop counterman, Bill Johnson (Jeff Daniels), takes in his newfound aptitude for painting and the affair with Betty to which it leads. But this moment also adds an entirely new layer of intimacy between mother and son, one that anticipates David's return to his own mother at the film's conclusion.

At the material level, this sequence's digital compositing reminds the viewer of the film's production. If *Pleasantville* concerns the process of social and representational change, its technical means call attention to the process through which the film takes form. Literally performing an inversion of the historical shift through which color replaces black-and-white stock on film and TV, this film *adds* black and white onto color. In its digital manipulation, color precedes black and white. The images that pass before us, then, register two times, both literally and metaphorically. In its material form, the film itself behaves like a screen memory, which forms a composite of elements from two or more memories and tends to lend striking vividness to apparently banal moments. Such memories derive their force from the memories with which they are overlaid and intermingled, and whose content they partially mask.[37] But this moment also resonates with David's simultaneous occupation of two temporalities, as he puts himself into the picture of a previous generation's media memory.

Of course, this sequence also metaphorically evokes "passing." Bill Johnson will soon convince Betty to stop "passing." In her newly colored state, she poses in the nude for him. This image, uniting color and sex in the nude female body, appears as a mural across the soda shop's window and becomes a central site of public outrage. Through this painting, the men's anxious agitation about the world of the sitcom escaping the father's control converges with striking images that recall the civil rights era. After a temporal ellipsis to the next morning, we discover a sign posted in a store window, "NO COLOREDS," just as we see the newsboy skid to a stop on his bike and fall down in front of the soda shop painting.

Allegorizing race through its color dynamics, and reminding us of white violence toward civil rights militants, the film produces a strikingly defamiliarized vocabulary here. A group of black-and-white boys led by the aptly named Whitey (David Tom) harass and menace Betty in terms that starkly recall white men's abuse and intimidation of black women as well as the eroticized nature of racial terrorism.[38] Strikingly, when Bud intervenes and punches Whitey, Bud himself becomes colored; it is not sexuality so much as the powerful effect of righteous anger on behalf of oppressed victims that seems to "colorize" the characters.

As violence escalates, its most compelling images emerge around the soda shop, a site that simultaneously recalls youth culture of the 1950s and segregated lunch counters as an arena of struggle. When the citizens of Pleasantville discover the nude that Bill has painted on the shop window, they gather outside in an angry mob. A handheld camera pans the mural, then the crowd, which it explores in abrupt, jerky motions. Its use of rack focus helps to suggest the effort to capture a moving crowd on film. Such a view might suggest the position of demonstrators facing an angry white mob. But the telephoto lens helps to hold us at a distance while allowing us an imaginative vantage point from within the crowd. Our view remains at some distance—outside and just beyond the confrontation. This perspective might also suggest that of TV cameras following agitated white crowds in civil rights confrontations, although news technology of the period would not have included this tool. It is as if the film were attempting to inscribe a point of view that was largely unattainable in news footage of the period it depicts.[39]

Scenes of vandalism in which the white men smash the window, destroying the offending image, and then trash the soda shop are shot in slow motion, highlighting the destructive frenzy. Significantly, when the teens and Bill and Betty return to the shop, the jukebox remains illuminated in neon colors, and they continue to play rock and roll on it in defiance of the Citizens' Council's new ordinances, which prohibit any music other than "Johnny Mathis, Perry Como, Jack Jones, the marches of John Philip Sousa and the Star Spangled Banner," as well as any color other than black, white, or gray, and any beds wider than thirty-eight inches.

Violating the new ordinances with another painting, Bill brings about the trial that finally resolves the color conflict. But now he moves into the domain of public art. On the wall of the police station, the law's concrete embodiment, he paints a mural that memorializes recent events. In one of the film's more clever conjunctions, social conflict appears as a battle of representations, as this mural's images present the repressed of the 1950s family sitcom that the men of the Citizens' Council are determined to inhabit. Equally important, Bill's style of painting evokes a long tradition of political mural art, stretching back to Diego Rivera's work of the 1930s. Director Gary Ross honors this tradition, and he reaches beyond the fictional frame of his film to commission Frank Romero, a Los Angeles Chicano artist, to paint the police station mural.[40]

Even as Bill and Bud finally emerge as "spokesmen" through the mural they protect against vandalism, *Pleasantville* makes girls and women the primary agents of the "colorization" that propels change. David/Bud still operates as a familiar sitcom figure: the white father who acts as anchor and commentator, whose bafflement gives way to wisdom as he interprets the behavior of other characters for himself and for us. Originally characterized by his sister Jennifer as a "hopeless geek," in posture and demeanor Bud recalls that preeminent sitcom paternal commentator, Ozzie Nelson.

But even as Bud's role requires him primarily to react to the cultural agency of the women and the girls who drive the changes around him, he also serves as paternal adviser to George, his TV dad, and as mentor to Bill Johnson, those even more perfect incarnations of the 1950s sitcom male. In highlighting the hapless befuddlement of its men, *Pleasantville* replays the gender dynamic that was at work in the sitcoms it recalls.[41] Reimagining that dynamic as a kind of protofeminist tendency, in the process it recognizes how the 1950s shows were registering and processing anxieties about women's agency.

Another figure of unstable ideological authority shadows the shaky sitcom dads in the film, as the TV itself intervenes through the repairman who appears on Bud's own set to reprimand him. Fuming, he performs just the kind of manic and impotent hysteria that characterized Barney Fife. Through this hysterical paternal figure, exhibiting the failure of his authority, this film also suggests an anxious 1950s spectator, fearful that the social world of difference could intervene in the domestic sphere through the TV. By the film's end, figuratively, TV has finally accomplished the repairman's threat to expel David from its "paradise." But it has also liquidated his nostalgia for the fictional world of 1950s innocence, as it erases the strictly black-and-white world of the sitcom. *Pleasantville* advances a wishful fantasy of eradicating racial conflict with the ease of "color adjustment" on a new TV set. More important, it stages the fantasy that if we contemporary viewers had only been in the historical picture, things might have been different.

If *Pleasantville* satisfyingly undermines paternal authority in its replay of the domestic sitcom's central generational issues, it does so by inverting the positions of parents and children. When David returns to his contemporary world, he emerges as a counselor to his own divorced mother, who has just broken off with her much younger boyfriend. He wipes his mother's tears and her smeared mascara, in a striking echo—and reversal—of his gestures with Betty after she has become "colorized." In each case, he helps the mother to regain her composure by fixing her makeup. Now he offers his mother life lessons, reassuring her by challenging her conviction that her life violates the norms of how "things are supposed to be": "They're not supposed to be *anything*." Having followed his own nostalgia for how things "are supposed to be" into a world where he is not supposed to belong, David has found that things there really were not *supposed* to be as he had supposed. Once this sentimental journey transforms into an ideological one, the generational framework collapses, just as temporality has evaporated (we realize that the duration of the events that develop the town's crisis and resolution has amounted to a brief compressed interval in "real" life).

David arrives home ahead of his mother, who needs him to put her back on track as a single woman in the 1990s. He is the one who can the answer the question, "What's a mother to do?" This poignant sequence seems to suggest that the best "father" might be an adolescent boy, and—even more perversely—that David might make a better boyfriend than the one his mother has just dumped. And what makes him so suitable is that his masculinity has been shaped through the benefit of history, as he straddles the moment of his mother's birth and his own proper historical moment.[42] But, in casting the white male as a sensitive 1990s type of guy who supports the women in their bid for more agency, more color, more feeling, *Pleasantville* may not have come as far from Ozzie Nelson as it has wished. And certainly, by this point, it has pushed issues of social color out of the picture, displacing them with the intergenerational melodrama to which it emphatically returns here.

And what of Mary Sue/Jennifer, who remains behind in the television world? By her own account, when she heads off for college in "Springfield," she's finished with the "slut thing," having traded sex for books and having come into her own intelligence through the exercise of her sexuality. But the film still leaves us to wonder what could possibly be in this for Jennifer. According to *Pleasantville*'s terms, she stays in the sitcom world because it is only there that she has a chance to attend college. But the film's last image of her shows her flirting with a handsome boy on the steps of the library. As a 1950s coed, she faces the statistical fate of dropping out for marriage. So within the film's generally refreshing circular logics, she gets marooned in the past David has "fixed" for her, and he gets the future. This splitting into two temporalities would seem to mark a residue of the traumatic history the film has sought to work through.

Pleasantville sharply highlights questions of race relations and racism as centrally important to the sanitized world of 1950s sitcoms, precisely by emphatically underscoring their absence. Its world juxtaposes color to black and white, thus both displacing and allegorizing the racial opposition of black to white that continues to organize much of our thinking about race. In the process, however, it may invite us to forget that struggles of the sort we witness in *Pleasantville* do not take place over just any change at all, or over change for its own sake. Paradoxically, in making visible the particular intersections that intermittently obtained between women's early efforts at liberation and youth culture and civil rights, the film may overgeneralize to the point of losing historical specificity. In casting white women and girls as heroic agents of social change, it may create a universe where color drops out, and race passes beyond the frame once again.

The Feminist Alibi

In the historical revisions to which these interracial melodramas contribute, perhaps women's visibility comes at the price of being transformed from the symptom of whiteness into its alibi. In revisiting the civil rights period, these nostalgic films perform complex representational work. A crucial component of this work makes explicit an understanding of the importance of representations—and especially, given the historical period in question, televisual representations—to social and political struggle. Equally important, these films advance the premise that history itself is a representational struggle that continues through permanent revisions in which popular melodramatic plots and fantasies continue to play a part. And one can find no better evidence to support this claim than the wild success of *The Help*. A persistent racial unconscious linked to the Poitier effect nonetheless underlies the films' critical efforts. In organizing narratives of political enlightenment transformation around white women's encounters with color, these films charge their singularity with representativeness. Whether sentimental or celebratory, this central focus on the progressive woman downplays white resistance to integration in general, since not only white men but also white collective racism and aggression recede into the background behind the protofeminist women protagonists.

Garnering political credit through their feminist sympathies, these films—like the contemporary iteration *The Help* offers—advance familiar false analogies between gender oppression and racial oppression that white consciousness so frequently entertains. Credit gained through this false analogy cannot be so easily transferred; the links the progressive women make between gender ideologies and racial ones do not automatically guar-antee the films' racial politics. As political alibi, then, these white women are symptomatic. Once the symptomatic site of white fantasies about the vulnerability of whiteness to blackness, these revised figures of white fem-ininity serve as the privileged medium of racial exchange in films that cast the protofeminist as a medium for the transformation of racial conscious-ness. These films accomplish this through their classic association of women with the figure of television, the medium for national racial exchange dur-ing the civil rights era. But where television brought social struggle into the private domestic sphere, these films' prosthetic memories of the 1950s and early 1960s rewrite public political conflicts as privatized, family affairs, screens for our fantasies of a better past, retroactively redeemed by a fem-inist future.

3

The Lure of Retrospectatorship

Hitting the False Notes in *Far from Heaven*

In their mass-mediated, "prosthetic" memories of the civil rights period, the films we have been examining screen that history through the prism of an idealized 1960s, which condenses the decade into a post-1968 moment. That idealized 1960s, imagined as already feminist and forgetting or smoothing over the period's conflicts, violence, and contradictions, rescues the 1950s and early 1960s, dissolving their repressions and curing their pathologies—racial segregation and institutionalized gender inequality. In *Far from Heaven* (2002), Todd Haynes is doing something different. He remembers the pathologization of homosexuality that also marked the period's cultural terrain as he opens the horizons of classic maternal melodrama to the world of racial melodrama, as well as to its sexual subtexts. This film represents perhaps the richest and most ambitious of these efforts to mobilize the resources of melodrama and its ironies to map historical cultural tensions.[1]

Most explicitly, this film's media memory pays homage to Douglas Sirk by consistently reworking his signature effects, evoking his 1950s melodramas of heterosexual longing and disappointment. But it deploys these effects in complex negotiations both with television—as cultural institution and as domestic consumer technology—and with a striking iteration of the Poitier effect. While foregrounding Sirk's particular awareness of melodrama's susceptibility to irony, however, *Far from Heaven* proves less critically ambitious in its deployment of the tropes that ground the Poitier effect and the films' engagement with race, as we will see.

Far from Heaven's densely complex approach to its media archive, its "prosthetic memories," may best be described as engaging the viewer in a form of the "retrospectatorship" that Patricia White analyzes in *Uninvited: Classical Hollywood Cinema and Lesbian Representability*. For White, "all spectatorship, insofar as it mobilizes subjective fantasy, revises memory traces and experiences, some of which are memories and experiences of other movies." Thus, "retrospectatorship" allows us to find new angles on our past and present media culture in our repeated viewings of the classical Hollywood movies that continue to fascinate us. White describes the importance of this process: "Classical Hollywood cinema belongs to the past but it is experienced in a present that affords us new ways of seeing" because "it preserves a structuring role culturally."[2]

Retrospectatorship allows us to disclose the fantasies our favorite films deployed on the subterranean level, retroactively providing access to what they repressed, to what they—and we—did not know they knew. In the special case of retrospectatorship that cinematic texts deliver, their reworking of images, tropes, and generic strategies from the films they cite amounts to an analytic bricolage that remains especially attentive to fantasy structures attending the symptoms of their repressions.[3] As *Far from Heaven* revisits the world of Sirk's melodramas, it engages with sexuality as a social—as well as familial—question. This transformation of the sexual from familial to social issue, from a private to a public difference, depends heavily on the parallels this film establishes with racial difference. In the process, the retrospectatorship it proposes extends to engage more broadly social fantasy structures.[4] But it engages these unevenly, vigorously reworking Sirk's favored gestures while leaving the tropes of Poitier's racial melodramas strangely unretouched. Indeed, *Far from Heaven* proves as unironic in its treatment of the Poitier effect as it remains ironic in its handling of Sirk's strategies.

Condensation and Displacement

From its credits through its opening sequence, *Far from Heaven* cites Sirk's *All That Heaven Allows* (1955) point by point. The opening establishing shot holds on a clock tower while a flowering branch obtrudes on a diagonal from the upper left frame. This image gives way in each film to a slow upward arc to a high-angle shot of the street in front of a train station, fixing on a two-tone blue-and-white station wagon. Yet, while the car in *All That Heaven Allows* belongs not to the heroine, Cary Scott (Jane Wyman), but to her best friend, Sara (Agnes Moorehead), *Far from Heaven* produces a slight displacement, putting its protagonist, Cathy Whitaker (Julianne Moore) at the wheel. We first pick up our heroine already in motion, rather than finding her at home awaiting a visit, like Cary. From the start, then, Haynes's film signals that it will work through subtle condensations and displacements.

Its plot closely follows the trajectory of *All That Heaven Allows,* whose affluent suburban widow risks scandal and ostracism on account of an unconventional love relationship with her gardener, the younger, "inner-directed" Thoreauvian Ron Kirby (Rock Hudson). In the almost electrifying network of condensation and displacement that structures it, *Far from Heaven* also amalgamates elements drawn from Sirk's *Imitation of Life* (1959) and *Written on the Wind* (1956). Cinematically, it shares with these Sirk productions an obtrusive score, a meticulous attention to color, strikingly truncated interiors, and a rhythm of hysterical eruptions. Yet, as this film substitutes Raymond Deagan (Dennis Haysbert) for Hudson's Ron Kirby, it establishes a sharp departure from the Sirk plot it partially reiterates. Not only is Deagan inflected by the intertextual reference to *Love Field* that Haysbert himself imports, but he also repeats the Poitier effect of that previous characterization.

But *Far from Heaven* also seeks to mark its distance from Sirk through its "project of articulating affect and analysis," in Mary Ann Doane's terms. For her, Haynes's film definitively rejects "a fear of the pathological as it yokes together pathos and logos, suffering and its analysis."[5] Consistently elaborating its difference from Sirk's universe, this film opens a social and historical perspective to explore the shaping effects of the 1950s on contemporary culture.[6] Lynne Joyrich makes a similar claim for the film: "Haynes's reworking of Sirk's reworking of melodrama's reworking of classical Hollywood film (and the social and personal issues it narrates) enacts a complex attitude toward, and position within, mediated culture." "This immersion," she continues, "indicates a deep involvement with mass culture—but one that is at the same time (and, indeed, because it *is* so involved) analytical."[7] Still, for all the ironic critical complexity of this film's "immersion" in mass culture—women's melodrama and television—the familiar tropes of Poitier's films largely escape its ironies. Thus, it leaves to Raymond the burden of a certain unironic authenticity, the weight of unmediated affect, and its narrative limits him to remaining a catalyst figure. He stands as Poitier's direct descendant, largely lacking the critical mediation that shapes *Far from Heaven*'s rewriting of Sirk.

Far from Heaven overlays *All That Heaven Allows* with *Written on the Wind*'s drama of heterosexual discontent. In the latter film, an upright geologist, Mitch Wayne, played by Rock Hudson—again—anguishes over his love for Lucy Moore Hadley (Lauren Bacall), the increasingly disappointed and disrespected wife of his wealthy and dissolute boyhood friend, oil heir Kyle Hadley (Robert Stack). Whereas the Hadleys' marriage founders on Kyle's fears about his own potency and his blindness to his wife's loyalty, *Far from Heaven* presents a drama of marital impasse between Cathy Whitaker, in her wishful heterosexual blindness, and her husband, Frank (Dennis Quaid), who struggles with the escalating unmanageability of his homosexual urges.

At the same time, because *Far from Heaven* filters its heterosexual disappointment and failure through Cathy's scandalous relationship with Raymond, it reframes the drama of the suburban middle-class wife and mother through a "racial angle." Thus, the film also borrows tropes from *Imitation of Life*, which stages its twin maternal melodramas within the framework of inter- and intraracial difference. That film turns on parallel mother–daughter conflicts. Ambitious single mother Lora Meredith (Lana Turner) pursues her acting career while remaining consistently indifferent to the concerns of her daughter, Susie (Sandra Dee). On the other side of the film's structuring racial divide, Lora's maid, Annie (Juanita Moore), as overattentive to her child as Lora is inattentive to hers, remains painfully and futilely hopeful that her mixed-race daughter, Sarah Jane (Susan Kohner), will eschew the desire to pass as white and accept her blackness. As it thus refracts the plot of *All That Heaven Allows* through the concerns of *Written on the Wind* and *Imitation of Life*, in a process that resembles nothing so much as filmic "dreamwork," *Far from Heaven* furnishes its viewer with a rich generational cinema archive anchored in Sirk's memorable 1950s melodramas. Cathy's maid, Sybil (Viola Davis) evokes Annie Johnson, and Raymond's daughter, Sarah (Jordan Puryear), shares a name with Annie's daughter and suffers similar racial violence. These characters encourage us to consider them in light of the representational work their predecessors performed. But when it comes to Raymond, it seems, his textual job remains much the same as that of Poitier's characters, and this complicates the film's archival effects.

To highlight the richness of this layered archive, we might recall a moment of striking self-reference in *Imitation of Life*. When Lora declines to appear in David Edwards's (Dan O'Herlihy) next comedy, his preferred genre, opting instead to do a drama, Edwards protests: "And that 'colored' angle in it. It's . . . absolutely controversial!"[8] Thus winking at its audience, Sirk's film calls attention to the status of its own "colored" angle as potentially a mere artifice or prop, a backdrop of "authenticity" that highlights Lora's fakeness, just as the diegetic play's "colored angle" endows it with a frisson of controversy and helps to code or package it as "serious drama." By similarly playing on this "angle," Haynes invites his viewer to wonder if race may be at risk of becoming a dramatic device for his film as well. But *Far from Heaven* elaborates its racial angle in complex ways. Set in a network of displacements and transfers of energy and affect, the status of its racialized representation remains unstable, and it often surreptitiously diffuses into the mise-en-scène. And we need to explore this instability through the film's representational work on both the visual and theoretical planes.

If we look at its striking technical departures from Sirk's cinematic vocabulary, we notice, for example, that *Far from Heaven* often abruptly introduces a canted frame. Regularly marking brutal shifts in perspective, the canted frame brusquely forces us into a different "angle of view" as it punctures the diegetic surface and disrupts the melodramatic atmosphere. Such angles, drawing our attention back to the frame itself and disaligning us from the character occupying screen space, remind us of the film's interpretive distance—and agency—at the level of the visual. Likewise, as the film articulates its sequences together with a strong inclination toward dissolves and fades, it suggests both film history and its own artifice. Its dissolves continually render a visual analog to its overlapping intertextual references—a montage of memory. Thus, the editing itself evokes the structure of condensation and displacement that is so crucial to the film's work.

In this regard, we note that *Far from Heaven* is as much an homage to film theory, and in particular to feminist film theory, as it is to Douglas

Sirk. It reads the 1950s melodrama (and beyond it, the 1950s in popular memory) through the lens of 1980s and 1990s feminist film theory. This feminist work cast Sirk into renewed prominence, as his films opened up new angles on the spurned genre of women's melodrama.[9] Furthermore, at the moment when feminist concerns and approaches took over the study of this genre almost completely, feminist theory also turned to explore the 1950s as something other than a regrettable period of regression in gender ideologies, intent on luring women back into the home, and began to reconfigure the period as one of intense contradiction around femininity, particularly in its relation to popular culture, especially television and consumerism.

But before achieving "almost legendary status in film studies" as the "'father' of melodrama theory and criticism," Barbara Klinger reminds us, Sirk produced quite different reactions among his contemporaries.[10] She writes: "During the 1950s, Universal-International Pictures presented Sirk's melodramas as slick, sexually explicit 'adult' films in accordance with the postwar culture's emphasis on sexual display in representation. At the same time, film reviewers decried his melodramas as 'soap operas,' typical not only of the crass commercialism of the film industry, but also of the frightening mediocrity of a mass culture with fascist tendencies" (xv). Disdained though they were by critics, Sirk's films nonetheless performed strongly at the box office, no doubt in part precisely because of the features the critics derided. Klinger quotes *Time* magazine's reviewer, who compared *All That Heaven Allows* to "radio daytime serials" and lamented that "the characters talk *Ladies Home Journal*ese and the screen glows like a page of *House Beautiful*. The moviegoer often has the sensation that he is drowning in a sea of melted butter, with nothing to hang on to but the clichés that float past" (78). Leaving aside the surreal imagery that elaborates the male viewer's plight here, these remarks capture the affinity between women and popular consumer culture that the film foregrounds and the critic decries.

Like the characters and viewers of soap operas, and the readers of ladies' magazines the *Time* critic imagines, and like the mothers in family sitcoms of the period, *Far from Heaven*'s Cathy Whitaker starts out "fixed" in a dense domestic consumer network, and she appears to be straining to perform a well-defined domestic script. As she gradually becomes "unfixed"

from the family household of which she is the pillar, her centrality organizes the plot's parallel worlds. We shall see the diverse consequences of
Cathy's structural position later. For now, we note that she thus appears
as the perfect icon for the contradictions that attend shifting boundaries
between public and private, and changing social relations within popular
and consumer culture. As her personal relationships turn political, she
introduces blacks, Jews, and homosexuality, as well as the specter of "com-
munism" to which McCarthyism linked them, into the suburban middle-
class family. Much like the television set itself, Cathy smuggles public
struggle into the domestic environment, where it transmutes into haunting "family secrets." Lynne Joyrich has explored the liminal status of television in U.S. culture, arguing that it is both conceptually and structurally
bound to the logic of the closet. She contends that "by both mediating
historic events for familial consumption and presenting the stuff of 'private life' to the viewing public, the institutional organization of U.S. broadcasting situates television precisely on the precarious border of public and
private, 'inside' and 'outside.'"[11]

Through its unstable family secrets, Haynes's film elaborates on the
social pressures that Sirk's films, like their historical milieu, repressed, marginalized, or "euphemized." We could describe its project as both archaeological and fantasy driven: archaeological because it seeks to restore the
social subtext whose anxieties Sirk's films captured in their exquisitely
overwrought dramas and decors; fantasy driven because *Far from Heaven*
lavishes obsessive attention on moments when the 1950s "unspeakables,"
the loves that dare not speak their names, homosexuality and interracial
desire, body forth in all their scandalous effects. Inviting the repressed to
return, the film represents the past as trauma. Both the archaeological and
the fantasmatic come together as this film searches out those tensions—
homoerotic, racial, and social—that Sirk's films held in check, or displaced,
in order to disclose them and to restore them to their "proper place." As
we will see, in *Far from Heaven* those tensions emerge in both the visual and
the discursive terrain.

It is indeed the question of proper place that incites such tensions, for
this film seems intent on imagining what would happen if "mother" devi-
ated from her popularly assigned tasks. What if she failed to manage her
man? What if she dropped the job of strictly regimenting masculinity into

the form of properly virile heterosexuality? What if she refused to collaborate in the management and repression of what lay just beneath the surface of her home and her culture? What if, instead, she sought not just to support equal rights in the abstract but to establish an actual connection across racial lines? And what if all these things were linked, and her personal politics exploded the heavily guarded boundaries of suburban middle-class convention? What if she made representable what Sirk's films could only hint at? Such a project of reelaboration or transcoding suggests a dream of filing in the gaps, of exposing underlying textual architecture, and ultimately of retrieving the fullness of the films'—and their period's— meanings. Can the dream of restoring plenitude ever be far from maternal metaphors?[12]

In its fantasy of maternal plenitude, *Far from Heaven* seems to pose the question: What kind of mother does the cinema of the 1950s make? More specifically, what happens if we understand 1950s film melodramas as offering oblique but active contestations of the world of television family sitcoms? Surely, Cathy Whitaker functions as an icon for such contradictions, as all her personal proclivities elaborate a certain politics. As Haynes reworks Sirk, de-oedipalizing the melodramas that inevitably turn on intergenerational conflict, he does so from a particular historical perspective. Born in 1961, Haynes comes from a generation for which his film's period, 1957–58, represents the historical moment just before his birth. Thus, we might imagine that period to function as a kind of historical primal scene for the filmmaker and his generation. And that scene remains profoundly marked by conflicts over civil rights.

The year 1957 saw the founding of the Southern Christian Leadership Conference, and it also witnessed the integration struggle at Little Rock Central High School, which began in August 1957 and continued into 1959. Significantly, *Far from Heaven*'s very precise historical detail centers on this crisis. For all the images of TV we find in the film, the one television broadcast we actually see and hear features President Eisenhower's speech of September 23, 1957. Eisenhower appears on national television to announce that he is sending federal troops to Little Rock Central High School: "I have today issued an executive order directing the use of troops under federal authority to aid in the execution of federal law at Little Rock."[13] At this point, the school remained surrounded by the Arkansas National

Guard troops that Governor Orval Faubus had posted on September 2 to prevent its integration.

This isolated televisual event in a text for which Hollywood and TV are centrally organizing figures tells us much about the film's angle of view. We can set this moment alongside the film's introduction of the 1957 release *The Three Faces of Eve* (Nunnally Johnson), playing at the Ritz Theater, where Frank discovers gay cruising at its screening. That film dramatizes a small-town southern woman's shifting identity—between mousy Eve "White" and sultry Eve "Black"—in the role that propelled Joanne Woodward to stardom. Thus, *Far from Heaven*'s studied historical accuracy carries significant political weight: this reference to film history displays the tense vibration in the period between the "visibility" both consciously and unconsciously granted to race relations in the public media and the rigidly segregated boundaries that conditioned private life, especially as represented in the TV sitcom.

Television: Image and Agency

Significantly, since *Far from Heaven* deploys television and the movies as technologies for the introduction of difference into the homogenized world of white suburbia, the period 1957–58 also registers as the peak of anxious rivalry between Hollywood and television. Hollywood studios struggled to regain ground lost to television—and on television in the form of the newly evolving genre of "telefilm" and archival films released for TV broadcast. Meanwhile, critics both inside and outside the television industry indicated that it had reached a nadir.[14] TV's crisis in programming, which is clearly related as well to the medium's negotiations with Hollywood, also connects with cinematic representations of telephobia that abound in the period.

Sirk himself appears systematically hostile to television, in keeping with Hollywood's generally paranoid vision of the rival medium in the 1950s as well as with his own affinities for the Frankfurt School position on the dangers of mass culture. In *All That Heaven Allows,* he savagely abases the medium in the memorable scene where Cary's children offer her a TV set as a replacement for the love relationship they have demanded that she relinquish. By contrast, Haynes's film, as we will see, seems more sanguine about the historical interpenetration of Hollywood and television.

Television figures powerfully in *Far from Heaven* as a dead zone within the living room and as a haunting symbolic presence that governs both the Whitaker family's own economy and its iconicity, while also reminding us of the world outside its suburban interior. TV secures a dense network of intertextual resonances. Among these, of course, are the connections among television, advertising, and consumer culture that *All That Heaven Allows* so aggressively criticizes. In *Far from Heaven,* by contrast, TV is much more basic: it is literally constitutive of the family's economy because Frank works as an advertising executive for a television manufacturer, Magnatech. Frank and Cathy thus embody precisely the consumer nexus that *All That Heaven Allows* rejects. We remember that Ron Kirby's friend Mick (Charles Drake) has abandoned the world of corporate advertising under Ron's ideological tutelage, following his inner voice out of the corporate world into the natural environment of the tree nursery, where he has time to read Walt Whitman's *Leaves of Grass.* Similarly, *Imitation of Life* presents Lora's suitor, photographer Steve Archer (John Gavin), as having betrayed his artistic ambitions and fallen back into a debased career in advertising.

Television may form the ground on which *Far from Heaven* operates, but the film never simply takes it for granted, as do its characters. For example, TV anchors a telling sequence in the master bedroom, where we see Frank in bed through the three-paneled mirror of Cathy's dressing table. As she probes him about the therapy he has undertaken to cure his homosexuality, he asserts his right to privacy. The television playing at the margins of the scene marks the erotic impasse, a substitute for sex and an icon of dysfunction. As the characters speak, we see at least two images of Cathy, from in front of and within the mirror. At other moments, this three-paneled mirror, so familiar from Sirk (and also evoking the intrapsychic partitioning of *The Three Faces of Eve*), allows us to see two angles on her face. And, as in Sirk's films, this split image disorients us as it displaces Cathy in relation to herself. Frank, on the other hand, is mirrored between her images, as if he is confined or framed there.

Strikingly, this is the only scene in which the film explicitly references the public/private divide, despite the centrality of gossip and rumor to its plot. Eisenhower's speech about Little Rock imports the central social conflict of the moment into the bedroom itself, in the *only* moment the TV is ever illuminated for the viewer to see as well as to hear. Elsewhere, TV reduces to background noise. Since neither character acknowledges the televisual discourse, it recedes into a kind of ghostly voice invading from the public sphere. Here the TV set seems to evoke a parallel—however distorted—between the private sexual impasse and the public racial impasse. Significantly, the broadcast that Frank and Cathy ignore has itself become historic. Sasha Torres cites Taylor Branch's characterization of the Little Rock crisis as "the first on-site news extravaganza of the modern television era." She goes on to contend that the kind of media events it inaugurated "allow network news not only to report, but also to intervene in, national culture in political discourse."[15]

But the television also acts as a catalyzing and binding force that actively organizes the film's condensations and displacements. It literally defines Cathy as corporate "wife and mother," since Mrs. Leacock (Bette Henritze) of the *Weekly Gazette*'s society page comes to interview her specifically as "Mrs. Magnatech." Frank's professional position thus defines Cathy as a "poster" wife and mother explicitly in relation to television. And this interview structurally propels Cathy's encounter with her gardener into the public view. As the *Gazette* article and Mrs. Leacock shadow Cathy through the film, the television—as product this time—will later propel civil rights to the foreground, since the Little Rock crisis emerges centrally in the conversation at Frank and Cathy's party for the launch of Magnatech's 1958 television models.

This party, then, intertwines the television set as consumer icon with its broadcast content, its news-reporting function. A woman guest announces that "what's happening in Little Rock couldn't happen in Hartford." Someone suggests that the reason might be that there is no Governor Faubus in Connecticut. But another man chimes in to assert that it is because "there are no Negroes here." After a jarring cut to a canted frame, the black wait staff at the buffet appear, startled and momentarily arrested by this astonishing comment. This scene reminds us of the moments of whites' obliviousness to the maids overhearing them in *The Long Walk Home* and, most recently, in *The Help*. But it retreats from this startling visual inscription of segregation's effects when guest Dick Dawson (Stevie Ray Dallimore) intervenes. "Still," he volunteers, "there are some rather dangerous pro-integration types here in Hartford," provoking general jocularity with this allusion to Mrs. Leacock's *Gazette* article describing Cathy as a "woman who is as devoted to her family as she is kind to Negroes." Dawson thus reminds us of the published interview that has generated a media picture of Cathy that her friends obsessively cite.

Visually the scene of the interview links the TV set to mirrors, screens, and surveillance in a dense condensation of its images and effects. A darkened television screen, like the oddly placed mirrors—objects that are not for viewing—emphasizes the film's ongoing interest in ways of seeing and not seeing. In a sequence that is overloaded with mirrors, Mrs. Leacock sneaks up on the Whitakers in their home, thereby recalling the ways that Sirk's mirrors act insistently to deny privacy, to promote spying. As we watch Cathy and Frank's morning good-bye kiss—in a pose reminiscent of sitcoms—a camera clicks and its bulb flashes as the newspaper photographer takes a "candid" shot. One of the many ironies of the sequence is the resemblance between this "candid" picture and later images of the family's life. Indeed, this candid image also suggests that it is posing that makes Frank and Cathy a family at all.

While the characters exchange pleasantries in the hallway, we first see Mrs. Leacock in the mirror, flanked by her photographer and by Sybil. In a departure from the position of black servants in Sirk's films, Sybil regularly exhibits an active gaze. For one thing, she can look directly into the mirror, unlike Annie Johnson in *Imitation of Life,* whose glance is always oblique to it. And, unlike the servants in *Written on the Wind,* who spy from their basement window on the comings and goings of the Hadley clan above, Sybil is frequently seen actively observing the family around her.

As the characters pass into the living room, we note the bizarre echo and rhyme between Mrs. Leacock's hat, the fringed brim of which replicates the shape of the mirrors on the living room wall, and the objects within Cathy's house. As a figure, Mrs. Leacock becomes a site around which to orchestrate echoes of Sirk's signature effects: the devastatingly grotesque hats that undercut feminine poise and self-containment, and the domestic artifacts that obtrude into a character's space, cutting shapes into her body or face. During the interview, Cathy sits beside the dark TV set, which is placed awkwardly in a corner between the couch and the fireplace. Above her head hangs a poster of Mr. and Mrs. Magnatech and their own TV. This image clearly bears a schematic resemblance to Cathy and

Frank; in other words, it abstracts them. In a sense, the couple is *only* this image. In a relationship entirely mediated by TV, the model couple exists only for and through advertising.[16]

But if television underwrites and occasions Cathy's performance as wife and mother in this sequence, it also calls our attention to the actual structure of the model family that surrounds the console. In doing so, *Far from Heaven* evokes a central moment in the intergenerational melodrama of *All That Heaven Allows*: the children's gift of a television to compensate Cary for the love she has relinquished. As the camera moves in to frame the set, we see Cary's face reflected on its surface. Across her ghostly image—the evanescence or maternal iconicity to which her children would condemn her—the TV deliveryman drones, "drama . . . comedy . . . life's parade at your fingertips." Sirk isolates the set as a mute—"dumb"—icon whose function as a "window on the world" is blacked out. The ghostliness of the darkened screen on which Cary's image floats reminds us that for her children, she is most useful as an image, and an image borrowed from the idealized repertoire of television.

Throughout Cathy's interview, a ceramic bird's tail intrudes across the poster, arching up from its perch on top of the TV set, to register the ironic discontinuity between this couple and their images, including the one that is under construction in this interview. Embracing the 1950s obsession with feminine definition, and with her own role as an advertisement for television as well as for the family, Cathy declares, "My life is like any other wife and mother's." She continues, elaborating, "I don't think I've ever wanted anything . . ." Her sentence trails off, at this point, as something offscreen catches her interest. We follow her gaze to the window. But the object of her gaze remains obscure.

After a cut, we follow her outside, where we discover the object of her curiosity and concern, Raymond. A shocking incongruous detail in the suburban yard, he punctuates Cathy's unfinished sentence. He may just be the "anything" she doesn't think she's "ever wanted." When he informs her that he is replacing his dead father as her gardener, Cathy puts her hand on his shoulder and apologizes for her previous tone. We see this image framed through a window from Mrs. Leacock's point of view. Framed under glass, as a picture emblematizing Cathy, this tableau will be frozen and publicized by Mrs. Leacock: "a woman who is as devoted to her family as she is kind to Negroes." Thus, the article creates a kind of slogan, a verbal echo of the Magnatech poster, and one that her friends continue to cite ironically.

After Cathy reenters the house, in a gesture reminiscent of Sirk, the camera pulls back to reveal a previously unseen observer. Sybil is framed in the kitchen doorway. The sequence ends punctuated by a look exchange between her and Raymond. Sybil's expressive gaze deploys suspicion and hostility, recalling Tillie from *Guess Who's Coming to Dinner*. Meanwhile, Dennis Haysbert evokes his own role as Paul Cater in *Love Field*. In his quiet watchfulness and gentle politeness he echoes that extraordinarily compassionate black partner and mentor to Lurene. He already promises a new iteration of the Poitier effect.

"The Only One"

While Sybil consistently evokes Sirk's black servants, Raymond emerges from a different movie archive altogether. He appears always as a surprise, a startling incursion into Cathy's white suburban environment from a world that remains off its map—"there are no Negroes in Hartford." And that world, effectively, stays off her map, as it does the film's, even though Raymond—as "the only one"—updates Poitier's pedagogical project for this wishful twenty-first-century contemporary moment. That project involves escorting Cathy on an ethnographic mission to Eagan's, a black restaurant and bar, so that she can see what it is like to the "the only one" of her race in a given context. The tour, however, as we will see, leaves Raymond's black community, and his relation to it, opaque. And his dislocation from community pointedly recalls the systematic isolation of Poitier's characters from black contexts. But Cathy's ignorance also underpins the film's image of parallel and analogous subcultural universes that remain outside white suburban territory, gay life and black life, since the film seems to equate her heteronormative wishfulness and the naïveté that feeds her racial curiosity about "being the only one in a room."

After their first awkward meeting on her porch, Cathy and Raymond come together again at Eleanor's art show. This moment establishes Raymond's radical—and alienated—visibility in the midst of segregated affluence. Of course, Cathy comes to occupy this same unpleasant visibility, while remaining strangely oblivious to it at first. Upon entering the gallery, she joins her friend Eleanor Fine (Patricia Clarkson), gossipy socialite Mona Lauder (Celia Weston), and Mona's uncle, Morris Farnsworth (J. B. Adams), a New York art dealer. Mona's unctuous introduction includes a reference to Cathy's "civic fancies," as detailed in the *Gazette*'s profile.

Morris, for whom Eleanor has previously expressed her distaste, on account of suspicions about his "masculinity," introduces a point of "deviance" that parallels Raymond's in this scene—almost. The appropriateness of Morris's presence in the gallery is guaranteed by his flamboyant gayness; his sexuality is framed, and contained, in a perfect fit with his professional expertise. But this figure serves another representational function: he is a flaming queen, and his niece Mona's sycophantic pandering to him casts her as a grotesquely clichéd "fag hag." By figuring this queen phobically, the film highlights its relative sympathy for Frank; likewise, Mona rescues Cathy from any hint of "fag hag" tendencies through the excess with which Mona occupies that position.[17]

When Cathy drifts away from this enclosed group to contemplate a painting, a flash interrupts her. Mrs. Leacock has had another picture snapped, and she is composing a caption for the image she is shaping of Cathy. Between their heads, Raymond is framed in the distance on the other side of the gallery. Like Mrs. Leacock's flash, he arrives to surprise Cathy. Spotting him, she crosses the gallery to greet him: "What a tremendous surprise, finding you here! How on earth did you find out about this show?" Raymond replies with irony, "I *do* read the papers," prompting Cathy to offer the following account of herself: "No, of course you do. I just meant that it's such a, it's a coincidence. Because, you know, I'm not prejudiced. . . . My husband and I have always believed in equal rights for the Negro and support the NAACP." Raymond responds politely, "I'm glad to hear it." When she continues, "I just wanted you to know," Raymond rescues her with an awkward, "Thank you."

This weirdly oblique conversation reveals Cathy's awkwardly liberal pose, her racial "angle," and suggests again the importance of angles to this film throughout. But the sequence that follows will transform Raymond from an enigma, in Cathy's eyes, into a teacher. As if to highlight this moment's awkwardness, the film cuts away to Sarah approaching the dreadful white boy, Hutch, and his friends, whom Raymond has improbably sent her to join. We return to the gallery to contemplate the Miró painting the camera is scanning from Raymond and Cathy's point of view. Shot/reverse shots alternate between the painting and its viewers. But another shot intervenes in this structure to triangulate the gazes in play: Mona and Morris huddle together glaring at the couple. We scan the painting's surface and then adopt its point of view as Raymond instructs Cathy, first helping her to pronounce Miró's name and then offering his view on the "modern art" before which she remains speechless. For him, abstract art "picks up where religious painting leaves off," "divinity pared down to shapes and colors."

This meditation ends abruptly when loud laughter punctuates the scene. A rapid pan follows Cathy and Raymond's turn toward its source: the tight little group around Morris and Mona. As Cathy moves to depart, Eleanor intervenes to reinscribe the parameters of normalcy, indicating to Cathy that her appearance with Raymond has the "whole place in a clamor." Occupying a pivotal position between the scene of conversational and sexual impasses in the Whitakers' bedroom and Frank's aggressive outburst at the Magnatech party, this art show sequence establishes both Raymond's pedagogical relationship to Cathy and the idea of being "the only one" that underwrites the film's parallel universes. Cathy's fascination with knowing how it feels to be "the only one" will lead to her excursion into Raymond's world, but it also operates as a figure for the parallel universes the film establishes as inhabited by the Whitakers in their heteronormative pose, Frank in his subcultural explorations, and the black community.

After Cathy's domestic world begins to crack, at the Magnatech party and in Frank's violent eruption in its aftermath, Raymond again surprises her by appearing in her yard. They decide to take a walk in the woods. He notices the bruise Frank's blow has left, a telling detail, and he connects it to the secrets she does not reveal: domestic strife and, behind it, Frank's sexuality. She deflects his concern: "I guess we all have our troubles . . . I'm sure you do yourself . . ." She trails off, indicating that she means to suggest an awkward analogy. Responding to his look of incomprehension, she ventures, "I keep wondering what it must be like to be the only one in the room . . . Colored or otherwise." She thus explicitly recalls the art show, where their mere appearance together produced a significant disturbance. Now he refers to a life that remains a "secret" for Cathy: "There *is* a world where everybody does indeed look like me. . . . Trouble is, most people never leave it." Raymond finds himself "the only one" so often, this exchange seems to suggest, because black people segregate themselves. Of course, in the Whitakers' home, Sybil is also "the only one," but her status never seems to have provoked similar curiosity for Cathy.

This moment again transforms Raymond from an enigma into a teacher. In order to allow Cathy to enact an identification with him as "the only one in the room," he escorts her to Eagan's, an implausible combination of restaurant and midafternoon nightclub—as if all his community's entertainments and culture have to be condensed into this one space to maximize authenticity. Even as Raymond functions as Cathy's tour guide here, he is obliged to *tell* as much as he *shows* in this ethnographic visit to a "black space." And the fact that he must continue telling and explaining suggests that, in *Far from Heaven*'s universe, "blackness" requires explanation, whereas gayness does not. Race, that is, seems more volatile than sexuality as both subject and object of knowledge.[18]

But Cathy troubles the sealed world of black leisure. She troubles it just as she and Raymond, by alighting from his truck together, have disrupted Mona Lauder's world, as a canted frame captures Mona's shocked, but smug, reaction when she spies them heading to the bar. When they enter Eagan's, Cathy and Raymond become tinged with lurid red and green lights as they cross its threshold, in a moment that precisely recalls the lighting at the gay bar Frank visits. Inside, a range of hostile gazes greet them. Not least of this sequence's false notes is its suggestion that hostility to white patrons in black establishments would function as an analogy with white hostility to blacks in segregated spaces. The scene's building tension culminates when an older male customer asks Raymond, "What the hell you doing, boy?" A white man will later echo this moment, addressing Raymond as "boy" when he interrupts Raymond and Cathy's interaction on the street. At this point, the film seems also to inscribe an equation between black and white hostility to interracial couples, in a forced comparison that hinges on the word "boy." But, of course, this is a false echo, since the white man uses the word as a racial epithet, whereas the black man uses it generationally. To the implausibility of this implied analogy, the scene in Eagan's adds other false notes.

As the couple sits, Raymond makes a toast to "being the only one," as if Cathy were now sharing his regular experience. Cathy abruptly poses a question: "Why don't you . . . ?" All expectations suggest that she is finally going to ask him to call her Cathy, instead of Mrs. Whitaker. One of the many features that mark this implausible intimacy is the asymmetry of Raymond's use of her title and her use of his first name, in a reflection of servant employer relations. Instead, Cathy finishes, "ask me to dance?" Eventually, as they dance to a full jazz ensemble (implausibly playing to a midafternoon dance crowd), they are melodramatically isolated at the center of the frame, in a pointed citation of Fassbinder's *Ali: Fear Eats the Soul* (1974), which begins with a German woman dancing with a Moroccan man in an Arab bar. They have become a pure spectacle for the now invisible black spectators. Thus, this sequence in the safe but deeply uncomfortable refuge of the all-black space ends with a fantasmatic utopian image. Though posed as ethnography, this scene, riddled with false details, strikes us more as a suburban white fantasy about segregated black spaces.

Far from Heaven nonetheless seeks to establish parallels between the violent repressions of racial mobility and repressions of sexual object choice. Its drama works through a play of visibility and invisibility. Raymond emerges from his invisibility as a service worker in this white suburb into scandalous hypervisibility when he appears in public with Cathy. Frank's "deviance," on the other hand, stays invisible as long as he remains with her and erupts as scandal and vulnerability when he ventures into illicit homosexual spaces. Cathy thus becomes the film's switch point, the central pivot that links its parallel repressed worlds: homosexual subculture and the black community. Equally important, however, this switch point forms an uneasy join between the 1950s world of Sirk's melodrama and Poitier's racial melodramas of the 1960s.

Cathy remains continually both disappointed and disappointing in her knowledge of Raymond's world. Significantly, the film disappoints on this point as well: Raymond's world is, for the film, far more invisible than the gay subculture whose margins Frank haunts, and with which it seems to strike a structural analogy. But that analogy proves false, because, for one thing, Frank shows himself to be far from "the only one." In the apparent structural parallel that emerges across Cathy as the switch point between Frank's subcultural life and Raymond's community, it is the former's struggles that capture significantly more of the film's attention. As it choreographs the two men around Cathy, *Far from Heaven* remains more interested in the failing couple than in the Poitier figure who sparks Cathy's curiosity and promotes her ideological explorations.

Sour Notes and False Details

Where *All That Heaven Allows* ironically casts the family's oedipal difficulties in the well-worn pop Freudian clichés of the period, *Far from Heaven*
insistently de-oedipalizes the family scene.[19] The Whitaker children inhabit
a parallel universe whose impact on the parental world is negligible. Ambas-
sadors of "normalcy," they strike us as nothing so much as emissaries from
the late 1950s television sitcom world that radically excludes the forbidden
cultural zones their parents increasingly frequent. Janice (Lindsay Andretta)
and David (Ryan Ward) remain oppressively normative in their gender-
appropriate interests: she takes ballet, he plays football. In the excruciatingly
picture-perfect Christmas scene that the family stages, Janice rhapsodizes
over new pink ballet slippers while David remains manically riveted to his
electric train set. Cathy is clad in a Mrs. Claus costume, while Frank relaxes
in a woolen sweater: the picture of the businessman at leisure, an echo of
Ozzie Nelson and Ward Cleaver in their "dens." This scene is framed like a
postcard of idealized family life: a Hallmark version of holiday cheer.[20]

Here, as elsewhere, the children appear as mere props. Their enthusiastic reports and whining demands alike are met with unrelenting parental
rebuffs and dismissals. Far from identifying with their plight, however, we
experience the children as oppressive. Their appearances operate as interruptions within the adult universe, where they invariably emerge as artificial details. And Cathy's emphatic resistance to providing maternal affection
figures a site of ambivalence. Even as its overarching project seems aimed
at restoring a fantasmatic maternal plenitude, at the level of narrative *Far
from Heaven* relentlessly undercuts the child-centered discourse that 1950s
popular culture advances in sitcoms, developmental psychology, parenting
manuals, and gender ideologies.

If we can describe Haynes's film as "turning up the volume" on Sirk,
exceeding Sirk's excesses, we can see this effect in its proliferation of just
such false details and moments of embarrassing strain. These emerge as
frequently on the aural plane as on the visual one. Elmer Bernstein's score
provides a more nuanced musical palette than we are accustomed to find
in Sirk, since it alternates among distinct solo piano, woodwind, and full
orchestral passages. But in its volume it often obtrudes aggressively into the
affective tonality of the unfolding sequences. Much the same effect obtains
in the film's dialogue. Where Sirk's characters may rely on euphemism and

suggestion, rarely are they inarticulate. By contrast, Haynes's characters experience regular verbal blockage and bypass. Their tense and embarrassed exchanges often stammer to a forced closure, trailing off in mutual disappointment. They sometimes remind us of Carol White's increasingly strangled discourse in Haynes's 1995 film *Safe*.

A similar effect marks *Far from Heaven*'s conclusion: the film ends on a pronounced false note. An isolated sour note floats free of the piano solo that punctuates the beginning of the credit sequence, and it holds long enough to disturb. A kind of aural pun, this tone reminds us that Sirk specialized in tingeing his happy endings with sour notes, even as it recalls the abundance of false details that shape Haynes's own film. As in Sirk's films, *Far from Heaven*'s false notes provide ironic punctuation or retreat from the affective texture that composes the melodramatic environment. In this film, however, these details not only destabilize the scene but also sometimes gesture tellingly toward a zone beyond the family, just as, for example, Sybil's judgmental gaze introduces the broader context of race relations into Cathy's first meeting with Raymond.

Specifically, these details help to mark Frank's "deviance," his affiliation with a subcultural world. Early on, when Cathy receives a call from the Hartford police to come and redeem her husband, the unspoken—and unspeakable—nature of his arrest figures in the soiled handkerchief that he clutches in his hand. Or we may think of the hideous salmon-colored bird-shaped lamp that his secretary quizzically presents to him on his arrival at his office one morning. We know, of course, that this broken lamp has been damaged in his lover's panicked flight upon Cathy's interruption of their office tryst. Frank has stuffed it in the closet, where his inquisitive secretary has found it. This false-note structure carries across and mediates between the specific and punctual embarrassments of private life and the more global scale of public discursive circulation and scandal. On the level of the film's thematics of social difference/deviance, the false-note structure helps to effect a transfer between two zones of transgression— homosexuality and interracial relationships.

Among the richest of the false notes are those that mark the central sequences of this melodrama, propelling its conflicts into a crisis. In a shockingly revelatory stroke of performance—by both the actor and the character—Frank disrupts the Magnatech celebration. In reply to a vacuous compliment about Cathy's beauty from one of their male guests, Frank erupts with the hysterical force of Kyle Hadley in *Written on the Wind*. Contorting his body back onto the couch and affecting a tone lifted directly from Paul Lynde, arguably TV's favorite unacknowledged queer of the 1970s, Frank blurts out, "It's all smoke and mirrors, fellas." Wrinkling his nose and baring his teeth in a Lynde grimace, while allowing his hands to hang limp in an additional flourish as his body convulses in disgust, he delivers this blow: "You should see her before she puts her face on!" This perfectly calibrated moment of stupefying inappropriateness and embarrassment provides one of several tense scenes that edge this melodrama from crisis to crisis.

With the 1950s housewifely poise exhibited by June Cleaver and Harriet Nelson, Cathy diffuses the shocked silence of the guests: "No. He's absolutely right. We ladies are never what we appear. Every girl has her secrets." Of course at this point, Cathy's well-guarded secret is her husband's sexuality. But soon the film will provide her with an "open" secret of her own: her relationship with Raymond. A community of hostile gazes around her will fix the "meaning" of this relationship as erotic even before Cathy herself discovers it.

In this transfer of secrets, the film retreats from the hysterical terrain of *Written on the Wind* to that of *All That Heaven Allows*. That film plays the emotional and ideological transformations that its heroine undergoes against a relentless physical stasis that completely belies the erotic theme it asserts narratively. By contrast, *Far from Heaven* sets the static interactions of Cathy and Raymond against the volatile kinetics that characterize Frank, and that make him such a compelling—perhaps the most compelling—site of visual and narrative interest. In his anguished hyperkinetic energy, Frank recalls the intensity not only of Kyle Hadley but also of Sarah Jane in *Imitation of Life*, both of whom seethe with erotic tension. Frank shudders and erupts in sharp contrast to the immobility, and even rigidity, of Cathy and Raymond. He alone, among this film's characters, is permitted erotic charges and affective release.

After this party, which occupies the film's temporal center, we find Cathy in the darkened living room, staring out the window. We follow her gaze as she turns abruptly; Frank enters the frame, a predatory look contorting his face. Embracing her brusquely, he leads her to the couch and begins to make love to her. But he breaks off suddenly, his discourse mimicking the sexual impasse, as he exclaims, "Jesus! What's happening? I can't even . . . God!" Cathy's attempts to reassure him are desperately stilted, and her tone reminds us of the therapeutic discourses that treat homosexuality as a pathology to be cured by "adjustment" that are beginning to dominate in the period depicted: "It's all right. The important thing is to keep trying."[21] Frank replies by taunting her—perhaps she wouldn't mind if Dick Dawson "could lend his services from time to time."

Here we confront the excessive overdetermination that makes *Far from Heaven* so much fun to watch and so semiotically complex: Dick Dawson's very name recalls Rock Hudson's, even as the sexual suggestion echoes that made by Kyle regarding his best friend and rival, Hudson's Mitch Wayne. Kyle's explosive episodes turn on his unraveling over his "sterility," a code word for "impotence," which, in turn, suggests the ultimately repressed term, homosexuality. For a contemporary viewer this character's rages seem barely to contain, let alone conceal, his homoerotic attachment to Mitch. *Far from Heaven* highlights this repression in Sirk's film. As with Kyle, one effect of Frank's erotic frustration is brutality toward his wife. He strikes her in the forehead after she desperately seeks to reassure him: "You're all men to me; you're *all man*." But unlike Kyle's violence, which directly brings about disaster, Frank's outburst has consequences that are more mysterious and pervasive; they diffuse into the mise-en-scène and across the relay of "false notes" the film consistently strikes.

The "Color" Angle: Cathy's Clothes

Just as *Far from Heaven* pays scrupulous attention to melodrama's musical effects, it also insists on the crucial importance of color to the genre, consistently referencing and amplifying Sirk's effects through its chromatic palette. As the literal and figural meanings of color continue to slide into each other, we can begin to read the elaborate effects of condensation and displacement that structure this film's reading of Sirk and his historical period. Through its gorgeous deployment of color as figure, this film seems frequently to displace the social "color" that Raymond's character imports into its world.

A key moment produces an abrupt shift in *Far from Heaven*'s color coding, and it is one that reverberates. The morning after the Magnatech party, Cathy has rearranged her hair to cover the bruise Frank's improbably placed blow has left on her forehead. As she puts it brightly to Eleanor, "I experimented." In the film's marvelously economical universe, this slight remark reminds us of Frank's "experiments," both with men and with the failed pose of heterosexuality, and it anticipates Cathy's future cross-racial bonding. But Eleanor calls attention to the bruise, a false detail that disrupts Cathy's pose of serenity and marital stability. Given away by the jarring detail of her new hairstyle, Cathy is betrayed by the telling mark. What renders this detail so arresting for the spectator is that we never see it. Instead, the effect that we do see is a startling—almost sickening—chromatic dissonance.

This is the first time that the clothes of the women on-screen do not match or harmonize in a pattern of analogous colors. In her mustard-colored coat, brown pants, and leaf-patterned blouse, Eleanor rhymes with the autumnal trees behind her. Cathy's attire, however, introduces a striking visual discordance—a cacophonous note. She wears a lavender sweater over a mint-green dress. Not only does her dress clash with Eleanor's, but it also introduces a new tonal range into the centrally important thematics of women's clothing, as her colors suggest a more 1960s palette. These colors also recall, by contrast, an earlier scene of almost claustrophobic feminine harmony.

Cathy's lavender-and-green outfit, with its striking contrast of near complementary color, recalls her signature lavender scarf, a key signifier in the film's metonymic and figural economies. One especially gorgeous scene—regularly referenced in popular critical response to this film—takes shape around the lavender scarf. Three of Cathy's friends have come for lunch, and the four women standing outside the house display across their harmonizing outfits a stunningly coordinated range from warm reds and oranges to gold. These colors, of course, echo the foliage around them and create an exaggerated replica of a common Sirk technique: he merges a woman into her environment by keying her colors to the setting.

One element interrupts the seamless texture of analogous colors here: Cathy's scarf. This cool accent stands out as the false note in the red-orange palette that unites the women and their surroundings. But it rhymes beautifully with the scene's narrative text. Eleanor reads from the *Gazette* article, and her tone turns ironic as she delivers the line that haunts Cathy throughout the film: "Wife and mother and Mrs. Magnatech herself, Cathleen Whitaker . . . a woman as devoted to her family as she is kind to Negroes." Eleanor goes on to mention that Cathy has always been a liberal, "ever since she did summer stock with all those steamy Jewish boys"; that's why they called her "Red." While Cathy jokes about going inside before Senator McCarthy hears them, her lavender scarf blows off and over the roof, leaving her clad entirely in red. As the red links Cathy to communists, the lavender suggests her sympathy for homosexuals, placing her at a nexus of ideological and social deviance for the period, as a central signifying knot within the film's political universe.[22]

After the friends' departure, the film cuts to a close-up of the lavender scarf in Raymond's hand, shot at waist level from behind his body—another of his surprise appearances. When Cathy acknowledges her scarf, he replies, "I had a feeling it might be yours." He has a feeling for "her color": "It was the color . . . it just seemed right." Like Poitier's characters, Raymond shows himself to be a practiced observer, with a "feeling" for white people and a gift for knowing enough about them to teach them about themselves. His feeling for her "color," of course, produces another chromatic pun. Beyond the metaphoric reference to race here, not only is Raymond right about Cathy's palette, which differs from that of other characters in its preference for complementary colors and its striking combinations of cool and warm, but he also registers this color as her signature. She wears this scarf to see him off at the train station in the film's poignant final moment, and her appearance in lavender and green, clashing with Eleanor, structurally precipitates her daring expedition with him into the public sphere, where she confronts skin color as an impossible obstacle. This expedition will generate the gossip that forces an end to their contact.

Cathy's sartorial palette consistently produces hypersignifying effects through its intra- and intertextual references. Her color spectrum both encodes her centrality to the film's structure and emphasizes her shifting relations to the diegetic world.[23] Often, the striking contrasts of her outfits seem to speak to her surroundings but also to lift her out of them by recalling other scenes. A dramatic example is her emerald-turquoise coat over a russet-red dress. We first see her in this ensemble, and this is also the outfit she wears on her ill-fated visit to Frank's office carrying his dinner in Tupperware.

Significantly, the basic complementary structure of this red–green ensemble relates to some of the film's most lurid effects of lighting as well as to the spaces it establishes beyond the home and the office. The movie theater lobby, where Frank notices the gay men he will follow, is cast in red and green lights, and these colors dramatically define both the gay bar and Eagan's. As Frank hesitates on the threshold of the gay bar, his passage through red and green light creates an uneasy effect and anticipates the color scheme of the bar itself and the entrance to Eagan's.

This garish red–green combination of lighting and interior seems to mark disciplinary or disciplined spaces: the movie theater as protected space for furtive private acts, the gay bar and the black club as spaces closed off from the heterosexual and white worlds. These ambiguous zones of semiprivacy carved out from the public sphere provide a certain privatized sanctuary at the expense of a segregation that consolidates difference in a site that is readily surveyed and policed.[24] Cathy's red–green ensemble, then, helps to establish a link between the spaces that attract and confine Frank and the space of African American leisure and entertainment, thus recasting the latter as a zone of furtiveness as well.

In this film's hyperrefined, nuanced chromatic orchestrations, the outfit Cathy sports for Frank's first visit to the therapist is also striking. Her coordinated dress, coat, and hat offer a subtle range of gray and purplish tones that harmonize perfectly with the color scheme of the doctor's waiting room. Thus, when Cathy retreats to the waiting room couch, she seems literally to become part of the therapeutic environment, part of its containing frame, its surveillance apparatus.[25] After the appointment, side by side with Frank in the claustrophobic space of the elevator, Cathy plays out this surveillance, rattling on nervously and plying him with questions until he bursts out in one of the verbal explosions that provide us a cathartic release from a moment of tense embarrassment: "I just want the whole fucking thing over with!" Cathy appears aligned with repressive apparatuses here, just as she does in her home, and a spectator with a rebellious inclination may take no small pleasure in Frank's outburst here—as elsewhere.

While Cathy's palette is defined by its vividness and its extensive range, as well as by its volatile relationship to the environment, Raymond's and Frank's restrained wardrobes are no less powerfully engaged in the film's chromatic metaphors. Frank appears only in shades of gray and blue—until the couple's trip to Miami, that is, where the palette contrasting pink to baby blue emphasizes gender opposition. Raymond, by contrast, appears entirely clad in earth tones and muted warm colors, as in the red-orange-yellow plaid wool shirt he wears with brown corduroy trousers for gardening. His uniform attire fixes him in place as a man centered by his own confidence, but also as visually static. Like Ron Kirby of *All That Heaven Allows,* whose clothes he seems to have borrowed, Raymond is resolutely bound to nature. In the scene in which a distraught Cathy encounters him behind the house the morning after her party, Raymond's torso emerges out of the bushes; he is figured as a tree blending into the foliage, as his shirt perfectly coordinates with the colors of the leaves.

As Cathy moves from the fall earth-tone palette into cool blues, mauves, and purples, her look parallels the change of seasons and reflects the increasingly frigid tone of her marriage. Her movement across the spectrum of color and hue also recalls Lora Meredith's increasingly icy color schemes in *Imitation of Life.* By the film's end, however, she appears in a tweed tailored suit, much like Marylee Hadley (Dorothy Malone) in *Written on the Wind,* who signals her transformation from freewheeling nymphomaniac into the businesslike spinster who will run the family business after her brother's death and Mitch's union with his widow. These tailored suits encode erotic disappointment and dead ends, as both these women exchange sexuality for finance (we see Cathy paying bills in the film's penultimate sequence).

Missed Encounters

If I have lavished particular attention on Cathy's wardrobe, this is because it secures her status as the film's captivating visual center. Rare are the moments when a scene does not focus on Cathy, and telling are those moments when the film's attention wanders from her or becomes urgently drawn away from her. As she alone traces a path of connection between the world of her husband and Raymond's world, her presence and absence seem to condition what we see, and this amounts to a narrative limitation. Although we see Cathy herself almost continually, often we do not see what she sees. Just as often, our view exceeds or anticipates hers, as in the scene in which Eleanor phones to warn her about the gossip surrounding her and Raymond. Before Cathy notices, we see Frank tensely approaching in the hall. The displacement of our view from Cathy's produces dramatic consequences that reverberate in camera work and framing as they shape encounters of impasse, blockage, or bypass among the characters.

Striking displacements also emerge in the montage. Among the most stunning of the film's dissolves is the one that propels Cathy out of her kitchen and into the revolving door of Frank's office building, where she will discover him embracing another man. This expressionistic image matches the rate and direction of Cathy's passage across her kitchen onto the flurry of the building door's revolution, literally precipitating her toward a moment of discovery and out of the illusory closure of her conventional domestic life. Here, both montage and camera work operate with an interpretive force and an obtrusiveness that rival the work of the film's imposing and fraught mise-en-scène. Whereas Sirk has been noted for the estranging effects he creates with the picture plane and its varying depths, Haynes reworks this technique through edgy focus pulling.[26] Shallow focus forces the figures into sharp relief against blurred backgrounds. Such an effect obliges continual reexamination of figure and ground relations, and it metaphorically destabilizes the characters' relation to their contexts.

Significantly, odd camera angles—markedly low or high in alternation—disturb our sense even of the size of the bodies on screen. As Raymond and Cathy speak in her yard after he has found her lavender scarf, for example, the two are framed together from varying angles. A low angle on Cathy alternates with a high angle on Raymond, and subsequent shots offer a low angle on him and a higher one on her. Our sense of perspective, of size, and of relations of power/dominance keeps shifting, suggesting an overall instability or indefiniteness to this relationship.

In two-shot compositions, strongly favored for Cathy and Raymond's interactions, rack focus pulls one figure into crisp definition while blurring the other into the background. Frequently, one of the two figures dominates the frame as a blur or a blob, as the camera shoots from behind the back or shoulder to capture the other frontally in medium shot. Thus, we could say that in *Far from Heaven, angles* of view predominate substantially over *points* of view. This means that subjective shots are largely replaced by distinct angles on the characters and their interactions—the view of a deeply interested and always interpreting third party.

Frank and Cathy's scenes together are marked by distance and almost never supported by shot/reverse-shot techniques of spatial continuity. Rack focus casts one into relief while the other fades into the background, as if to inscribe the characters' inability to inhabit the same plane. Often, their encounters begin with our realizing, along with Cathy, that Frank hovers near, just out of frame. We hear him before we see him; we anticipate him from the sound of his metal cigarette lighter and the clink of ice as he pours his drinks. Frequently lurking, he links the classic 1950s "dad" presence—offstage, consuming something—to the homosexual cruising in the gay bar. Equally important, and in marked contrast to Sirk's characters, Frank and Cathy engage in dialogues that could best be described as haltingly inarticulate, stammering in bypasses.

Perhaps the most striking conversational bypass emerges when Frank comes out to Cathy. After her shocking discovery at his office, she is sitting in darkness in their living room beside the dark TV set. Her household small talk gives way to the following "exchange":

FRANK: You see, uh . . . once a long time ago, a long, long time ago, I had, uh . . . problems. . . . I just figured that was . . . that was it. I mean, I never imagined . . .

CATHY: You never spoke to anyone? . . . A doctor?

FRANK: No.

CATHY: I don't understand.

FRANK: Neither do I.

CATHY: What if? . . . I mean, there must be people . . .

FRANK: I don't know.

CATHY: Because, otherwise, I don't know what I . . .

In this last line, Cathy employs the same locution she uses when expressing exasperation at her son's refusal to heed her instructions. And Frank finally capitulates to her unspoken demand: "All right." In the densely charged silences that bear the meaning between words here, the impasse of discursive exchange reminds us of what Eve Kosofsky Sedgwick has argued in relation to the "open secret" structure of the closet: "The fact that silence is rendered as pointed and performative as speech, in relations around the closet, depends on and highlights more broadly the fact that ignorance is as potent and as multiple a thing there as knowledge."[27] From this point Frank and Cathy's "dialogues" become increasingly stilted and blocked, as the unspeakable haunts their speech.

By contrast, the film tracks the development of intimacy between Cathy and Raymond in conversations where he draws her out, filling in the gaps in her truncated discourse, and supplying her with a vocabulary for things she has difficulty conceptualizing. Like Paul Cater, Raymond provides Cathy with a lexicon for the previously unspeakable, in much the same way that Poitier's characters instruct their white interlocutors. *Far from Heaven* handles this effect without irony, however. It folds Cathy's increasingly fluent conversations with Raymond into a symmetrical opposition with her ever more strained exchanges with Frank. In a way, Raymond's representational job as the film's primary black figure is to highlight the white marriage's decline, providing a melodramatic foil in the hint of an alternative—an elsewhere—to the troubled domestic scene.

Just as stammering discourse arrests narrative flow, canted frames function to puncture the diegetic surface, calling our attention to interruption or impasse. They introduce a trauma around the emergence of "deviance," or transgression, in the public visual field. The abrupt dislocation of the frame, and of our perspective, suggests the trauma that the transgressive figure or couple experiences in public. But it also suggests the traumatized hostility of the segregated or heteronormative public sphere when it is interrupted by the spectacle of its "others." Through the canted frame that marks our view of Cathy's panicked flight when she surprises her husband with another man, for example, the film both highlights and mimics her shock.

Because *Far from Heaven* provides us with few conventional point-of-view shots, we confront a universe where characters uneasily inhabit ambiguous spaces. Since most conversations are captured in two-shots rather than shot/reverse-shot structures, we read their effects through reaction shots. Notable point-of-view shots do occur, however, and they form a striking pattern. When Cathy enters Frank's office on that fateful evening, a "swish" pan follows her inquisitive gaze as it picks up the men's kiss. This visual pun evokes a larger pattern within the film. Camera work visually inscribes its characters' "deviations." The camera's swerves, like the abrupt shifts of the frame from its normal vertical axis to canted angles, mime the characters' own wrong turns.

Another urgent pan marks a sequence that briefly detours the film's attention from Cathy to Raymond's daughter, Sarah. Three white boys interrupt her trip home from school, taunting her about her father's "white girlfriend" and forcing her into a detour. As she flees in terror, the camera inscribes her fear, abruptly panning to the boys and dislocating the point of view it has momentarily assigned her. Having chased her into an alley from which there is no issue, the boys continue to taunt her: "Daddy's girl took a wrong turn . . . she took a wrong turn . . . just like her Daddy." This scene concludes with Sarah lying unconscious in the alley, having been hit in the forehead by a rock.

A dark percussive piano on the sound track amplifies the scene's tension and violence, and it recalls the driving jazz rhythm of the scene it echoes from *Imitation of Life*. In a moment of shocking violence, Sarah Jane's boyfriend, Frankie, played by teen heartthrob Troy Donahue, slaps her repeatedly until she falls into the gutter at his feet. Frankie explodes in violence because of rumors of her mother's blackness, and he beats Sarah Jane for "passing," for attempting to repeat the miscegenation of her ancestry. In its echo of this scene, *Far from Heaven* evokes a displacement from parent to child, again in terms of racial mixing. But while Sarah Jane's beating propels her definitive separation from her mother, Sarah's victimization reunites Cathy and Raymond one last time, and it emphasizes the impasse to which each character's wrong turn leads.

Far from Heaven punctuates its narrative through sharp turns and swerves that operate at the level of both characters and intertexts. Frank's visit to the Ritz Theater, and later to a gay bar, provides the most sustained, and stunning, derailment of the film's attention to Cathy. The only sequence in which we see him alone also creates a particularly pointed and dense intertextual kernel. Days after his arrest for "loitering," a drunken Frank leaves his coworkers after a business dinner and wanders into the Ritz. From the lobby, as he is catching a sequence in *The Three Faces of Eve*, that drama of repression and dissolute behavior, he also observes a dandified young man ascending to the balcony, followed at a discreet distance by another man. These are the men he later follows to a bar.[28] Under lurid blue light reflecting on the wet pavement, Frank scuttles along, framed in a sharply canted angle, which marks his "wrong turn," the altered perspective that leads him to this gay bar, where he picks up the fellow with whom Cathy will later catch him.

The Three Faces of Eve premiered in September 1957, its appearance co-inciding historically, as Haynes's film registers explicitly, with the Little Rock integration crisis. "In light of the film's historical context," Allison Graham argues, "the story of the battle between 'Eve White' and 'Eve Black' for the 'mastery' (in the narrator's words) of one woman's 'character' seems an almost blatant indicator of the era's racial hysteria."[29] Eve Black, of course, is the sexually aggressive and assertive personality repressed by dowdy, sub-missive, and naive Eve White. For Graham, Eve Black represents the "scandal of the 'sexualized' white woman, a metaphorically blackened image which hints at miscegenation" (46). At the same time, however, because it is Eve Black who can emerge at will, and who is aware of her other personality, the film organizes itself around metaphors of both "passing" and "coming out," as she regularly emerges to displace and impersonate Eve White.[30] This film's intertwined metaphors prove especially apt for *Far from Heaven*'s examination of the 1950s. As it tells the story of psychological adjustment through the integration of psychically segregated and strictly opposed personalities, *The Three Faces of Eve* pointedly evokes the thera-peutic tone of popular liberal discourses around both sexuality and race in its period. Thus, it provides a representational and intertextual anchor—but also an alibi—for *Far from Heaven*'s structures of intersection and hom-ology between sexual and racial passing, between homosexuality and mis-cegenation. Cinema, here, displaces history to provide a too-neat analogy between the zones of transgression Cathy joins.

Switch Points

Within its architecture, *Far from Heaven* carefully constructs a symmetry between racial and sexual oppression, bringing together the violent repres-sions of both racial mobility and sexual choice. Not surprisingly, to render oppression in the visual field, the film focuses on forbidden couples: on one side the homosexual couple, "unnatural" because of their nonrepro-ductive erotics, and on the other the interracial couple, who scandalize because their sexuality might reproduce the "wrong" children.

In this transfer from invisible to visible "vice," or difference, Cathy be-comes the film's switch point, much as Eve Black acts as a bridge between Eve White and Jane, the fully "integrated" personality who emerges when *The Three Faces of Eve* ends in a cure for multiple personality disorder.

Cathy's function as a switch point, as the central fulcrum upon which the film constructs its parallel worlds, first emerges in a striking conversation between Cathy and Eleanor, who gossips cattily about Mona Lauder and her uncle Morris, musing at length: "A bit flowery for my taste. . . . A touch light on his feet? . . . Yes, darling, he's one of *those*. Of course, I could be mistaken. It's just an impression I got." Their next exchange highlights the ignorant knowingness that makes Eleanor such a comfortable inhabitant of her era, while simultaneously underlining Cathy's discomfort and alienation when she asks, "You don't care for them particularly?" Eleanor's reply generates pointed irony: "Not particularly. Not that I actually know any."

Just like the good liberal that she aspires to be (and, of course, in keeping with the 1950s popular appetite for analyses of deviance), Cathy indicates that she has done some reading on the subject. Eleanor remarks that she is taking an interest in "another civic cause" and imagines society-page news copy about "Cathy Whitaker and her kindness to Negroes and homosexuals." Meanwhile, Eleanor's confident assertion that she knows no homosexuals counterpoints her anxious policing of Cathy's public interaction with Raymond at the art show and her urgent concerns about the gossip that Mona later circulates about their interracial dalliance. Her carefully guarded ignorance forges another link—of disavowal—between Frank and Cathy's transgressions, and this, in turn, contributes to a growing parallel between their bad object choices.

Of course, both of Cathy's object choices are "bad." In her last encounter with Eleanor, she confesses the reasons for her marriage's failure. Eleanor's sympathetic response remains entirely consistent with "enlightened" 1950s white middle-class heteronormativity. Cathy is the victim of Frank's tragically incurable sexuality. She cannot be blamed for failing to uncover his deeply occulted secret, unknowable to those around him; Eleanor certainly didn't know she knew any of *those*. When Cathy goes on to confess her feelings for Raymond, "the only one" to whom she can really talk, Eleanor cuts her off. This voluntary interracial association is unthinkable, and unspeakable; it puts an end to all possible discourse. Cathy's doubled disappointment here seems to reinforce the parallels the film has established between her impossible male object choices. But they are not impossible in the same terms, and this is where the film's logic falters.

Each of the two men is condemned and endangered if he finds himself in the wrong place, takes a wrong turn. And the wrong place may be the segregated space of the art show or the company of a white woman, or it may be the gay bar, the cruising zone, or the arms of another man. The striking difference between the two men's positions turns on visibility. Raymond is consistently surveyed by the social gaze as he traverses the film's predominantly white terrains. Frank, on the other hand, becomes visible only if he enters a gay zone or appears coupled with a man. Of course, the paradox is that Frank enters the gay zones precisely in an effort to become invisible.

Only when Raymond enters the black club, the one space in the film where we see a population of black characters, might he shed his hyper-visibility. But he cannot, because he has brought Cathy along with him, thus reproducing a version of the effects he encounters in the white world. Signally important here, this scene sketches a parallel black universe that the film wants to imagine but also segregates. This scene itself conjures not so much a metonym of a different cultural world as it does a stage set (much like the "foreigners'" bar in *Ali: Fear Eats the Soul*). Even amid the stunning effects of mise-en-scène that inscribe the artificiality of Cathy's melodramatic world, this hermetically sealed scene stands out for its emphasis on artifice and performance. Equally important, we never gain access to Raymond independent of Cathy's presence and agency. This peculiar limitation of our access strikingly recalls the Poitier effect, mediating Raymond, as it does, through the white characters' responses to him. By marked contrast, we do see Frank, independent of Cathy, in the key sequence that "outs" him to us, which also takes place in a subcultural bar.

As the film produces more striking incidents involving social difference, it becomes especially attentive to gaze structures, introducing relatively rare subjective point-of-view shots and emphasizing the kind of collective gaze that Fassbinder strikingly depicts. In *Far from Heaven*, an especially poignant moment structurally links imposed homosexual furtiveness with racial segregation. When Frank and Cathy take a "second honeymoon" in Miami, they are reclining by the hotel pool as a little black boy dips his foot in the water. Horrified white women desperately urge their children out of the pool and scramble away, demonstrating the kind of visceral terror of contamination that a Jim Crow system built and sustained. When a black man dressed in hotel livery berates the child aggressively, the incident introduces a brutally realist cast into the film's melodramatic texture.

But this scene also recalls the metaphors of pathology and contamination surrounding the homosexuality that is segregated out of Frank and Cathy's world of white suburban families. This awful incident ruptures the serene Miami setting by revealing one structural subtext, the segregation to which it is hysterically bound, in terms of another. In the same sequence, Frank's look subtly tracks the movement of a pretty teenage boy (Nicholas Joy) whom he has noticed the night before. After spotting the young man again, Frank volunteers to fetch Cathy's forgotten book, her "Miss Mitchell," as she calls it. The reference to *Gone with the Wind* reverberates. It suggests that Cathy has put aside the "civic issues" that interest her in favor of the iconic text of white popular culture's romanticized segregation in nostalgic fantasies about plantation life.

When Frank reaches the hotel room, we see him captured in an oblique angle through the mirror, from a point just outside the door, which stands ajar. In the next shot, from a vantage point just behind his shoulder, the camera reveals the pretty young man's face in an opposing oblique angle through the mirror. Recalling Sirk's marvelous play with mirrors to indicate invasions of privacy and both revelation and masking, this shot casts us as intimate voyeurs. The slow movement of the young man's hand across his torso and down into his swim trunks constitutes what is unquestionably the film's most emphatically erotic moment. Significantly, this scene combines the most intense sexual charge in the film with the most sustained shot/reverse-shot look exchange that is not hostile. Indicating where the real eroticism lies, these shots remind us of its absence between Cathy and Raymond. And they remind us that the film rarely grants Raymond a point of view.

But this furtive erotic connection takes place against the background of the brutally interrupted contact between black and white at the pool. Thus, the visible and public violation of social rules sets the stage for the unseen private transgression. Significantly, the young man strongly resembles Frankie, played by Troy Donohue, the all-American white boy, who beats Sarah Jane in a shockingly brutal scene in *Imitation of Life*. Later in the film, the lover for whom Frank has left Cathy turns out to be this very same flat, superficial character. At this point, the man's blank indifference suggests that, like the characters in *Imitation of Life* who come together in the end, at Annie's funeral, Frank may not live happily ever after; his story may well lead to disappointment.

Disappointments and False Analogies

Like Sirk's work, *Far from Heaven* exploits the layered texture of melodramatic form to elaborate both affect and irony. This film understands that the imposition of affective tonality native to melodrama guarantees and embeds ironic potential that the form itself can never fully control. As in Sirk, it is the moments of referential "breakthrough," those instances where the film incorporates contemporary social issues of race and sexuality, that remain problematic, and that trouble—or disappoint—the film's logic.[31] Such referential breakthroughs, of course, are precisely the moments that Poitier's films fail to accommodate as well. But *Far from Heaven* seems to confine itself to examining the terms of Sirk's model rather than those of interracial melodrama.

If this film follows Sirk's 1950s melodramas in sustaining a fragile balance between irony and sentiment, and between cool aesthetic distance and affect, it also maintains the ambition of exposing the complex workings of repression and resistance in that period's cultural representations of race, gender, and sexuality. As *Far from Heaven* elaborates its intertextual relay of aesthetic and theoretical insights, it also allows affect to sneak up on us. Several moments invite our affective investment and release, but the ways they function, and the relations among them, tell us much about the film's governing logic, as well as about what may escape it.

Raymond and Cathy's final meeting at the train station mobilizes a surprising level of pathos within the film's generally cool tonality. This wordless scene, filmed in rare shot/reverse-shot structure, offers the spectator sustained subjective views as it captures the exchange of looks upon which it turns. And the scene does turn, literally, as the camera pivots to follow Cathy's gaze on Raymond as the train pulls past her and then turns to frame her on the platform, watching her recede from Raymond's point of view as the train departs. Thus establishing point of view to control the scene and then withdrawing, like Raymond, the film emphasizes Cathy's solitude as it highlights the actors' performances in facial expression and body language. Significantly, this is also the only time Raymond's point of view is not registering the hostility of others. He comes fully into possession of active point of view only as he passes out of view.

This compelling moment, however, also gains force by its contrast to other, less successful, instances of pathos. One of these is the moment when Cathy breaks off her relationship with Raymond. At her request, he has come to meet her in a diner. Once they are seated, the camera frames a reaction shot containing the waiter and, across the counter, several customers. At the center of the frame, separating the hostile onlookers, we see the cash register bearing the sign "We reserve the right to refuse service to anyone at anytime," clearly referencing the struggles over segregated lunch counters. While Cathy and Raymond are driven from the diner by the concert of aggressive gazes, we are left with a false note of implausibility, so unimaginable is it that a man like Raymond would ever have ventured to meet Cathy in such a place at that time.

Subsequently, Cathy delivers her decision under the Ritz Theater marquee. "It isn't *plausible* for me to be friends with you. You've been so very kind to me, and I've been perfectly reckless and foolish in return." Here we note the significance of plausibility in this film's extended reflection on melodrama. In her essay "Written on the Screen," Lynne Joyrich shrewdly notes that Cathy speaks here like a critic. She reads her relationship with Raymond "through the discourse of realist narrative—one that positions her as merely a spectator, rather than an active participant, within her own life," since she "describes their situation more in terms of narrative credibility, of character motivation and diegetic consistency, than in terms of interior emotion" (194). But what about Raymond, apparently left mired in the diegetic world from which Cathy takes this critical distance?

His response bears all of the scene's affective force. As Cathy trails off, apologizing for "thinking . . . ," he picks up her thought. "Thinking what? That one person could reach out to another, take an interest in another? That maybe, for one fleeting instant, we could manage to see beyond the surface, beyond the color of things?" He is obliged here to speak the language of white liberal discourse, with its metaphors of "color blindness," much like his predecessors in Poitier's films. But Cathy asks if "we ever really do . . . see beyond those things . . . the surfaces," suggesting that she herself cannot. We are reminded that, as a figure, Cathy is all external appearances, her clothing a dazzling carapace that codes her interior as surface. Raymond, who, by contrast, asserts that he doesn't "really have a choice" but to see beyond the surface, remains the one who is confined, constricted, and policed purely on account of the visual surface of things. The cinematic self-reflexivity at play in this scene, likewise, does not extend to Raymond's iteration of the Poitier effect. Were he similarly to be granted the status of a critic, he would have to conclude that he is in a different movie altogether.

This pedagogical moment fails, though Cathy has nonetheless acquired something of a sentimental education through Raymond. But this is not really an education about racial difference so much as about her capacity for feminine autonomy. And in this failed encounter, the film highlights the questions it cannot answer: What draws Raymond to Cathy? Is it desire? Identification? Is his attraction erotic or pedagogical? Does he identify with the social circumscription of her life? Tellingly, because the film never clarifies Raymond's motives, it limits the story it can tell about him to the curiosity he provokes in Cathy and to the vague analogies through which she tries to imagine his world. Raymond's story, then, faithfully reproduces the Poitier effect, faithfully reproduces the racial imaginary of its diegetic period, in which the innocent black character remains a cipher, a screen for white projections.

And this effect emerges immediately as the conversation breaks off. As Cathy turns to leave, Raymond places his hand on her arm to retain her. At this point, the film interrupts the couple: a white man across the street yells to Raymond, "You, *boy*, hands off." Subsequent shots frame groups of white spectators in canted angles, as if shifting the balance of the world, leaving everyone else on the opposite side of the frame, isolating Cathy and Raymond. But the canted angle also suggests potential violence. Here, as elsewhere, the film emphasizes the displacement of erotic tension into an aggressive response to the couple's interaction. The violent response of these diegetic spectators inscribes a displaced intensity; the erotic affect that has remained suppressed between Cathy and Raymond rebounds upon them from the outside.

In other words, no tension emerges between Raymond and Cathy, though it emerges all around them. Conversely, nothing but tension marks Cathy and Frank's interactions, coming across his suppressed aggression and tortured expressions. By contrast to Sirk's films, in which women tend to function as sites of tension, both in relation to men and between men, the men in *Far from Heaven* remain the primary sites of Cathy's erotic curiosity, and they establish the sharpest contrasts.

As a model 1950s "wife and mother," Cathy remains assertively attentive to her children's and husband's physical and mental health and hygiene, alternating between therapeutic and managerial styles, figuring a "mom" caught in a web of discourses of expert advice and saddled with the task of managing everyone. In this world, Frank's eruptions reveal the false details in the picture the family is expected to uphold. Indeed, we might say that the moments of most intense and gratifying affect the film offers come when Frank explodes. Because his vulgar diatribes produce unseemly interruptions in the wholesome family sitcom environment that Cathy struggles to preserve, they constitute moments of sheer discharge, momentarily lifting repression to exhibit just how oppressive this domestic life remains.

Cathy fails to live up to the image of the 1950s dream mother, who has fully internalized the repression that she imposes on the family whose domestic stability and boundaries she is charged with maintaining. And because she continually disappoints her role even in its performance, she might appear to be the ideal figure for feminist sympathy, alignment, or projection. But this film offers only the most fragile, tenuous structures of potential identification, limited as they are by its paucity of point-of-view shots, its preference for reaction shots, and its commitment to emphasizing aesthetic distance. Frank is the character who displays and deploys the uncontrolled rage, the uncontainable erotic energy, and the affective protest that we wish to find in Cathy. In this splitting of repression and affect, Frank seems to offer the most satisfying, if intermittent and fragile, points of identification.

If the film stages the decline of Cathy and Frank's marriage, as it sputters to its final breakdown, in the strangled inarticulateness of their dialogues, by contrast, Raymond stands out as the film's most fluent character. He is the one who stimulates the flow of Cathy's speech and thought. However, eloquent as he is, Raymond can only *tell*. Unlike Frank, who can *show* us his most private world, Raymond never appears without Cathy in this film. As the two men pivot around Cathy, never appearing at the same time in any given space, her figure anchors them in an opposition that also establishes a parallel, since they both remain opaque for her. But *Far from Heaven* never takes an ironic distance from the Poitier effect that Raymond enacts. Consequently, its two melodramatic tracks intersect in sharp dissonance, replicating the false analogy of parallel worlds it establishes through Cathy.

Raymond, in the end, remains the film's abiding mystery, like that alluring cinema balcony that Frank does not dare to investigate, and like his own neighborhood, which Cathy visits furtively, and which the film does not explore. We remember that he has spoken explicitly about his other world, a world that the film constructs in parallel to Frank's "secret." This is a world that Cathy seems unable to imagine, despite her daily contact with Sybil. Strikingly, in the sequence that immediately follows her visit to Eagan's, she asks Sybil, apparently apropos of nothing in particular, about black churches to which she might donate old clothes. Her surprise at learning that Sybil remains active in several churches indicates a resolute ignorance about Sybil's life that directly echoes Lora's astonishment on learning that Annie has friends in *Imitation of Life*. But Cathy's surprise does not end there, because when she opens the door to exit, two NAACP representatives appear before her. In her haste to end this encounter, she accepts their literature and passes it to Sybil without even examining it. Pushing past the visitors, she leaves her perplexed maid to sign her name to their roster.

Apart from Raymond, Cathy's exchanges with blacks inevitably come to an impasse. Later, when she finally takes the initiative to call the NAACP about "volunteering," her call is interrupted by Frank's early return from work. The impasse of her communication with the NAACP—a first gesture toward public politics—directly connects to the definitive impasse of her marriage, since Frank interrupts her call to announce that he has fallen in love with a man. Neither Cathy nor the film can pick up that thread again; as far as we know, she retreats from the civil rights front after this aborted gesture.

Cathy's last dialogue with Raymond sharply foregrounds an impasse of racial understanding—the implausibility of their relationship—in a conversation that is itself marked by implausibility. Sybil has belatedly delivered to Cathy the news about Sarah's assault, news that apparently travels only through *black* channels, a dispatch from a parallel universe. This announcement precipitates Cathy's urgent mission to Raymond's home as an emissary of white guilt and sympathy. Of course, she must again rely on Sybil's insider knowledge to learn his address. A cut delivers us seamlessly to the exterior of his house, eliding any passage through the neighborhood that surrounds it. His domestic world, like his community, lies off Cathy's—and the film's—map. Even at home, then, Raymond remains as decontextualized as any of the characters Poitier played.

In a striking evocation of the service entrances that household help were often required to use, Raymond asks Cathy to meet him at the side door. He explains that his business has been ruined by the scandal of their relationship, which is plausible enough, since he relies on white patronage for much of his livelihood. What he tells her next, however, distinctly stretches plausibility. He declares that the rocks that have broken his windows "were thrown by Negroes," concluding, "that's one place that whites and colored are in perfect harmony." His facile assertion of analogy between hostility and violence on each side of the racial divide rings false. This intrusion of the "real" defies both realism and history.

Despite striving for tragic pathos, the scene derails on its stunningly unlikely premise, failing to acknowledge, let alone capture, the historical complexity and nuance of African American communities' responses to interracial relationships. As it strains for a racial analogy here, the film stumbles on a referential breakthrough. It cannot, in other words, consistently rely on the referential force of the civil rights movement in the years 1957–58 and then go on to strike an unbelievable parallel between black and white reactions to racial mixing. In this moment, the tensions the film deploys between realism and melodrama reach their most extreme. At this point, perhaps more than at any other, one is aware that the film aligns itself with Cathy, persists in relaying an identification with her. But here, its viewpoint seems to slide into hers, as if it believes for a moment what Cathy herself wants to believe.

In a world where everyone's longings and desires are disappointed, Raymond's is surely the harshest fate: he must liquidate business and property and move to Baltimore to start over. He is expelled from his world—both the white world of his business and the black one of his community. Of course, Frank is expelled from his family and from heteronormativity, and Cathy is expelled from suburban wifely normalcy. But we see that Frank has ended up with his lover, and Cathy has taken full charge of her household, sharing its management with Sybil (in a neat condensation of Marylee

Hadley taking over the family business in *Written on the Wind* and *Imitation of Life*'s black–white female domestic arrangements). Neither of them ends up as bereft as Raymond. He is literally pushed out of the film's world, and off its map. But he moves off his own map as well, since, by his account, he has never even been to Baltimore.

Because the film builds its parallels around Cathy, her fascination with the mystery and inaccessibility of both men maintains a false equivalence between them. Perhaps more to the point, it constructs the men as the "secret," the mysterious depth to be investigated and penetrated, and leaves Cathy herself as very much a surface and a vehicle for the spectator's, and its own, interest in the men. This web of fascination, secrets, and disappointments also splits into separate, noncommunicating worlds. All the sexuality and desire coalesces in the homosexual sphere, while the interracial couple is drained of erotics. Equally important, racial difference becomes accessible only through structural analogy founded on coupling, by which we return to the lens of heteronormativity. Ultimately, the film disappoints its own logic because its analogy between racism/segregation and homophobia fails through its very visual organization. It cannot go beyond the boundaries it has set for Cathy in terms of racialized geography and spaces. And it cannot grant Raymond the independence it permits Frank because it has not endowed him with his own point of view.

As in so many Poitier films, race here is displaced into the interracial bond and replaced by the white–black couple. Thus, the film's "racial angle" ultimately fades into a *white* angle of fascination with the ongoing mystery of a black world that remains persistently elsewhere. Like Cathy, the protofeminist mother, whose complex and contradictory political plenitude it seeks to restore, this film proceeds by the analogies she favors: *Far from Heaven* seems bound, by the very project it so lovingly elaborates, to disappoint.

In concluding, *Far from Heaven* circles back on itself; its closing scene visually replicates its opening as it follows Cathy driving away from the train station at which the film had first picked her up. But, perhaps recalling the kind of ambiguous ironic restorations or resolutions that Sirk's melodramas so often delivered, this film also suggests something else. Its sound track interrupts the fullness of this melancholy moment in a single sour note the piano strikes to punctuate the transition to the final credits.

This note signals an ambiguous distance as it musically marks the moment with disappointment. Affect here seems to displace analysis at the point of loss.

Like Poitier's characters, Raymond passes on from the diegetic world; but unlike them, he seems to leave this white context largely untouched— untouched, that is, except for Cathy, mournfully isolated against the cold gray stone of the train platform. Her melancholy mood shapes the sound track. Even the one false note, recalling the film's frequent shifts to ironic perspective, does not diminish the melancholic tone that establishes Raymond as its lost object. That loss may be the price of privileging Sirkian women's melodrama over the interracial melodramas this film's iteration of the Poitier effect evokes, or of trying to make two dissonant modes cohere. Even as the Poitier figure here provides an angle through which to pry open the complex ironies and repressions of Sirk's world, *Far from Heaven* does not bring its analytic irony to bear on the affective and ideological charges of the effect that grounded those interracial melodramas. Like Homer Smith, Virgil Tibbs, and John Prentice, Raymond Deagan, it turns out, was just passing through.

4

Black Authenticity and the Ambivalent Icon

Keeping It Real in *Talk to Me*

Mediations

Perhaps by coincidence, perhaps not, Kasi Lemmons's *Talk to Me* (2007) seems to offer a rejoinder to the nostalgic representations of the civil rights movement that we have been considering. Sidney Poitier anchors the dense web of popular references through which it remembers a certain black cultural history of the 1960s and 1970s. But *Talk to Me* remembers not the Poitier effect so much as its impact within and on the popular cultural lexicon. This film's fictionalized account of the career of the historical figure Ralph Waldo "Petey" Greene, a popular disc jockey on WOL radio in Washington, D.C., deploys black performances that are not addressed to white audiences or interlocutors. Where *Pleasantville* highlights musical crossover, privileging and even idealizing its progressive cultural and political force, *Talk to Me* focuses on black production for black audiences; others may be overhearing, but they are not the privileged point of address.

Talk to Me also privileges a different form of mass mediation in its memory. The nostalgic melodramas that "remembered" civil rights, shaped by a projective gaze from the "feminist future," all concerned themselves, in one way or another, with television's increasingly central claim on national attention. But in this film radio is central. Set in the period during which television expands and definitively consolidates itself as the primary vehicle of the national "imagined community," *Talk to Me* emphasizes radio's rootedness in the local. As television steadfastly homogenizes the image and the sound of "Americanness," radio keeps its local and racial accent. Indeed, this film's narrative reaches its crisis when Petey definitively refuses to perform on the national stage of *The Tonight Show,* explicitly rejecting its forum in favor of his Washington-based radio show and his local-affiliate TV show.[1]

Tracking the complicated relationship between Petey (Don Cheadle) and Dewey Hughes (Chiwetel Ejiofor), his friend and the programming manager at WOL, this film juxtaposes the hustler ex-con with the steadfastly middle-class and ambitious manager. It thus plays on an opposition between the hardworking, upwardly mobile, responsible "civil rights subject" and the "poor and disenfranchised members of the black community" that Herman Gray identifies as so crucial in representations that seek to "rewrite and readjust the dominant cultural story of the black presence in post–World War II America."[2]

But the film quickly disrupts that formula. While representing Petey's transformation into a "Washington, D.C., icon," *Talk to Me* steadily resists creating its own iconicity, refusing to freeze into fixity the polarities Petey and Dewey themselves exhibit in their initial encounters. That opposition—between repressed and uncensored, deliberate and spontaneous, artificial and authentic, copy and "original" simply will not hold. At the same time, the film examines the significance of the mass-mediated black voice in the context of a shifting landscape of media reception and ownership, remembering for us the historical importance of the radio for African American populations.

Exploring the multilayered and contradictory masculine identities that here contend, the film also reanimates iconic images of the late 1960s and 1970s that circulate in collective media memory, while crucially anchoring them to Poitier. Interestingly, it deploys the Poitier of interracial melodrama in a new mediascape that is responding to black cultural politics. Taking 1968 as its structurally central pivot, *Talk to Me* foregrounds the moment just after Poitier's box-office popularity culminates in 1967. This is the moment when he rather abruptly passes beyond the mainstream screen, and when some critics and audiences express sharp ambivalence, if not outright hostility, toward *Variety*'s "useful Negro." To viewers more disposed toward the activist stance—and style—advanced by the Black Panther Party, for instance, Poitier could stand as an icon of conciliation, compliance, and even complicity, packaged by white productions as black authenticity. To take one example, for Clifford Mason, a black playwright and critic, writing in the *New York Times* (September 10, 1967) under the title "Why Does White America Love Sidney Poitier So?," Poitier's characters supported the ideological assertion "that the Negro is best served by being a black version of the man in the gray flannel suit, taking on white problems in a white man's world."[3] *Talk to Me* redeploys the Poitier icon as a decidedly ambivalent site around which the film explores the questions of black authenticity that helped to shape the period it remembers.

Centering on the contests over meaning and identity that marked 1968, this film tracks the development of African American style and speech attending and responding to the emergence of black power, the Black Arts Movement, and blaxploitation cinema. Curator Thelma Golden, who organized the 1993 *Black Male* exhibition at the Whitney Museum, cites black power's emergence in 1968 as one of the key "cultural signposts" around which she organized this show. Golden emphasizes that "Black Power brought with it codifiable images of masculinity." And she stresses the power of visibility: "The black leather jackets, dark sunglasses, big afros, and bigger guns made visual the myths of uncontrollable aggression and rampant sexuality."[4] But, just as the Black Panthers manipulated signs, codes, and images in the production of media spectacle, this film sets familiar slogans and clichés in dialogue with Petey's own public and private discourse, consistently reframing and interrogating postures of masculinity.

Remembering the turbulence of 1968, *Talk to Me* both overtly and obliquely echoes African American cultural productions of the period. And Poitier circulates most explicitly through this film as part of the lexicon of playful aggression and serious insult its characters deploy and as an image at play in Petey's signifying. When Dewey initially refuses to hire him as a DJ, Petey attacks him: "I thought you was *real*. You're nothing but another white boy with a tan . . . you Sidney Poitier–ass nigger . . ." In this scene, Petey's spectacular red velvet suit, with wide paisley lapels, creates a stunning contrast to Dewey's light-silver-gray pinstriped suit. That suit is directly modeled, as costume designer Gersha Philips declares on the DVD commentary, on that of Mr. Tibbs in *In the Heat of the Night*. Tibbs is, in many ways, the most perfect incarnation of Poitier's civil rights subject, since he doubles his ideological commitment to the law of the land with a professional one. And Tibbs is the character against which Petey will so aggressively assert his own status as an *anti*-Poitier.

This juxtaposition foregrounds their opposing styles and highlights their reciprocally stereotyped readings of appearance. In their complex pre-occupations with truth telling—"telling it like it is" and their discourse of "keeping it real"—Petey and Dewey endlessly evoke questions of authenticity. In its polyphonic layerings, the film itself works through issues of the "real" and "authentic" on the terrain of speech. Foregrounding the technological mediations of speech in its repeated focus on the period's media apparatus itself—from the broadcast booth to the television—this film explores the ways performance and artifice play against claims to truth and authenticity. Such claims become particularly contentious in this period, linked as they are to African American identities under construction in the public sphere.[5]

At the same time, this film clearly recalls more broadly the breakthrough moment in black cinematic production that displaced Poitier's regular returns. Some months before *Sweet Sweetback's Baadasssss Song* (1971) delivered a protagonist who addressed white fantasy as its "bad object," *Cotton Comes to Harlem* (Ossie Davis, 1970) reworked the cinematic possibilities for racially based humor. This film, according to Donald Bogle, "seemed to be telling black audiences that it was now alright to laugh at the old dum-dum characters which would have infuriated audiences of the 1960s." "Now the old ethnic humor," he writes, "seemed blessed with a double consciousness: rather than cooning or tomming it up to please whites (as Fetchit had to do), the black comic characters joked or laughed or acted the fool with one another." Far from pitching their comedy to white laughter, Bogle notes, "sometimes they used humor combatively to outwit the white characters."[6]

Talk to Me submits Poitier himself to a comic retooling, demonstrating the persistence of his "usefulness" as an icon, now deployed ironically in an evolving black cultural vernacular. But while this film explicitly evokes Poitier and his role as Mr. Tibbs, Lemmons cites as a key model his *Uptown Saturday Night* (1974), in which he starred with Bill Cosby.[7] This was the first of three buddy films (the others were *Let's Do It Again*, 1975, and *A Piece of the Action*, 1977) that Poitier directed in which he plays Cosby's straight man. These films—like the period that *Talk to Me* frames—mark Poitier's migration out of mainstream interracial melodramas and into comedies aimed at the black audiences that Hollywood had newly rediscovered. Deploying ensembles of noted black actors and comedians, these films seem implicitly to answer back to the history of Poitier's previous roles, which cast him in isolation from a community, fixing him firmly in inter-racial encounters, often organized by buddy pairings. Lemmons's film plays on, but recasts, the intraracial buddy thematics of these 1970s films in a fraternal melodrama as it examines the bond that emerges from antago-nism between two men of radically divergent styles and class affiliations.

Unlike Poitier's white-authored films, *Talk to Me* reaches no magical trans-formation. Instead, maintaining a balance of power and impact between its buddies, this film explores the cultural landscape that shapes its protag-onists while they themselves gain some access to the means of cultural production. Their discursive understanding develops across diametrically opposed styles in clothing, speech, and posture, in a shared aural environ-ment that brings together a range of voices and sounds, as the film expands its arena into the terrain of the surrounding community as well as into the broader historical moment.

Remembering the civil rights period from 1966 forward, *Talk to Me* fore-grounds its own mass-mediated memory. Restaging the look and sound of the late 1960s through the 1970s, it incorporates images from film and tele-vision. Music of the period, whether in original or covered form, shapes and drives its progress, punctuating the scenes it unfolds. But throughout, the performing voice—both on and off the air—structures the film's con-flicts and resolutions, foregrounding the centrality of performance to any assertion of authenticity. To elaborate its premise that authenticity, and specifically black masculine authenticity, emerges as performance, this film consistently produces collisions of style and idiom.

Montage

Beginning with a parallel editing sequence that leads to its protagon-ists' first confrontation, *Talk to Me* establishes its emphasis on editing and cinematic technique. After Petey places an LP on his turntable and dons headphones in his Lorton prison broadcast studio, he orders, "Wake up, Goddamn it!" The film cuts to Dewey, fallen asleep at his desk.[8] As the sound track carries the song Petey has selected, James Brown's "It's a Man's

Man's Man's World," we watch Dewey dress and drive to the prison.[9] It is as if this sound has already extended its reach into Dewey's home and along the length of his route. The song's lyrics emphasize the polarization of overwhelmingly *men's* worlds, that of corporate media and that of the prison. But they also invite our attention to the troubled complexity of the male relationships we are about to encounter. When Dewey settles in at the prison for a visit with his incarcerated brother, Milo (Mike Epps), the music recedes into a backdrop for Petey's patter, itself the subject of their conversation.

Characteristically eschewing classic realist fictional space as constructed through shot/reverse-shot structures, *Talk to Me* stresses the relationship of bodies in space. A key example occurs when Dewey first encounters Petey and his girlfriend, Vernell Watson (Taraji P. Henson), during this prison visit. Keeping all three in frame throughout this exchange, the handheld camera continues to move slightly, as if joining this uneasy group. Constantly asserting its presence, the camera regularly reminds us of the limitations of its view, sharing as it does so closely the space of the characters. In stressing limited view, calling attention to what lies out of sight, of course, the camera figures the question of point of view more broadly. And it emphasizes the significance of what is not immediately given to sight, or what appearances do not reveal. But the scene also establishes the weight of words because Dewey reinforces the class barrier between himself and Petey with a lexical one. To Petey's consternation, Dewey pronounces him to be a "miscreant."

When Dewey strides away in blurred focus, Arthur Conley's "Sweet Soul Music" comes up on the sound track, as if prompting the cut to WOL, where "Nighthawk" Bob Terry (Cedric the Entertainer) is playing the song on his show in progress.[10] Musical flow here liquidates distance and dissolves barriers, but it also functions figuratively, evoking accounts of early radio's impact on social spaces, its tendency to "blur" their boundaries. Where "public and private have temporarily merged to form an . . . *intimate public,*" according to Jason Loviglio, considerable ambivalence arose around the proliferating radio technology. "Accounts of shared radio reception," he writes, "also reinforce the notion of distinct spaces, spaces whose difference becomes most apparent at moments . . . when the listener's mobility across the lines of public and private space makes the boundaries seem clearer and more porous at the same time."[11] Radio's blurring of public and private, and its articulation of individual with community, will become central to this film's development, as well as to its complex meditations on the status of voice and identity.[12]

Continuing to trouble the sharp opposition it has established between prisoner and businessman, in the next sequence the film allows Petey's voice to break into Dewey's world. A scene in which Dewey is promoted over his white counterparts to head of programming ends with Petey's voice-over, broadcasting to his fellow inmates. "I found out today I'm not a con, you all . . . No. I am a miscreant." He has gleefully taken up the foreign term and incorporated it into his own repertoire, accessorizing it within his own stylistic vernacular. Now he deploys it in a rhetorical turn that figuratively bridges the distance Dewey sought to create through vocabulary.

As parallel editing juxtaposes him moving along the cell block greeting other inmates and Dewey receiving congratulations as he walks the halls of his office, Petey continues to play with words. He ruminates over the power of euphemism, of calling a thing by one name rather than another, as in "correctional facility" for "prison," concluding that this is all "wordplay." Here the film cuts back to Dewey settling in to watch *The Tonight Show.* That show's master of wordplay, Johnny Carson, has crucially influenced Dewey's own particular vernacular and style, through which he accentuates his distinction from Petey.

We have already begun to see the importance of style and pose as Petey moves through his prison environment. When a group of inmates report for conjugal visits, the camera first captures only their legs, wearing identical jeans and black sneakers—except for Petey. His burnished orange leather shoes create striking relief in the drab parade. At this point the camera moves up his body to show his paisley ascot; it cuts him out from the crowd, and, in foregrounding him, it structurally replicates his own strategies of distinction. At the same time, of course, this moment amusingly evokes such blaxploitation heroes as Shaft and Priest from *Superfly,* whom we come to recognize and read by their shoes.

Upon Petey's release, we are abruptly transported outside the prison walls into contemporary Washington, D.C. A shot of spectacular shoes marks the end of the stunning montage that elides the passage of time and the change of location. A scene of prisoners cheering Petey from behind bars dissolves into several crowd sequences showing antiwar protesters on the National Mall (probably the October 21, 1967, demonstration at the Lincoln Memorial). We hear President Lyndon Johnson in voice-over, and then we see him in contemporary TV footage. His image gives way to a televisual image of Martin Luther King calling for an end to the bombing. This image, in turn, dissolves into a shot of a newspaper kiosk; we can read part of the headline on the *Washington Post*: "Tens of Thousands Stage . . . March from White House." Into this frame comes a pointy red leather toe, and Petey and Vernell appear from behind the kiosk, at first visible only as legs and shoes. A rapid pan upward brings their deliciously extravagant costumes and Vernell's voluminous Afro into view.

In its assertive combination of natural texture and cultivated artifice of shape, her hair emblematizes the elements of style this film will deploy and examine. Kobena Mercer argues for the interest of "rereading" this period's "transformative political movements in terms of style and dress." Asserting that "as they filtered through mass media, such as magazines, music, or television, these styles contributed to the increasing visibility of black struggles in the 1960s," he contends that, "as elements of everyday life, the black styles in hair and dress helped to underline massive shifts in popular aspirations among black people and participated in a populist logic of rupture."[13] It is this terrain of everyday political discourse, in all its semiotic volatility, that the film explores through Petey's performances.

Montage has propelled Petey from the prison yard directly to his first approach to WOL. Significantly, the news images that fill the gap left by his invisible trajectory anchor him, and us, in history and in the specific turmoil of the moment, as the civil rights and antiwar movements converge in Washington. In his flashy red velvet suit, Petey looks very much like a blaxploitation character. As Vernell describes him: "You're the man with the *pants,* the shit talkin', pimp walkin', good lovin' man." Although at this point Petey seems to have missed the historical events the montage registers, subsequent scenes will show that his view is deeply marked by politics.

His first visit to WOL dramatizes a clash of cultures, as the film plays with limitations of the visual field. A meeting of management begins with an establishing shot of the length of the conference table as station owner

E. G. Sonderling (Martin Sheen) stands at its head, the white coworkers all aligned on one side of the table, across from Dewey. As Sonderling paces to the right, Dewey slips out of frame. When Sonderling inquires about the station's loss of audience share, we hear Dewey responding before we see him. "The problem is that we've lost touch with the *real* D.C. in our attempts to win over the Beltway . . ." As he speaks, the camera pans so rapidly to the left that it blurs the image, thus miming the turn of a human head, until it brings Dewey back into focus on the beat of the word "real." Emphasizing Dewey's claim to speak for the "real D.C." over and against his white colleagues, this camera also figures him as "off their map," much like the black audience they are losing. The camera here establishes a strategy that will mark the film throughout: it frequently races to catch up with unexpected developments just out of sight. It continually revises and reframes the visual terrain, pointing to the "overlooked," to what we have not quite taken into account.

These effects dramatize the scene of Petey's arrival. Dewey abruptly interrupts himself, and a cut brings the cause of his consternation into view, as Petey and Vernell enter, framed in the office window. When Nighthawk begins his broadcast, Vernell's whoop of enthusiasm penetrates the meeting room. As the secretary, Freda (Alison Sealy-Smith), anxiously calls in to the meeting on the (superfluous) intercom, her voice joins Vernell's shrieks, now doubled as they are channeled through the audio technology; this relay of aural effects disrupts the visual field as the meeting degenerates into a scramble for the door. An effect emerges to which the film will frequently return: sound precedes sight, and the radio voice figuratively enters the conversation.

Body rejoins voice as we take in, with Dewey, the spectacle of Petey and Vernell dancing to the broadcast. When all the characters assemble in the main hallway, the camera frames them in tight medium shots, so that our view of each character is marked by the bodily presence of others. Barreling up to encounter these disruptive characters, Sonderling exclaims, "What in blue blazes . . . !" Petey reacts to the anachronism of expression and the inhibition it signals with hilarity, repeating the phrase incredulously, as Vernell howls with glee. Hijacking the phrase through repetition and ironic expression, Petey's verbal performance "signifies" on it.[14] He will permanently claim "Blue Blazes" as his personal nickname for Sonderling.

Throughout the tense argument that organizes this scene, the film highlights performance, both verbal and physical. While the men argue, Vernell continues dancing to Nighthawk's show. Consistent with their steadfast commitment to inappropriateness, she and Petey spew obscenities, and her dancing violates the protocols of the professional space, where the other characters behave as if they hear nothing. Radio heard in the office—on-site—is not radio heard at home or on the street. In their exaggerated, aggressive performance, of course, these characters intend to provoke and mock both the white and the black behavioral styles arrayed before them, in a spectacular performance that comically disrupts the professional space, casting its conventions as "uptight."

But the film will eventually undercut this effect. Conferring privately with Petey, Dewey tries to enlighten him about his prospects: "Even if I could get you a job, it would be as a janitor or a window washer." Petey retorts with rage, "Man, I thought you was *real*. But you're just a white boy with a tan . . . Shit, I expect to get rejected by Whitey." As Petey establishes an equation of realness with his own "black" performance, this scene sets up a rigidly stereotypical opposition of the black middle class as repressed, censorious, and punitive superego to the black working class as ecstatic, chaotic, and aggressive id. While the characters will negotiate beyond this limiting equation, their initial confrontation consistently foregrounds competing styles, underscoring their crucial importance to the film's development. Kobena Mercer offers a subtle account of the emergence of certain African American styles and "stylization" in the mid-twentieth century, following on migrations from the rural South to cities in the North: "Shut out from access to illusions of 'making it,' this marginalized urban formation of modern diaspora culture sponsored a sense of style which answered back against these conditions of existence."[15]

At the same time, this sequence displays the film's consistent musical inflection of scenes and space. Music amplifies or mutes, intensifies or attenuates. It makes unexpected connections, and it highlights jarring juxtapositions rather than smoothing them out. After Petey's raucous departure from the station, as Dewey and his white management colleagues regroup, the Chambers Brothers' "Time Has Come Today" emerges on the sound track and bridges the cut to Dewey's well-manicured hand reaching to collect the *Washington Post*. This song, whose lyrics emphasize that "the rules have changed" and repeat the title line assertively, seems to propel and to pace the next sequence as well as to underline the political news that anchors it.

The *Post*'s headline reads, "Johnson Deploys 50,000 Additional Troops, Draft Call Doubled." We follow Dewey in medium close-up as he crosses the street to his office. In the long distance, a small picket line circles. Dressed in an open-necked shiny red shirt, striped bell bottoms, and a long leather vest, Petey leads the group, carrying a sign that puns on the station's call letters: "Washington's Original Liar." We follow Petey's placard as he walks out of frame. But as the placard disappears from sight, what emerges from behind it is another shot of Dewey's arm in a different expensive suit, picking up another newspaper. "U.S. Continues Lull on Raids in North." A smooth continuity elides time and space through the camera's steady circling, as it tracks the intersection of national and global conflict with this local struggle. Dewey crosses the street once again, and the camera circles around his head to catch the black man in the newspaper kiosk observing the whole scene, and to align itself with his view for a moment. We hear the picketers before we see them; the emphasis has shifted from visual signs to voice. Significantly, Petey has transformed his attire; he now wears all black. His expanded picket line chants, "WOL go straight to hell." But as the group of protesters has become more tightly organized, their message has become no more readily legible.

Again the camera circles with Petey, and then the film cuts to pick up the newspaper again. Under a photograph of police officers bending over a prone body, we read, "Civil Rights Leaders Call For Investigation into Negro Boy's Death." As the protesters chant, "Dewey Hughes is in bed with the Man," the camera, located within the protesting group, reveals Petey with a bullhorn, and we catch Dewey's look of alarm at this interpellation. Now dressed in the Panthers' signature black turtleneck and beret, Petey has mobilized the bullhorn technology to lead a much larger group. One of the most prominent of their placards reads, "Stop the Killing," a double message that can apply to both the Vietnam War and local police brutality. Another sign announces, "WOL is for the Power NOT the People." When Dewey appeals to the crowd, saying, "Our goal is to speak for and unite the community," Petey replies by asking why the station isn't "speaking about that black boy that got shot down by the pigs the other day?" Montage here figures the imbrication of local and global issues, increasing political focus, and solidarity growing through collective voice.

So this sequence captures a distinct shift in rhetoric and style. Petey appears as a bricoleur who deploys the period's galvanizing slogans and vocabulary along with its style politics. As a figure, he recalls the dexterity with which the Black Panthers staged and manipulated media spectacle.[16] But he also resonates with heroes of the blaxploitation genre, with its central concern with appearance, its premium on "looking good." Charles Kronengold contends that "if a political act succeeds in a black action film, it is because the characters look good doing it." "Black action films," he argues, "suggest that the performance of everyday acts with style has political consequences. The flip side, however, is that explicitly political words and acts cannot be privileged, nor can they be understood independent of the nuances of performance."[17] Much the same, we will see, might be said of Petey's own performative style.

Reframings

Talk to Me remains preoccupied with the space offscreen, what lies just beyond the camera's view. Continuously alert to what unfolds just out of sight—ambient but unseen—the film's visual strategy suggests its expectations of surprise events, reversals, and reframings of its perspective. Metaphorically, of course, the space out of view is occupied by history, always outstripping our observations. But likewise, the radio community Petey addresses, by its very nature as a mass-media community, remains largely invisible—until it emerges as a protesting crowd at a concert after Martin Luther King's assassination.

Editing strikingly foregrounds the relationship between the seen/known and the unseen/uncertain, as the film elides distance and telescopes time, again and again introducing an unsettling "foreign" element into a scene that it will quickly reshape. Equally powerful are the film's effects of aural editing: its sound track regularly bridges disparate places, particularly as it articulates the radio station and broadcast booth into the public sphere of the street. Establishing connections but also partitioning spaces, this film's musical track functions, like the music in blaxploitation films, to challenge, undermine, or enhance the moods and claims of the narrative, and thus to reframe our view.[18] But music also frequently splits our attention, gathering additional connotations that may undermine explicit discourse.

At the end of the montage that tracks Petey's evolving protest strategy, the film overturns the dynamics of the first scene at WOL. Cutting from the moment when Dewey finally gives Petey his phone number, the film moves into a pool hall. We follow a billiard ball that Petey has just shot to Dewey's hand. If his appearance on the scene provokes a slight visual surprise for the viewer, Petey emphasizes his unexpected "looks" in this context. "You're a little outta your element around here, ain't you, Mr. Tibbs?" Poitier's image organizes this pivotal scene, as ironies multiply. We remember that *In the Heat of the Night* is built on Mr. Tibbs being out of his element, constantly surprised and surprising. At the same time, of course, Petey invokes Poitier as an icon for "inauthentic" blackness, for "acting white." In Petey's world, the roles that established the actor as the figure of black authenticity for the white gaze register as precisely the opposite. Poitier functions as the measure of the inauthenticity that Petey polices.

These questions of appearance and acting will shape the film's progress from this scene forward. What follows overturns Petey's view of things, when Dewey responds to his public protest as a spectacle that calls for a display in return. This display takes shape when Petey challenges Dewey to a game of pool. The stakes are extreme: in addition to a bet of five hundred dollars, Petey proposes to "Tibbs" that he wager a job at the station. As Petey warms up, Dewey adds a bet against Petey's sinking a ball on his first shot. Squaring off for reciprocal insults, Petey mocks Dewey with an imitation of Sidney Poitier's accent and diction: "I like your style, Tibbs." But Dewey shows himself to be equal to this exchange, and he launches into a series of jokes that undermine Petey's composure. The camera holds Dewey at the edge of the frame as Petey shoots.

After he fails to sink his ball, Dewey takes over, and the camera follows in a series of smooth rapid pans the ever more complicated shots he successfully makes, cutting away after each to reaction shots of Petey and Vernell, while evidence of his virtuoso skills accumulates. He begins a muted tirade, one that gradually undoes any resemblance he may bear to a Poitier character. "You see, Negroes always think that if you speak correct English or you wear clothes other than clown suits, that you're not real," he asserts. "Now, for you, what's real," he continues, "is a nigger loud mouth, telling everybody how *bad* he is . . ." Rounding the space as it glides across Dewey's body to follow his shots, blurring the background as it circles, the camera shapes him as a central pivot. "You were so busy running your mouth you never really asked yourself *why* I chose a pool hall to meet," he continues, indicating the limitations of Petey's view of him. "'Cause this uppity nigger could *never* have grown up in these projects, or made his way through school hustling dumbass niggers who thought he wasn't down," he concludes with his last shot.

Inverting the dynamics of the scene at WOL, this chiasmatic sequence answers performance with performance, and in the process it calls radically into question the concept of the "real." When Dewey's speech shifts his diction, intonation, rhythm, and vocabulary to match Petey's, he asserts his own "realness" in ways that call attention to the performative nature of Petey's vaunted "keeping it real." Dewey rips the veil off his performance as "Mr. Tibbs" to reveal, beneath it, another performance, and perhaps to call into question Poitier's status, for a certain black audience, as the icon of black inauthenticity against which to perform its own authentic identity.

Addressing Petey indirectly through the relay of a third person, "Negroes," and without specifying his inclusion in that group, Dewey's discourse plays on a kind of identity politics. This oblique address is a form of "signifying"; it uses Petey's own vocabulary against him while not explicitly identifying him as the target of the critique.[19] Henry Louis Gates Jr. sums up the observations of a series of commentators on "signifying" as follows: "Signifying depends on the signifier *repeating* what someone else has said about a third person, in order to *reverse* the status of a relationship heretofore harmonious; signifying can also be employed to *reverse* or *undermine* pretense or even one's opinion about one's own status. This use of repetition and reversal (chiasmus) constitutes an implicit parody of a subject's own complicity in illusion."[20]

But Dewey's performance also reframes the competing masculinities we have been watching. Phillip Brian Harper comments on masculine verbal display in *Are We Not Men?*: "If verbal facility is considered an identifying mark of masculinity in certain African-American contexts, however, this is so only when it is demonstrated specifically through the use of the vernacular." "Indeed," he emphasizes, "a too-evident facility in the standard white idiom can quickly identify one as not a strong black man, but rather as a white-identified Uncle Tom. Simply put, within some African-American communities, the 'professional' or 'intellectual' black male inevitably endangers his status both as black and as male whenever he evidences a facility with Received Standard English" (11).[21] This is the diction, precisely, that characterizes every iteration of the Poitier figure in his interracial melodramas. And for many, it seems to dovetail with his desexualization: Clifford Mason describes him as a "good guy in a totally white world, with no wife, no sweetheart, no woman to love or kiss . . . the antiseptic, one-dimensional hero."[22]

In this key sequence, Dewey demonstrates his "authenticity" through performance. (A bonus of pleasure in this code-switching scene accrues to the spectator who knows that Ejiofor is British.) But authenticity as performance does not reduce to the "performance of authenticity" in the sense of revealing a hidden core and stabilizing it.[23] This performance does not equate to "performing" black authenticity for dominant media and its largely white audience. Rather, this assertion of authenticity as artifice or style doubles as a claim on identity, and on American identity at that.

Writing in 1964, in the introduction to *Shadow and Act*, Ralph Ellison remembers his youthful group of friends appropriating elements of style from the movies and "the vague and shifting figures" they paraded. "The proper response to these figures was, we felt, to develop ourselves for the performance of the many and diverse roles, and the fact that certain limitations had been imposed upon our freedom did not lessen our sense of obligation." "Not only were we to prepare," he writes, "but we were to perform—not with mere competence but with an almost reckless verve; with, may we say (without evoking the quaint and questionable term of *negritude*), Negro American style?"[24] Performance and style are linked here: "We recognized and were proud of our group's own style wherever we discerned it—in jazzmen and prizefighters, ball players and tap dancers; in gesture, inflection, intonation, timbre and phrasing" (xvii). Style depends crucially on appropriation for Ellison: "Part of our boyish activity expressed a yearning to make any- and everything of quality *Negro American*; to appropriate it, possess it, re-create it in our own group and individual images" (xvii). Ellison stresses the art of style as appropriation and refashioning. But here as elsewhere, he refuses to disarticulate black identity from American identity, situating blackness at the heart of Americanness.

Perhaps nowhere does (Ralph Waldo) Petey Greene's namesake make this point more forcefully than in his essay "Change the Joke and Slip the Yoke" in *Shadow and Act*, in which he argues that the trickster figure so closely associated with African American literature is far from exclusively native to that tradition; rather, it is a central trope of American culture. "I knew the trickster Ulysses just as early as I knew the wily rabbit of Negro American lore," Ellison asserts (58). He explains: "I use folklore in my work not because I am Negro, but because writers like Eliot and Joyce made me conscious of the literary value of my folk inheritance." Then he goes on to add, with wry reference to his namesake, that pillar of American literary tradition, Emerson: "My cultural background, like that of most Americans, is dual (my middle name, sadly enough, is Waldo)" (58). Ellison's remarks seem especially apposite for a reading of this pool hall sequence, since Dewey shows himself to be as much of a "trickster" as Petey, organizing this whole sequence around his performance as trickster. Performance and style remain central to the film's unfolding, as it interrogates the status of authenticity elaborated through competing versions of black masculinity.

Petey's first radio "appearance" brings questions of style and performance together with issues of truth and rhetoric. This sequence immediately follows Dewey's stunning vernacular performance, and it opens with his pitch to Mr. Sonderling to replace DJ Sunny Jim Kelsey (Vondie Curtis Hall) on the morning show.[25] "But Sunny Jim is a D.C. icon," Sonderling protests. "We're not playing Nat King Cole and the Drifters anymore," Dewey insists. His boss objects: "I'm not turning this into some kinda teenie bopper American Bandstand. We're a respectable R and B station." At this point Dewey begins to play on the terms of respect: "With all due respect, sir, this is not a *respectable* town. This is D.C. You see them out on the mall every day protesting the so-called respectable establishment. We can't become the establishment or they'll turn on us." No longer a matter only of generational opposition, the program's playlist and design reflect an overlay of class, style, and politics, which *is* the 1960s.

This is, of course, where Petey comes in, as the man who will become a different kind of "D.C. icon." Dewey explains that he has found an out-of-town DJ. As he speaks, a quick cut reveals feet striding in pointy-toed white shoes, and the camera moves up Petey's body to examine his striped suit and paisley shirt. Playfully cued to the cut, "Hold On, I'm Coming" (performed by Sam and Dave) fills the sound track in the kind of aural design that propels this film's transitions and introduces ironic distances and shifting tonalities into its texture. Edgy camera work once again captures and maps Petey's disruptive impact on the workplace. Linguistic competition and conflict immediately come into play, with Petey greeting Sonderling as "Blue Blazes" and the latter mistaking Petey's name as "Mr. *Brown*." Because Sunny Jim has already stormed off in a rage, Sonderling is forced to put Petey on the air. Dewey introduces him in an oddly stilted voice, which closely resembles that of an FM classical music announcer. But Petey appears paralyzed by performance anxiety. Halting of speech and belching with nervous nausea, he falters. After a break, during which we hear "Knock on Wood," in an ironic tweak that voices the men's internal anxiety, Petey finds his verbal stride.[26]

He begins by announcing his commitment to "tell it like it is." "I am an all around hustler, and some of my best friends is pimps, whores and gamblers. But I guess that don't make me no different than Berry Gordy. . . . So this is me, y'all, and you ain't gotta worry about me giving you nothing but the sho' nuff, 'cause that's *all* I know." Throughout this speech, the camera has returned to Sonderling's and Dewey's increasingly exasperated and alarmed reactions.

When Petey obeys their order to apologize for his remarks, the camera comes to rest on him in static medium close-up. This stilled moment of verbal performance stands out against the sequence's rapid editing and reaction shots. Apologizing to Gordy for "making him out to be a hustler and a pimp," Petey asserts: "I love the way he takes the little brothers and sisters . . . downtrodden from the projects . . . and he gets them off the streets. Then he puts a few dollars in their pockets, teaches them how to walk and talk, and sends them right back out there to bring him a whole lot of money. So I'm sorry if in any way I made him out to be a pimp."[27]

Thus repeating his original charge through disavowal and providing ample evidence for the conclusion he claims to want to attenuate, Petey leans back in satisfaction. His claim only to be saying "what black folks already know" directly challenges the station's commercial concerns about offending "Motown," which Dewey loudly advances. As the sequence concludes, Dewey and Petey clash over this issue, trading insults that invoke stereotypes of "house" and "field." Petey concludes with another declaration of his authenticity: "At least I know who I am! I'm Petey Greene and I'ma keep talking shit!"

A cut transports us into a bar, where we hear Nighthawk's voice on the radio. This space is multilayered, both visually and aurally. After the camera examines some groups of customers, it eventually finds Dewey seated alone. At the end of the bar, which is shot in shallow focus, we spot a television set, its image blurred. We recognize the profile of Martin Luther King Jr.; his silent, ghostly image inhabits the center of the frame. Because it occupies the end of the sharp diagonal formed by the bar's edge, this image constitutes the vanishing point of the screen's imaginary horizon line. But while King's voice remains inaudible, we begin to catch snatches of conversation from across the bar.

Dewey's attention, like ours, picks up speech and then seeks its source. We watch three men chatting as Dewey eavesdrops and registers excited recognition that Petey's voice has reached them. "Why do you think they snatched him off the air so fast if he wasn't telling the truth . . ." "Petey Greene was cool," a voice chimes in from just offscreen. This, the camera reveals in a quick pan left, is the bartender, who opines, "But that white boy he was with?" This amusing misapprehension of Dewey's race, through his "white" sound, continues the film's reflection on voice and on the play of performance and identification that radio DJs' invisibility enables. It may thus remind us of the "racial ventriloquy" that had spread on radio in the postwar period, with white DJs masquerading verbally as black, playing the music of African American artists for crossover audiences.[28] As media scholar William Barlow puts it: "As an invisible 'theater of the mind,' [radio] was the ideal medium for such voice impersonations."[29] Laughing out loud at this evidence of his inadvertent verbal masquerade, Dewey buys the men a drink and exits. He moves left across the screen and continues in a match on action, reappearing across the cut walking left into the pool hall.

This pivotal moment, where Dewey attempts to persuade Petey to make another effort on the radio, sets out the central terms of their relationship. "Why should I give up all of this right here to take a chance on you?" Petey inquires, ironically indicating the seediness of his surroundings. "I guess I need you to say things I'm afraid to say," Dewey ventures.

"And you need me to do the things you're afraid to do." Having established their opposition in style, manner, and idiom as coded for their class positions, the film overlays on it a dichotomy between "doing" and "saying."

But Dewey also introduces a notion of complementarity: each protagonist supplies what the other lacks and desires in his own character. Together, they add up to a "whole." However, this equation immediately dissolves in irony. "Man, that was deep," Petey declares. Framing him in isolation here, the film deploys one of its few classic shot/reverse shots. "Should put that shit on a greeting card," he concludes with affectionate derision. Refusing easy categories, even apparently dialectical ones, this film prefers instead to examine the complexity that relates evident differences, and it resolutely undermines any stable opposition between the well-educated, ambitious professional, speaking his Standard English, and the "street-smart" trickster, employing a vernacular register and talking his "trash."

In his own way, each talks for his living, and each knows profoundly the power of speech and voice. But, far from being simply complementary, these characters are tensely and densely intertwined, mutually overlapping in unpredictable ways. Each knows far more about the other than the other imagines, but he also knows less, and each understands the other more intimately than he realizes. In their mutual fascination with—and commitment to—voice and speech, the neat opposition Dewey proposes between saying and doing quickly collapses. As it does, a complex and overdetermined relationship develops between speech and action, and between talking and acting. This overdetermination, in turn, extends to complicate any conclusions the characters, or the film, might reach about the relationship of saying and doing to being.

Compared to What?

Inspired by the enthusiasm of the working guys at the bar, then, Dewey connives to reinstate Petey on the morning show. He helps Petey sneak into the broadcast booth by masquerading as a janitor, pretending to perform the very work to which Dewey originally suggested he aspire. This disguise resonates with the moment in *Shaft* when a group of militants infiltrate a mob-controlled hotel dressed as service people. But it also recalls Ivan Dixon's 1973 film *The Spook Who Sat by the Door*, scripted by Sam Greenlee, based on his novel of the same title. Its protagonist, Dan Freeman (Lawrence

Cook), an ex-CIA agent turned revolutionary, at one point instructs members of an African American street gang in techniques of stealing from white people rather than from each other. "Remember," he admonishes them, "a black man with a mop, tray, or broom in his hand can go damn near anyplace in this country. And a smiling black man is *invisible.*"

Extradiegetic instrumentals produce an accelerating rhythm to this sequence and enhance the episode's action-driven quality; it appears as the kind of caper that structures blaxploitation plots. The music ends abruptly once Petey is positioned at his microphone, with Dewey outside the booth as producer. This sequence's suspense, and the excitement it generates, turns on the question of whether Petey's voice can produce an audience response that secures his position before the management cuts him off. As station employees dash around frantically and Sonderling yells from offscreen, Petey discusses his previous dismissal on the air. Invoking Muhammad Ali, he asserts: "A black man can only say so much in this so-called free country, til they break you down. Well, guess what? I'm telling it. That's right, and I'ma keep on telling it!" "Telling it," of course, becomes a key category for Petey, as he makes himself a switchboard for critical dissent that lacks access to any other public media forum. He aims to draw out vices from the margins, from locally contained, "privatized" public spheres where black people gather: "If you got something to say, give me a call . . . I'm tired of hearing fools complaining in barber chairs and beauty shops. Let your opinion out."

As he speaks these words, we see Dewey in close-up. Offscreen noise has caught his attention, and the camera follows his gaze to Sonderling, Sunny Jim, and a white producer all crammed together looking through the window of the production room. Sonderling's and Petey's voices vie for our attention, alternately coming into the foreground and receding into the background, as the sound follows the image. This aural layering echoes in the sequence's predominant visual effect; because everyone is shot through windows, all their images are mediated by the reflections the glass picks up. These effects of superimposition suggest a palimpsest: multiple layers of messages compete and interfere in an image that condenses the effects of broadcast media.

While the outraged Sonderling points his finger ineffectually, Petey segues into music. "Now, I'm gonna play a little *non*-Motown for you."

Rejecting Motown in favor of Gene McDaniels's "Compared to What," performed by Les McCann, produces broader political associations. Though it introduces a slight anachronism here, since the song was written after Martin Luther King's assassination, it acts here to anticipate that event, to connect it to the antiwar movement, as well as to shape the technologically mediated conversation Petey conducts. But this moment also clearly situates Petey as avidly participating in the significant shift of popular radio's black musical culture from Motown to the grittier, edgier Stax Records that marked this historical moment.

"Compared to What" links the Vietnam War with urban poverty and oppression.[30] In a remarkable essay on realism, representation, and race, Wahneema Lubiano returns to this song's key line ("Tryin' to make it real—compared to what?") to interrogate its ambiguities. She explores the claims or injunctions to represent the "real" that continue to mark or haunt African American cultural productions and their reception. Producers who successfully gain access to the means of cultural production, she argues, are the ones whose versions of black authenticity meet dominant white expectations. She asks: "Trying to make *what* real? . . . Trying to make African Americans' complicated existence in the minds of others real in their own minds? Trying to make real the possibility of a counter-hegemonic discourse on race, a critique of race?" Emphasizing the ideological nature of what a culture constructs and understands as real, as shared reality, Lubiano goes on to ask: "But compared to what? . . . Compared to whatever else exists, has existed, or might be able to exist within the present terms of cultural production, or under terms that might be changed by our examination of what is real?"[31] Her point, of course, is that the "real" is not self-generating and stable, but rather a site of contest in an evolving cultural context.

In the framework that *Talk to Me* establishes for it, the song's repeated chorus, "Tryin' to make it real—compared to what?" places Petey's claims to "telling it" under interrogation. "Compared to What" foregrounds his assertion of "authenticity" while questioning what grounds it. As the instrumental introduction builds, the camera holds on the producer's instrument panel and the telephone in close-up. Petey begins taking a stream of calls, and slapstick action accelerates. Dewey struggles to hold the door closed against a growing crowd of station employees. Sounds multiply as the music amplifies, Sonderling continues yelling, and Petey talks with a listener. When a caller turns the conversation to politics, asking about the recent police slaying of a black boy, Sonderling and his crew finally break in. The musical sound track seems to have faded out, but as Freda joins the group to say that the phone lines are flooded, we hear the saxophone solo that provides the instrumental climax to "Compared to What" rising to prominence again. A pan brings us back to the telephone in medium close-up, all its switches flashing. When Sonderling answers it, the song's lyrics begin again. Centering Sonderling in frame as he hangs up the call, the camera slowly pans left back to Dewey, drawn by his voice.

At this moment, Les McCann's voice reaches the lyrics "Tryin' to make it real—compared to what?" And Dewey continues: "Because WOL is a station of the people, for the people, by the people." "*I'm* the people," Petey chimes in. In this moment, Petey's populist appeal to a community of shared tastes becomes overlaid with commercial concerns: his audience, "the people," is simultaneously a market. Completing this pitch, Dewey successfully commodifies Petey's authenticity and his immediate connection with the community in a way that the song's lyrics instantly ironize. Shaping and inflecting this sequence, "Compared to What" generates friction against the image and dialogue; it implicitly interrogates the status and grounding of abstract truth claims and of authenticity as assertion. Authenticity and the "real," here, must be negotiated through style, taste, and culture as commodity.

When we hear the last repetition of the words "Tryin' to make it real—compared to what?" Petey has settled into his seat before the microphone, and we see Dewey under striking reflections through the glass, backing away. Sly and the Family Stone's "I Want to Take You Higher" begins as he takes a satisfied drag on his cigarette and starts to dance in his chair.[32] His movement and the song carry through the next scene, a freestanding musical number in which he and Vernell dance in 1970s period underwear. This exuberant moment of pure performativity bridges the public sphere of the radio station into the space of private intimacy. As the song continues, this sequence flows into the next, back at WOL.

Cutting from the radio station to the street as Petey tells an extended joke, the film produces a montage of distinct groups of people. Panning to follow a girl on a bike, the camera moves past people gathered near portable or car radios while Petey continues his monologue. After we watch a group of women appreciating Petey's stated appreciation for a "sister with big hips . . . and a big old 'fro," the film cuts back to the station, where Freda, wearing a new wig styled in a smooth bob that represents the opposite of the Afro's "natural" effect, contemplates the huge bag of fan mail Petey has received. This montage trajectory suggests a breadth and diversity of community across both geography and style. Its camera echoes the radio's circulation through an "intimate public sphere."

In her history of radio, *Listening In: Radio and the American Imagination*, Susan Douglas remarks on the power of disc jockeys to shape audiences as communities: "DJs around the country became switchboards on the air for their young listeners, making themselves privileged conduits within their listeners' imagined communities." This kind of address, she continues, "constituted listeners as in on things together, as sharing a common experience on the air, while it acknowledged that the audience was not monolithic, not some 'mass' as the TV often treated it, but made up of individuals with their own particular autobiographies" (230–31). But Douglas also notes portable radio technology's transformative effect on public space: "At work, in the car, on the beach, people—especially the young— brought radio with them to stake out their social space by blanketing a particular area with their music, their sportscasts, their announcers. With transistors, sound redefined public space" (221).[33] This sequence clearly emphasizes the specificity of radio's address and its reach as distinctly different from television's.

Significantly, Martin Luther King Jr. himself had stressed the centrality of radio both to the African American public sphere and to the civil rights movement in a 1967 address to the National Association of Radio and Television Announcers. "The masses of African Americans who have been deprived of educational and economic opportunity are almost totally dependent on radio as their means of relating to society at large," King remarked. "They do not read the newspapers, though they may occasionally thumb through *Jet*. Television speaks not to their needs, but to upper middle class America." He continued, citing recent events: "One need only recall the Watts tragedy and the quick adaptation of the 'Burn Baby Burn' slogan to illustrate the pervasive influence of the radio announcer on the community." And he concluded by pointing to the power of radio's cross-over appeal and its bridging functions: "In a real sense you have paved the way for social and political change by creating a powerful cultural bridge between black and white."[34] King's words here uncannily anticipate the response of black radio to his assassination.

Media Memory/Live Broadcast

Just prior to that historic public trauma, we find Petey and Dewey arriving together at WOL. Because Vernell has thrown him out, having caught him in flagrante, Petey has taken refuge with Dewey, from whom he is obliged to borrow clothing. His appearance works to thoroughly comic effect in this scene, and we take the measure of his difference from Dewey, a difference foregrounded by the conservative suit, sizes too large, that flaps around his body. Petey assumes an awkward stiff-legged gait and produces an exaggerated imitation of his friend's voice and diction, apparently invoking once again the characteristics that constitute his resemblance to the iconic Poitier. Dewey's protest that he does not talk that way brings this response: "Yeah, you talk exactly like that, and you walk like you got a stick broke off in your ass." "I walk with confidence," Dewey asserts, "like Johnny Carson. You could learn something from him." Television enters the radio station through Dewey's acknowledgment of a different iconic model, which also displaces the question of cultural style.

As he utters this last sentence, the camera leaves him behind to keep up with Petey, who pauses on the threshold contemplating the sight of his own clothes strewn across the floor. Once they enter the office, the handheld camera parallels Dewey and Petey's progress, and we hear "Tainted Love" on the sound track.[35] This song ironically anticipates their discovery that Vernell is having revenge sex with Nighthawk in his office. At this point, the music's relationship to the diegesis remains unclear—is it part of the current broadcast? Could we hear it in the office, or does it confine itself to implicit commentary? This song carries over into the moment of trauma, when completely nondiegetic instrumentals displace it from the sound track—much as a shocking event can produce the effect of reducing the world to silence, of blotting out all ambient sound. The rest of the sequence is marked, in striking contrast to most of the film's flow, by the steadfastly nondiegetic status of its music.

This moment marks the film's temporal center, where a shocking reversal erupts. While Petey and Nighthawk are engaged in a hilariously naturalistic clumsy brawl, the rest of the station's crew haplessly attempts to separate them. But history intervenes, brutally rupturing the comic ambiance and interrupting the spectator's amusement. As we watch them scramble awkwardly, the camera jostles with the characters in the crowded frame. This frantic activity is arrested when the film cuts to a medium close-up shot of Sonderling absorbed in reading a document. His inscrutable expression suggests that he will deliver yet another reprimand to the rambunctious Petey, which would only extend the comic mood. But when he reaches the group, his arrival immobilizes them and silences their contending voices. A handheld camera wavers and wobbles as it moves in among the characters to catch their reactions to Sonderling's document. News of Martin Luther King's assassination arrives first through the silent, grief-stricken reactions that we observe.

As the personnel receive this shocking news, solemn instrumentals on the sound track provide a rhythmic structure, but this music's unusual extradiegetic status also holds us at a distance from the scene. While we hear the music clearly, the characters' speech is whispered, fragmentary; it is as if we are trying to hear through a glass partition. Only once the camera reaches the end of its shaky, agitated round among the characters does Petey's voice-over bridge into the broadcast booth, where we see him in close-up at his microphone, addressing his audience. Sharply in focus, we see King's image in a photograph pinned to the wall among handwritten instructions and reminders for DJs. This photograph forms part of the material texture of daily life and work in the booth.

Abruptly shifting from frenetic and chaotic movement to stillness, from loud clamoring voices to stunned silence, shocking the spectator out of amusement, the film inscribes the impossible suspended point between "before" and "after," the unsituated and unprocessed gap of trauma. From the incoherent murmuring around him, Petey's voice emerges clear and amplified. "Dr. Martin Luther King, Jr., winner of the Nobel Peace Prize and chief orchestrator of the civil rights movement . . ." Returning when it does, Petey's voice restarts time, stabilizes the scene, plunging it into history as it is happening.

But beneath and beyond Petey's voice resides another, remembered voice. Kasi Lemmons recalled her experience of the news of King's assassination in an interview on National Public Radio's *All Things Considered* on

July 13, 2007. Lemmons, who was seven years old in 1968, recounted hearing her mother scream: "And she kept screaming, and as a little child, what that felt like, and that I thought she said, 'the king is dead.' And I was wondering, 'What king? Do we have a king?' . . . I didn't really relate to who he was, but that sound that my mother made—that I'd never heard before or since—it's like the world must be ending if my mother's screaming, and how bone-chilling it was."[36]

Both acoustically and visually the film emphasizes the rupture in the sequence, impressing it on us through the violent reversal of our affective expectations, jolting us out of the moment. Thus does it evoke the effects of the childhood trauma marked by the mother's unprecedented and unparalleled scream. Petey's voice, then, literally and metaphorically, diffuses this personal memory of historical trauma into the broader social terrain of his radio reception. Likewise, in the film's contemporary moment of 1968, Petey will continue to broadcast through the riots that ensue, seeking to defuse the violence.

Petey concludes his emotional announcement: "I don't know if I'm more sad or angry. I'm tired of them taking our leader. I know you are too." We follow his gaze to the booth's window, where darkened, blurred figures move in agitation, and we hear a voice report, "They're burning it down!" Once again, the film calls our attention to events just out of sight, to the spontaneous movement outside. As we move outside, the music disappears; we find ourselves in the longest sequence—by far—that is void of music. In its place emerge the sounds of a riot, shouts, cries, minor explosions, windows shattering, flames erupting. Visually, the shoulder-mounted camera propels us into the vortex of pandemonium as we follow Dewey and Petey agitatedly surveying the scene and then running to help a white shopkeeper who is being assaulted. In its edgy documentary style, the camera captures with graphic naturalism the violence and panic of such events. Its naturalism reminds us of riot scenes in both *Medium Cool* (Haskell Wexler, 1969) and Ivan Dixon's *The Spook Who Sat by the Door.*

As the sequence concludes, the camera centers Dewey and Petey as the still point around which it follows the spinning chaos. King's voice comes up on the sound track, from his "I Have a Dream" speech: "I may not get there with you . . ." From the image of a flag burning and subsequent views of police beating rioters, the film cuts back to Petey's booth, where he has returned in hopes of calming his audience. The extradiegetic music that marked the sequence that delivered the first news has returned; it serves to frame the riot sequence that has risen as violently from the film's texture as it has from the characters' daily lives. The camera pans back and forth edgily between Dewey outside the booth and Petey inside, until he begins to take calls and to address his listeners. At this point, its anxious movement ceases when Petey enjoins his listeners: "Go look out your windows, those of you that got 'em, and tell me what you see. You see a city on fire. Now that's your city, our city."

While he speaks, a split screen shows images of destruction alongside his face, which occupies the left half of the frame. These images move across left to take up the entire frame, as if the voice were making them available to our view. Footage of fire, violence, and chaos passes. Some of this appears to be stock news footage, some retains the film's own texture, but all of it suggests the documentary form. This footage certainly evokes the news coverage from the "Long, Hot Summer" of 1967; through their repetition, such images quickly became iconic of the period. And this is the same disturbing footage from which, *Variety* declared, *In the Heat of the Night* provided some "comforting" relief.[37] It was the Poitier effect, of course, that delivered this relief.

But where television news footage of the riots of 1967 and 1968 despecified these images through repeated replays that merged them into an ongoing spectacle, held at a distance, this film reframes them through Petey's voice. His speech provides a shaping intervention. Televisual spectacles of traumatic events may forestall or even foreclose their working through. The stuttering effect of their endless repetition as spectacle may provoke instead various forms of acting out, whether physical or ideological. In their apparent simultaneity, such repeated spectacles seem almost to refuse to pass—either into the past or into discourse.[38]

As this riot sequence develops, returning to the split screen, we watch a montage repeating images from the riot we have just seen. But this split screen merges them into Petey's space, superimposing them, as if he himself has become a projection screen. In this montage, the film articulates together distant images of violence with medium shots of anonymous observers watching anxiously, and it progresses from these to shots of Lorton prison, where Dewey's brother appears to be listening to Petey's broadcast, and it concludes by reaching a medium close-up of Sonderling, staring pensively. It is as if the voice brought all of these images, spaces, and agents into contact.

Petey's appeals and injunctions to his audience to remain calm echo those of DJs on black radio across the nation at this historical moment. In this climactic moment, the film opens its vista onto a broader history of African American cultural workers' use of this medium to intervene in, and perhaps shape, ongoing events. In *Voice Over: The Making of Black Radio,* William Barlow cites a number of DJs who remember the events similarly, including Del Shields of WLIB-FM in New York City. "On the night that Dr. King was killed . . . on that night, all across the country, the black disc jockey went on the microphone and talked to the people," he reports. "It was black radio that doused the incendiary flames burning all across America" (216). In Shields's account, "the people were listening in to us to find out what was going on. They weren't tuned into NBC or CBS—no way. . . . Had we not been on, telling the people—'Don't burn, baby'—and all of that, it would have been a lot worse" (217).[39]

Barlow emphasizes the regular interventions of African American disc jockeys in moments of unrest: "They worked around the clock. . . . Over the airwaves, they urged restraint and caution, implored people to stay off the streets, and gave out information on the location and extent of each disturbance." But they also "stayed in touch with local police, politicians, and civil rights leaders, giving them access to the audience as part of an effort to quell the burning, looting, and killing" (213). Thus, these cultural workers constructed and staged new networks for rapid communication across starkly partitioned spaces and among diverse, even antagonistic agents. Maintaining a constant point of address from within their outraged and embattled communities, these voices opened different channels of address. The ad hoc "switchboards" they created echo an effect that Susan Douglas, among others, has noted in distinguishing radio from television: "Many radio stations provided a trading zone between the two cultures" (223). But as these DJs talked through the riots, like their representative Petey, they were making the events available to and as discourse at the local level. Alongside the national spectacles offered by TV, they constructed an arena for talking through and processing events as experience, urging people to speak rather than to act out.

In the riot sequence's concluding moments, Petey falls briefly silent, and the camera slowly pans across the wall of his booth, lingering on a poster of a hand giving the black power salute, framed by the words "Resist Racism. You Can't Stop the Revolution." Petey signs off by citing Martin Luther King Jr.: "The ultimate measure of a man is not where he stands in moments of comfort and convenience, but where he stands in times of challenge and controversy." Here, as elsewhere, the film represents the overlapping of the civil rights movement and black power in powerful condensations of image. Under Petey's final words, music swells up on the sound track. Sam Cooke's "A Change Is Gonna Come" plays through the sequence's conclusion. This 1964 single had become a civil rights anthem, and here its melancholic tone intensifies and transforms into elegy.[40] The song's elegiac quality is only enhanced by the recollection of Cooke's own death in the year of its release.

"It's been a long, long time coming, but I know, a change is gonna come." This line repeats as we follow Petey past his assembled coworkers and out into the street. A very slow panning shot from his point of view lingers on the detritus that remains in the riot's wake. Among the most prominent of the visual effects in this desolate scene is the sheer accumulation of paper strewn across the street and still fluttering with the passage of air. Describing her research for this sequence in a commentary for the film's DVD, Lemmons remarks on the effect of all the paper she discovered in the historical photographs she examined: "All the paper blowing . . . was eerie and beautiful in horrible kind of way."[41]

But cinematic resources enhance the haunting aesthetic beauty of the scene here, capturing the slight movement of the paper against the general stillness of the empty street. It is as if the sheets provide the scene's only animation. This moment inverts the shape of the moment that revealed the news of King's assassination. At that point, the film abruptly halted a scene of frantic motion, freezing its shocked characters into a tableau. Here, the camera adopts Petey's stunned gaze upon a scene whose stasis is marked by the tiny movements of paper, until a military truck on patrol reestablishes directional motion. During the pause it imposes here, the film invites us to contemplate the debris. These papers are trash, ephemera or waste dumped from public bins on the street. Or they are documents from various establishments that have been looted. Either they have spilled out of their proper receptacles or they have been pulled or blown from their proper storage. Either way, they represent a turning inside out. Documents or records of commercial and institutional activity, torn out of place and thrown out of order, now they are archives liberated and lost. What an image of the problem of recording history, and of historical memory in film.[42]

"The Revolution Will Not Be Televised"

Significantly, Lemmons speaks only of photographs when discussing this scene and the riots it recalls. Yet her film powerfully incorporates motion picture memories—from both film and television. Not only does *Talk to Me* allude to cinematic productions of this period, but it also regularly— and pointedly—refers to TV. Martin Luther King's ghostly image seen in poor resolution on a tiny portable TV forms the vanishing point of the scene in the bar Dewey visits. Johnny Carson, Dewey's model of style, comes up repeatedly, and we see snippets of *The Tonight Show.* Subsequent to the assassination and its aftermath, in fact, the film, like the protagonists whose careers it follows, becomes increasingly preoccupied with television. With Dewey as his manager, Petey follows a career arc that moves him into stand-up comedy before integrated, though largely black, audiences, and he becomes the host of his own TV show, *Petey Greene's Washington.* (This show aired from 1976 to 1982, first on local TV station WDCA and later on BET.) Throughout, Dewey remains obsessed with propelling Petey into the arena of national TV, and specifically to an appearance on *The Tonight Show.* When they finally reach that iconic venue, Petey's deliberately aborted performance ruptures their partnership.

Reference to Gil Scott-Heron's 1970 "The Revolution Will Not Be Televised" seems apt here, since the song excoriates television as a medium hostile to political change and to African American cultural aspirations. Lines from one verse suffice to capture its poetic ferocity: "The revolution will not be right back after a message / . . . The revolution will not go better with Coke. / The revolution will not fight germs that may cause bad breath. / The revolution will put you in the driver's seat." In conclusion, the song repeats its refrain: "The revolution will not be televised. The revolution will be no re-run, brothers; the revolution will be live."[43]

In the introduction to their edited collection *The Revolution Wasn't Televised: Sixties Television and Social Conflict,* Lynn Spigel and Michael Curtin concede that Scott-Heron "did have a point, because even though numerous revolutions were televised in the 1960s . . . television preferred to label such rebellions as senseless 'riots' staged by unruly mobs who reveled in self-destructive violence." "So too," they argue, "the networks presented the social movements of the 1960s less as a break with television's general entertainment logic than as part of the flow of its 'something for everyone' programming philosophy, from the 'zany' military comedy of *Gomer Pyle USMC* to the Vietnam protest music of Joan Baez that played, after considerable doses of network censorship, on *The Smothers Brothers Comedy Hour* at the end of the decade."[44] Of course, their book's raison d'être is to demonstrate that the situation was much more complex: television witnessed and participated in contests over representation and meaning along with the culture in which it is embedded.

I want to suggest that those contests, however muted or even repressed in television's everyday flow during the period, nevertheless continually broke through. In a way, the revolution was televised, if intermittently and obliquely, at least for white middle-class suburban and rural families, and especially for a whole generation of us who were yet too young to participate in public political events. Not only did news coverage of riots like those in Chicago at the Democratic National Convention in 1968 burst through in all their violent liveness, as did nightly images from Vietnam, but also various events and appearances on the "entertainment" front pointed to or tracked historical shifts. Perhaps the "revolution" was not exactly televised, but its effects were. In its intermittent and often deeply conflicted glimpses of social and cultural struggle, perhaps television could show us, if not history, then its symptoms.

Henry Louis Gates Jr. provides a vivid memory of Harry Belafonte's stint as guest host of *The Tonight Show* for a week in February 1968. "Night after night," he recalls, "my father and I stayed up late to watch a black man host the highest rated show in its time slot—history in the making." "Who," he asks, "had ever seen so many famous black folks (Sidney Poitier, Lena Horne, Wilt Chamberlain, for starters) on the *Tonight Show*?"[45] He does not mention it, but the power of their appearance is significantly enhanced because they come as speaking guests, and not just as performers. And perhaps this moment helps to explain Poitier's passage from the screen stage of interracial melodrama. The actor largely passed out of mainstream cinematic view, but, as we have seen, his iconic effect continued to recur with remarkable persistence.

But there was even more to the "history in the making" that Gates observed. He recalls Martin Luther King Jr.'s appearance on the second night: "'What do you have in store for us *this* summer?' Belafonte asked him, flashing a provocative smile: white folks were still reeling from the riots that had come with the previous year's long hot summer. The studio audience laughed nervously" (156). Against Belafonte's bemused provocativeness, playing on white people's fears of rioting and confusion about its origins and agents, King spoke of a new project and a new direction. Gates reports that he "announced that he was shifting his emphasis from strictly racial issues. 'The time has come to bring to bear the power of the nonviolent direct-action movement on the basic economic conditions that we face all over the country'" (156).

"He pointed out," Gates continues, "that poverty among blacks, Mexican-Americans, Puerto Ricans, American Indians, and Appalachian whites had reached 'Depression levels,'" and he "went on to argue that the war in Vietnam was at odds with the war on poverty" (156). King's plans would realize themselves in the Poor People's Campaign, which began on May 12, 1968, some weeks after his assassination, and lasted until mid-June, as demonstrators inhabited "Resurrection City," a tent encampment on the National Mall in Washington. Haskell Wexler visited this site to shoot footage that he included in *Medium Cool,* his film about the politics of media representation, which centered on the riots at the Democratic National Convention in August 1968.[46] This is the history in the making that *Talk to Me* also tracks, from its oblique angle in the radio station. But this film likewise registers "history in the making" in terms of access to national television representation—precisely the dream that Dewey Hughes formulates for Petey. Like Gates, Lemmons foregrounds the enormous symbolic importance of appearing on national television in this classic mainstream venue. Unlike the technological retrofitting of history that allows *Forrest Gump* to put contemporary spectators—along with its protagonist—in the picture, and on the right side, this film's "reverse engineering" into *The Tonight Show* seems intent on foregrounding broadcast media's historical effects.

In a variation on the *Pleasantville* fantasy of a child viewer entering the diegesis of his favorite TV show, *Talk to Me* places itself on *The Tonight*

Show, Dewey's ideal televisual world. In a DVD commentary, Lemmons notes that she picked a show with guests she liked, including Bette Midler, and one that aired just before Carson's famous 1972 move away from the show's roots in New York City to California. Cinematographer J. Miles Dale explains that "we reverse engineered ourselves into an existing show."[47] By this he means that they filmed clips of that original broadcast playing on television monitors. In a technically complex mise-en-scène, *Talk to Me* puts itself into the historical scene of television. Continuity holds because the camera returns us regularly to a TV screen as the show progresses. This set becomes a hall of mirrors in which television breaks up the space, puncturing the cinematic world, as the telemediated image inhabits the space of the show in the process of its taping. Ed McMahon's voice holds the scene together as he reads the names we see on the screen—"Gig Young, Joe Garagiola, Bette Midler, Los Indios Trabajaras [*sic*], and comedian, Petey Greene"—in a guest list that constitutes a veritable ethnic medley.

But this sequence also produces a curious effect: it doubles Dewey's obsession with *The Tonight Show* at the level of the film's own production, as *Talk to Me*'s crew re-creates a set that is ghosted by the original images playing within it. This shared fascination with *The Tonight Show* points to its iconic status for several generations. The longest-running talk show on television, it premiered in 1954 with Steve Allen as host. Based in New York until its move in 1972 to California, it emerged as a central icon of American middlebrow, middle-class culture, with its aspirations to witty, urbane modernity. And, according to literary critic and comedy theorist John Limon in *Stand-up Comedy in Theory, or, Abjection in America*, it had a shaping impact on "our postwar national humor."[48] Limon describes the structure of the late-night talk show, inaugurated by *The Tonight Show,* as ethnically "chiasmatic." "The hick visitor in New York is the 'host' of the show," he writes, "and the city kid . . . is the 'guest'" (5). *The Tonight Show*'s "star must be a pseudo-hick with attitude arriving in New York from the heartland; he hosts Jewishness there, and the chiasmus is the genius of the genre" (80). But Limon emphasizes that while the "city" kid might originally have been Jewish, and is playing his Jewishness, any ethnicity may fill this role. Ethnicity comes centrally into play, as long as it plays itself.

Limon makes a subtle point about the framework that structured the interplay between the "host" comedians and the guest comics, arguing that "comedians like Johnny Carson and David Letterman brought their honed talent for abstraction—in their heads, jokes become jokes about jokes—to the city in search of the bodies their minds had thrown off; they found there an abjection that was particularly congenial and complementary" (8). It is the role of the abject, of the performer performing his own embodiment, it seems, that Petey refuses when Dewey's highest aspiration for him realizes itself in an appearance on *The Tonight Show.*

While the film has throughout calibrated the passage of time in the nuanced detail of characters' wardrobes, here it accents their ascent into the mainstream with the expansion of the men's hair, mustaches, and sideburns, as well as of their lapels. Petey's jacket has elongated to coat length; Dewey now sports bold plaid trousers beneath his conservative blazer; Vernell's Afro has become huge, and her tight, cut-out jumpsuit is her most spectacular outfit yet. But the ensuing sequence issues in a botched performance. Petey's aborted stand-up number comes as the culmination of a building crisis that turns on performance itself—as spontaneous and as staged.

An anxious sequence building up to Petey's performance keeps Vernell centrally in focus as she struggles to mediate between the friends, making a futile effort to head off disaster. Her efforts to persuade Dewey that he has misrecognized Petey's desires and aspirations, confusing them with his own through a kind of misplaced identification, are bracketed by two unscripted performances: Petey's resistant, resolutely noncomic confrontation with the audience and Dewey's own performance on the soundstage before the show begins.

When the characters pass across the empty *Tonight Show* stage on their way to the green room, Dewey hangs back, explores the space, and then ducks behind the curtain. From there, he makes a Carson entrance, laughing self-deprecatingly and quieting his imaginary audience. Taking up the host's chair, he grips his coffee cup and begins an imaginary interview, imitating Carson's characteristic full-body chortles. This awkward moment of exaggerated performance ends even more awkwardly as Dewey spots a technician observing him and sheepishly bolts from the seat. In its awkwardness, this performance reminds us of Dewey's stated debt to Carson, from whom he "learned how to talk, how to walk." Its stilted quality high-lights the seamlessness of Dewey's normal performance, and it reminds us that the construction of identity takes place on a stage set before reassur-ingly empty "houses" in the theaters of our imagination. This embarrass-ingly interrupted performance will acquire a certain poignancy in light of one of the film's last developments, which it anticipates, and where Vernell once again serves as intermediary between the now estranged friends.

When Petey finally takes the stage, he stalls his performance quite will-fully. After some standard *Tonight Show* lead-in music, he steps onstage, and the sound track falls into an uneasy quiet. The camera remains close to him, capturing the nervous look frozen on his face, and then shooting over his shoulder. We see the blurred crowd of faces he confronts. "You all are gonna have to forgive me if I'm a little nervous. I just ain't never been in front of this many white folks before." Muted, hesitant titters mark the strain of the moment. "Well, the truth is, I'm just an ex-con, and the people that live in the world that I come from, well, most of them can't even afford TVs. They listen to me on the radio."

As he speaks the camera holds him first in tight close-up, squeezed to the right side of the frame, in an image reminiscent of his radio booth. After cutting away to Dewey's nervous agitated reaction, the film returns to Petey, now framed in extreme long shot under the boom, indicating his distance from the dark blob of the audience and starkly figuring his perspective, dwarfed by and alienated from his surroundings. "And they do that," he continues, "because I keeps it real." "And when they're laughin', I know they're laughing with me, not at me." At this point, the film cuts abruptly to Dewey backstage, facing off with Petey's image on a tiny TV monitor. Things remain off scale, out of kilter, throughout this sequence. "But I look at you all, and all I see is a room full of white folk, waiting to hear some nigger jokes." In the awful silence that follows, broken only by murmurs and coughs, we see Dewey crumpling with despair. "I ain't got nothing to say to you people. You all ain't ready for P-Town," he con-cludes, and the camera once again emphasizes his isolation visually, keep-ing him in close-up against a blurred background, where we barely make out the outline of Johnny Carson at his desk. Refusing the national net-work stage, Petey also challenges and interrupts its imagined community, in a dramatic reversal of the Poitier effect.

Not only does Petey refuse to entertain this audience, but he also forces them uncomfortably out of the position of spectator, revealing them to themselves as objects of his own view. While the camera work reminds us of Petey's first sessions in the broadcast booth, in this *appearance,* which we must take literally, since he does not perform his act, he reverses the gaze, casting his audience as object of scrutiny. Having just declared his "realness," he refuses to *perform* this authenticity. This discomfiting anti-performance suggests W. E. B. Du Bois's "double consciousness," as Petey shares his uncomfortable sense of what it means to "be looking at himself through the eyes of others,"[49] even as he submits his audience to a similar effect: "I look at you all . . ."

But as the moment ends suspended, this performance jars us, the screen audience, and perhaps produces an echo of the moment Gates remembers, when Belafonte joked provocatively with Dr. King. Was Belafonte self-consciously playing against the reassuring Poitier effect that *Variety* had so clumsily foregrounded? Harshly foregrounding his hypervisibility, isolated onstage, the moment reveals Petey's uncomfortable self-consciousness in his exposure as unwilling spectacle. His failed, suspended performance mirrors Dewey's interrupted improvisation at the sequence's beginning.

As Petey leaves the stage to feeble applause, Dewey confronts him with a punch. The ensuing brawl gets them both arrested. From this point, their friendship dissolves in mutual disappointment that turns on identification and misrecognition. Dewey identifies Petey with his idolized older brother, who has failed him by becoming a criminal. But Petey refuses this identification, emphasizing how obstinately Dewey has misidentified him, seeing in his place his own idealized image.

If *The Tonight Show* literally becomes the stage on which the men's friendship falls apart, it also figures in their rapprochement. We are transported from 1972 to 1982, and Vernell is once again attempting to mediate between the two, calling on Dewey at his office at WOL, which he now owns.[50] As they talk about Petey's failing health and his desire to see his friend, Dewey turns on the TV, where Johnny Carson appears, effectively producing a triangular gaze relay. "See this show? My whole fucking life is this show. I learned how to walk, talk, and dress watching *The Tonight Show.*" "It showed me that there was a world far away from the Anacostia projects," he continues meditatively, indicating Carson: "He reminds me of my brothers, loud-ass shit talkers, funny as hell. Always had me cracking up." Significantly, while citing the nationally broadcast show as his model for codes of style in dress, speech, and demeanor, Dewey quickly moves from its liberating space back to the particularity of place, the projects, and, metonymically, to his brother.

Across the triangulated relay created by the TV in this scene, Johnny Carson evokes Milo, the lifetime inmate who introduced him to Petey, the surrogate brother from whom he has become likewise estranged. "Milo was my hero. He could say anything, do anything." Here the formerly juxtaposed and opposed terms of saying and doing become reconciled in the figure of the lost brother, but across the image of Johnny Carson, who provokes his memory. This charismatic structure highlights the centrality of style to social identity and suggests the instability of racial difference. As the sequence ends with Vernell's departure, the camera lingers on Dewey, whose gaze lingers on the muted image of Carson performing his opening monologue. In the scene that follows, *Talk to Me* reunites its protagonists in the pool hall, where they reconcile through the performative repetition of difference: Dewey acts, and Petey speaks.

We next find the friends strolling on the National Mall. They approach in long shot, and we can see them talking, but their speech remains nearly inaudible—a sharply distinct effect in a film that is all about talk. Soon the visual field admits another camera, as Vernell enters the frame videotaping the men on her camcorder. Grainy video stock takes over the image as her camera work, zooming in to close-ups and panning rapidly and edgily to follow its subjects' movement, creates an intimate portrait that clearly means to memorialize the moment. Vernell's camera obtrudes, calling attention to its mediation of the scene. In its edgy proximity, this camera mimics the visual style of the film that contains it. Recalling the film's eccentric effects in this way, Vernell's camera suggests that its own overarching point of view may well be anchored to hers. She functions here as the director's stand-in, reminding us that a female spectator's point of view has shaped this nuanced examination of masculine style and pose.

Whatever sound Vernell might have recorded goes missing in favor of Petey's voice-over: "I ain't up here trying to be nobody's preacher. I'm just trying to tell the truth to you all like I promised I would." Video gives way to the film camera moving in on a newspaper announcement of Greene's death as Dewey's voice takes over: "Petey liked to say that he was just a con, telling it like it is." Through a dissolve, the film moves to Lorton prison, where Dewey now visits his brother Milo. Across Dewey's voice-over, then, the film bridges from the newspaper image to the prison interview. But voice pulls away from image, since Dewey's mouth is no longer moving. This brief sequence of reconciliation between the brothers is shaped by the restoration of voice to body. In voice-over, Dewey asserts, "He said the things we were afraid to say." And then, now speaking in synchronized voice to his brother, he says what he has heretofore been unable to say: "I'm sorry."

This elegiac sequence gathers up the narrative threads in a movement of commemoration and restoration at the same time that it emphasizes a preoccupation with technological mediation. As the privatized domain of the videotape opens onto the public sphere of the news, and as Petey's words pass from one disembodied voice to another, the film gathers into the arena of private exchange its central concerns with voice, giving voice, and with the radio voice's capacity to bridge divergent spaces. As the film passes from Vernell's private commemoration across the prison reconciliation, Dewey's voice again bridges the cut, carrying us into the public scene of collective grief at Petey's funeral, and we become aware that his voice-over has bled into the eulogy he is delivering.

In closing, Dewey once again cites Petey, repeating the signature conclusion to his shows. At this point, a dissolve takes us back to the broadcast booth as the film superimposes Petey's image over Dewey's. Petey takes over: "I'll tell it to the hot, I'll tell it to the cold, I'll tell it to the young, I'll tell it to the old. I don't want no laughin', I don't want no cryin', and most of all, no signifyin'." Another dissolve brings Dewey back into view as he chimes in to speak the last word, "signifyin,'" with Petey. Their images and voices superimpose and dissolve into each other, inscribing a figure of the complex play of identifications that compose their divergent styles of masculinity.

While Dewey ventriloquizes Petey here, the film has now established his own complex relationship to authenticity and to "signifying," as well as the ambivalence of his identifications. Through the triangular relay of identification that brings Johnny Carson into resemblance with Milo, that makes Carson's image recall the lost brother—both literally and figuratively—the film has established Dewey's "authenticity" as a web of identifications and appropriations. By this point, his own image accommodates an identification with Carson that does not require a disidentification from, or abjection of, his brother. No longer necessarily displaced by the idealized television image, the fantasmatically idealized brother no longer qualifies as abject; his loss can provoke mourning.

As Dewey concludes his eulogy, the camera pulls back to extreme long shot, finally revealing the full size of the crowd he addresses. (The film's end titles reveal that some ten thousand people attended Petey's funeral, a record crowd for a nonstate funeral in Washington.) But, rather than conclude with the scene of public mourning, the film chooses instead to return to an image of Petey in his radio booth, quietly enjoining us to "be cool." This closing image of the familiar routine, of the banal, produces interesting effects. Pulling away from the scene of public commemoration and narrowing its focus to the public privacy of the radio booth, the film turns away from the hagiographic possibilities of the vast crowd scene. In doing so, it registers its commitment to exploring the imbrications of public and private memory and of their shaping mediations across each other and across media technologies. Surely, not the least of these mediated memories emerges in the Poitier figure, which this film "repurposes" and thereby reclaims for its study of African American style politics of the period.

And like Vernell's videotape, stitched into the broader public arena of the movie screen, Lemmons's private memory of her traumatic reaction to her mother's unprecedented screaming at King's assassination weaves through this film. In its attempt to work through the ways that we seek to manage both trauma and identity through media culture, this film resists heroicizing and idealizing the past through a nostalgic gaze from the "feminist future." *Talk to Me*'s resistance to redeeming the past as a screen for contemporary fantasies seems entirely consonant with its insistence on picturing Poitier without the Poitier *effect*, remembering and reclaiming the icon for a self-conscious and critical African American vernacular culture.

Conclusion

Chasing Sidney

Poitier seems unable to escape his iconic usefulness—particularly, though not exclusively, to white liberal discourse. By way of epilogue, I want to explore the afterlife of the Poitier effect as it continues across a variety of popular discussions and cinematic projects.[1] In 2008, Poitier returns vigorously to the national media stage—or, at least, the spectral image of his 1960s star persona does. The Poitier effect seems to mark a number of accounts of Barack Obama's political ascendency, which emphasize his exceptional singularity as the quintessential "civil rights subject" who might instruct us in preparing for a "postracial" moment, a fantasy clearly descended from 1960s liberal fantasies of "color blindness." But Poitier himself sometimes figures quite literally in such accounts. He emerges significantly in Jabari Asim's *What Obama Means . . . for Our Culture, Our Politics, Our Future* as an important media "ancestor" of the president and an anchor for repeated comparisons.[2] In a chapter titled "Leading Men," Asim provides a list of celebrity precursors who contribute, in his estimation, to Obama's media appeal. He begins with Poitier in *Guess Who's Coming to Dinner*. Noting that one of the central objections expressed by the film's white liberal father to his daughter's interracial marriage concerns "any children that might result from the union," Asim reminds us that "the black intellectual assured his future father-in-law that the bride-to-be had no such concerns," quoting John Prentice: "She feels that every single one of our children will be president of the United States" (96–97).

Asim goes on to cite Obama's memoir *Dreams from My Father: A Story of Race and Inheritance,* finding in it a scene that mirrors the Poitier film.[3] Suggesting that Obama's white grandfather "had been forced to ponder the same dilemma" as the one facing Spencer Tracy in *Guess Who's Coming to Dinner,* Asim turns to the moment when Obama is imagining his grandparents first meeting his father: "'When the evening is over, they'll both remark on how intelligent the young man seems, so dignified, with the measured gestures, the graceful draping of one leg over the other—and how about that accent?'" (98). But Asim quickly transposes father and son, emphasizing Obama's own resemblance to Poitier's John Prentice, described by Joey Drayton as "so calm and sure of everything. He doesn't have any tensions in him" (102). "By 1967," Asim writes, "Poitier's smooth exterior had become a trademark." Contending that "an absence of tension often means the presence of cool," he suggests that "notwithstanding criticisms that his characters were sexually repressed, his apparent serenity radiates its own kind of seduction" (102–3). Having made this point, Asim again moves back to consideration of Obama's persona. Shuttling back and forth between the two figures, his analysis constructs a sustained analogy between them.

Tellingly, in a November 2008 *New York Times* op-ed column titled "Guess Who's Coming to Dinner," Frank Rich revisits the very same remarks concerning the "calm" of Poitier's character and his fiancée's aspirations for their children. In an uncharacteristic logical lapse, Rich compares Obama to Poitier's character, but then immediately fastens on the coincidence that Obama's parents met at the University of Hawaii, like the movie couple. He seems, in some kind of primal scene fantasy, to locate Obama in two generations simultaneously, both as a reincarnation of the Poitier character and as his offspring.

But perhaps this is not a slip. Rich notes that "what's most startling about this archaic film is the sole element in it that proves inadvertently contemporary." "Faced with a black man in the mold of the Poitier character," he writes, "white liberals can make utter fools of themselves." And he goes on to describe Joe Biden's hapless remark that Obama was "clean" and "articulate" as "recycling Spencer Tracy's lines."[4] Biden reproduces the awkward white liberal discourse of the 1960s that marks all of Poitier's films of the period, both diegetically and extradiegetically. Reading Obama through the cinematic past, Rich does not rewrite history to construct a triumphalist story of steady progress. Refusing the lure of anticipatory nostalgia, he insists on remembering the persistence of the past in the present, refusing the fantasmatic lure of the "postracial." At the same time, perhaps not inadvertently, he suggests that Obama brings out repressed tensions that become manifest in white uneasiness and awkwardness.

Strikingly, *New York Times* film critics Manohla Dargis and A. O. Scott pursue a project similar to Jabari Asim's in mapping a cinematic teleology that culminates in Obama's election. They offer a survey of how "evolving cinematic roles have prepared America to have a black man in charge." After an opening disclaimer, "Make no mistake: Hollywood's historic refusal to embrace black artists and its insistence on racist caricatures and stereotypes linger to this day," they continue on a surprisingly sanguine note. "Yet in the past 50 years—or, to be precise, in the 47 years since Obama was born—black men in the movies have traveled from the ghetto to the boardroom, from supporting roles in kitchens, liveries and social-problem movies to the rarefied summit of the Hollywood A-list." "In those years," the critics continue, "the movies have helped images of black popular life emerge from behind what W. E. B. Du Bois called 'a vast veil,' creating public spaces in which we could glimpse who we are and what we might become." Framing a brief survey of the past half century of film, they admit that the movies "hardly prophesy the present moment." Yet Dargis and Scott press on to contend that films "offer intriguing premonitions, quick-sketch pictures and sometimes richly idealized portraits of black men grappling with issues of identity and the possibilities of power. They have helped to write the pre-history of the Obama presidency."[5] Much the same wishfulness that characterizes their account of these cinematic images of black males also marks the feminist-centered civil rights nostalgia films we have been examining.

In the inventory of film figures Dargis and Scott present, which is organized strictly by types, Poitier figures prominently. He embodies the "series of firsts" that has tended to mark "modern African-American history": "the first black movie star" as well as "the first to win an Oscar in a lead role and the first to see his name featured above the title in movie advertisements." Thus, Poitier inaugurates the march of modern black history in the movies, introducing the first type of black man: "the Black Everyman." The article formats its list in boldface, as if to facilitate our embrace of its categories: "Black Outlaw" (Morgan Freeman in *Street Smart* [Jerry Schatzberg, 1987], Denzel Washington in *Training Day* [Antoine Fuqua, 2001]), "Black Provocateur" (Richard Pryor, Eddie Murphy), "Black Father" (Bill Cosby as Cliff Huxtable, Bernie Mac), "Black Yoda" (James Earl Jones and, later, Morgan Freeman), "Black Messiah" (Joe Morton in *Terminator 2* [James Cameron, 1991], Michael Clarke Duncan in *The Green Mile* [Frank Darabont, 1999]). Developing the outlaw category, the critics note: "It seems telling that in 2002 Denzel Washington became the second African-American man to win an Oscar for best actor playing a dirty Los Angeles police detective in the thriller *Training Day*." "Mr. Washington brought a queasy erotic charge to his character's violence," they continue, "that seemed intended to erase every last trace of his stoic, heroic, Poitieresque profile in films like *Philadelphia* and *Remember the Titans*. This was Denzel the Bad, with his black leather jacket and pumping big guns, cinematic soul brother to Samuel L. Jackson in *Pulp Fiction*" (9). In this reading, Washington's previous roles become defined by Poitier. These are his "good objects," the anchors against which his anti-Poitier character plays in *Training Day*.

These critics' reflections proceed as if Poitier were a harbinger of social change they presume to have been already accomplished, as if his roles bore its seeds, and as if his career had both mapped and produced progress toward racial equality. What a curious undoing of that figure's representational history! This account ascribes steady representational progress to a career that unfolded in compulsively repeated reenactments of the same scenario, as Poitier reappeared to exhibit the same characteristics across his roles. In its reclamation of this cinematic past as anticipating a racially progressive future, the story Dargis and Scott tell strikingly reproduces the gestures of civil rights nostalgia films, and it renders Poitier's recent reappearance more than a little uncanny.

In his own celebration of the progressive drive forward in racial representations that he sees in Poitier's career, Asim also highlights the Washington comparison. He revisits the scene of Poitier's previous return to the limelight, at the 2002 Academy Awards, where he received the Lifetime Achievement Award. At this ceremony, Denzel Washington treated his Best Actor win in Poitier's presence as a symbolic passing of the torch. "Forty years I've been chasin' Sidney," Asim quotes him as saying. "They finally give it to me and then what'd they do? They give it to him the same night. I'll always be chasing you Sidney. I'll always be following in your footsteps. There's nothing I would rather do, sir" (100). For Asim, "this simple, touching gesture expressed an unassailable truth," which he elaborates as follows: "No Poitier, no Washington. No Poitier, no Jamie Foxx, no Forest Whitaker. And, quite possibly, no Barack Obama" (101). I want here to explore the strange afterlife of the Poitier effect that persists not only in the curious genealogy that Asim constructs, leading from actors to the president, but also through the work honored at this ceremony.

In his memory of this historic Academy Awards moment, Asim has erased Halle Berry, who became the first African American to win in the Best Actress category. And this elision seems all the more odd because Berry, in receiving her award, pointedly emphasized her historical legacy, recalling Hattie McDaniel, the first African American ever to win an Oscar: Best Supporting Actress for her performance in *Gone with the Wind* (Victor Fleming, 1939). Strangely, the legacy Asim celebrates, then, stretches back only to Poitier, and it admits no women. But it is also curious that he makes no mention of the actual performance for which Washington gained recognition. As Poitier's presence works to enhance the impact of these two best acting awards, so does the ceremony's projected memory of his many roles as "good object" throw into relief the force of Berry's and Washington's performances as decidedly "bad" ones.

In Antoine Fuqua's *Training Day*, Washington's performance as Alonzo Harris, the demonic mentor to a white rookie cop, inverts the beneficent pedagogical formula Poitier's films enact. In the course of the twenty-four-hour training day that the film follows, Alonzo leads his pupil, Jake Hoyt (Ethan Hawke), through a series of harrowing episodes of intimidation and violence. Even as Alonzo attacks and terrorizes drug dealers and members of the surrounding community in South Central Los Angeles, he consistently puts Jake himself in a position to be subjected to threats and to increasingly horrifying violence. By the film's end, Jake has been spectacularly battered and threatened with even more horrific violence, like Mel Gibson's character in the *Lethal Weapon* series. But with this difference: nearly all of Jake's assailants and those who menace and taunt him are men of color, usually operating in groups. *Training Day* plays on white fears of urban men of color, elaborately putting these to rest when the members of a particularly menacing street gang rally to Jake's assistance in a final standoff with Alonzo. This vehicle of Washington's Best Actor award seems to depend for its force precisely on recasting the black mentor figure as vicious tormenter.

Contemplating this Academy Awards ceremony in his article "The Ruse of Engagement: Black Masculinity and the Cinema of Policing," African American studies scholar Jared Sexton asks pointedly: "What footsteps are these to follow? Who, or moreover, what is Sidney Poitier for Denzel Washington to chase?" Sexton notes that "several critics suggested that the historic top prize, only the second to go to a black actor, provided a sort of belated vindication for a long-recognized talent whose efforts . . . were sorely unrewarded," and that they especially cited his performance in Spike Lee's *Malcolm X* (1992).[6] But he goes on to connect Washington's Oscar for this particular performance *not* to Poitier's own win for the singularly peculiar and sentimental *Lilies of the Field* but rather to Virgil Tibbs, his character in *In the Heat of the Night*.

"Poitier," he writes, "at the height of his powers, introduced to the big screen a bizarre figure whose prominence grew steadily in the following years and whose appearance proliferated wildly in the closing decades of the twentieth century. Mr. Tibbs is, of course, the first significant black cop in U.S. film history and, as such, predecessor to a considerable list of creatures whose careers can scarcely be labeled as salutary" (42). Sexton produces an extensive genealogy running from Mr. Tibbs to Richard Roundtree's John Shaft to Roger Murtaugh of the *Lethal Weapon* films to Russell Stevens (Laurence Fishburne) in *Deep Cover* (Bill Duke, 1992) to Washington's own Nick Styles in *Ricochet* (Russell Mulcahy, 1991) and Lincoln Rhyme in *The Bone Collector* (Phillip Noyce, 1999). While I would dispute that the meanings of all these figures converge so neatly, if at all—Alonzo Harris, for one, is clearly deranged—I note with interest that the thrust of Sexton's argument is to contend that black filmmakers, like Fuqua, are as guilty as white ones of exploiting the characteristics of the black cop figure that Mr. Tibbs inaugurated. But I am also struck that the function of this figure as he describes it bears more than a passing resemblance to the Poitier effect. Sexton's black cop is a figure "involved in the image management of an emergent and uncertain black middle class or, rather, the profoundly convoluted focus on class stratification . . . among the black population."

For him this stratification produces a "cultural politics" that is "related to the widespread vindication of policing black people in contemporary law and society" (42).

But it is in *Monster's Ball* (Marc Forster, 2001), the film that earned Halle Berry the Best Actress Oscar in this historic Academy Awards year, that the Poitier effect most interestingly marks its persistent hold on Hollywood's racial imagination. So, I conclude this project with an analysis of that film's complex handling of interracial melodrama, which is much more complicated than any we can find in Poitier's own films. Berry's character, Leticia Musgrove, a quintessentially "bad" mother, struggles to provide for her shockingly obese son, Tyrell (Coronji Calhoun), whom she also verbally abuses and spectacularly beats. After he is killed she falls into an affair with a white prison guard, Hank Grotowski (Billy Bob Thornton), who has participated in her husband's execution. They bond, apparently, over their shared mourning for dead sons, hers killed by a hit-and-run driver, his dead by suicide. Like so many moments of interracial "intimacy" and "understanding" in Poitier's oeuvre, this bond remains thinly motivated. A bleak and desolate landscape of grinding poverty provides the setting for Berry's performance as a destitute and failed mother who spins hysterically out of control.

It seems the Academy rewards Berry for playing so spectacularly against her previous roles—much as Washington does in *Training Day*—and against what it imagines her physical type should suggest. But this performance has its lurid side, which emphatically and utterly transforms her body through the spectacle of hysterical abjection. In producing such a figure, Berry's performance plays not only against her own "type" but also against the *typing* that straitjacketed earlier black woman performers, like Hattie McDaniel. And this is why it is so striking that Poitier's appearance at the ceremony, alongside its reprise of his films, provides the framework of good objects for celebrating two "bad objects."

Failing Melodrama

Monster's Ball seems systematically to rehearse the tropes of Poitier's interracial melodramas while scrambling them, undoing them, and emptying them out. It fractures the Poitier effect, diffusing it across Leticia and her husband, Lawrence Musgrove (Sean aka Puffy aka Diddy Combs), whose execution early in the film anchors the plot. Evoking the fantasy of salutary

chance encounters between black and white on which Poitier's films depend, this film voids these encounters of development or content. While
it rehearses the tropes of interracial melodramas, this film resolutely rejects
the pedagogical turn that tends to structure them. Nothing positive happens
or pretends to happen in this frozen world, where race is consistently displaced. In this film, no one learns anything. Its interracial couple, formed
by accident, ends suspended before the blank screen of the future, suggesting that we might have reached a welcome impasse for racial melodramas
of redemption, as it starkly foregrounds—and recognizes—the aporia that
ends most Poitier films.

Monster's Ball replays interracial melodrama's familiar tropes through
exaggeration, inversion, and undercutting, ultimately pushing that form
to a breaking point in mute blockage and stasis. This film's fragmented
plot proceeds convulsively; its episodes alternately amplify melodramatic
affect to pitches of hysteria and flatten it to benumbed mutism. Its world
seems temporally static; though it is marked by history, it seems to admit
neither memory nor development. Its uneasy and opaque relationship
to history comes across forcefully in the vehicles its characters drive and
the televisions, constantly playing, that anchor domestic spaces. All these
objects are dated, but diversely so; they do not clearly establish a precise
temporal environment.

Like history, geography, for this film, remains scrambled: though it is
explicitly set in Georgia, its prison scenes take place in what is recognizably
Louisiana's Angola State Prison. Literary critic Sharon Holland argues
persuasively that these effects are "crucial to the psychic life of the film,"
which takes "southern culture's history of violence as its primal scene." In
so doing, she contends, *Monster's Ball* casts "the South" as "the perpetual
past of American history." Because that South is "mired in the past," she
continues, "it can never be part of our future."[7] Cultural studies scholar
Aimee Carrillo Rowe makes a similar argument that, in this film, "the South
comes to signify a racial 'border zone' . . . as the abject other to the alibi
of U.S. multicultural nationalism."[8] This is the paradigmatic and timeless
"South" that organizes *The Defiant Ones* and *In the Heat of the Night. Monster's Ball* takes the temporal uncertainties and spatial vagueness that tend
to mark Poitier's films to an extreme; history becomes a fantasmatic primal
scene that grounds the melodrama it stages.

Even within its family plots, history is problematic. Change eventuates only through tragic accidents. While Hank and his father and son, three generations of prison guards, forcefully assert radically different racial attitudes, whatever contexts have shaped these attitudes remain obscure. History seems embedded in this family as a symptom. While the family wants to organize itself by aggressive claims to continuity and resemblance, violent disidentifications consistently displace those claims. By contrast, Leticia's family seems sealed into its broken nuclearity; it reveals no generational past at all.

Like historical context, spatial continuity is deficient in the film. Space fragments and permits us to establish no clear relations. Hank's and Leticia's depressingly worn claustrophobic interiors remain hermetically sealed theaters of intergenerational conflict. We are unable to discern their houses' surroundings. Significantly, we do not see that Leticia's house is situated in a neighborhood until her eviction, at which point her neighbors emerge as predatory witnesses to her misfortune. *Monster's Ball*'s only public space is a diner whose near-empty expanse and harsh fluorescent lighting emphasize its resemblance to the institutional settings—the prison, the hospital, and the nursing home—that provide the only outside to its protagonists' drab and suffocating houses. In this shrunken and closed world, interracial proximity and distance alike remain largely unmotivated, coincidental.

Billing itself as "a hard hitting southern drama tempered by a story of powerful, life-changing love" (this melodramatic hook is the first line of copy on the DVD packaging), *Monster's Ball* presents an utterly implausible interracial affair—as implausible, in its own way, as any of the gentler encounters in Poitier's films—in a narrative that suggests a central concern with race and racism.[9] It pointedly introduces Hank's father, in sordidly exaggerated terms, as an unreconstructed racist. Buck Grotowski (Peter Boyle) first appears complaining bitterly about two preadolescent black boys who have come onto his property, referring to them as "porch monkeys" and invoking Hank's mother's memory—"she hated niggers, too." Hank placates the old man by approaching the boys, gun in hand, to evict them. We are struck both by his willingness to menace such young boys and by the odd fact that these boys have come to visit Hank's grown son, Sonny (Heath Ledger), who thereby registers as not racist. But the very tension of these unexplained approaches to identity and difference highlight this film's uneasy and erratic self-consciousness about race. Here it registers a marginally more self-conscious approach than *The Help* takes, at least suggesting that even an unenlightened character might pause to think about race relations.

More strikingly, perhaps, we soon learn that these boys are sons of the Grotowskis' only neighbor, a black mechanic played by Mos Def. In other words, this incident refuses to make sense. This brutally explicit setup establishes that the film will be able to approach racial difference only asymptotically. Its story can only obscurely motivate the relationship between the executioner and the widow of the prisoner he has helped to kill. *Monster's Ball* embraces, however uneasily, tropes that organize the Poitier melodramas of racial reconciliation: an accident propels black and white contact and leads to white enlightenment and redemption. But it fragments and jumbles these melodramatic gestures, as if to mark the genre's exhaustion. Moreover, as we will see, this central "redemptive" relationship is anything but. Proceeding by violently evicting all the other characters, the film leaves us with a couple haunted by the violent past and unable to envision the future in a populated space. Hank and Leticia come together under the sign of failed reproduction; their miscegenation occurs after their children's extinction. Unlike the Poitier films whose effects it borrows, this film offers scant hope for a better future. It proceeds as if it were recasting *Guess Who's Coming to Dinner* from romantic comedy to naturalist tragedy.

Perhaps this bleakness is part of the film's attempt to create an air of authenticity that Poitier's films so often lack. In his DVD commentary, Marc Forster insists on the authenticity he seeks to establish through practical location shooting. Though set in Georgia, the film is shot in Louisiana, where it uses a working motel and diner, local housing, and, most significantly, the notorious Angola penitentiary, with special emphasis on shooting in the actual execution room. This film is also scrupulous in the detailed realism of its interiors. But despite its obsessive concern for authenticity in the geographic locale and in mise-en-scène, the film's commitment to aesthetic artifice consistently reframes its project. It continually overlays its realism with spectacle, asserting its melodramatic cinematicity in the images that reverberate, the frames that proliferate. Dialogue withdraws in favor of gesture as space and mise-en-scène become narrative agents.

For all of its obsession with realist detail, this film's space also remains curiously abstracted, as inexplicable spatially as it is narratively. Its camera refuses to decide if it stands inside or outside the spaces the characters inhabit. Nor can it connect the spaces it explores. This story happens nowhere: we have no sense of a real locale, where traffic and people circulate, and roads connect things. Instead, we confront either an abstracted "South" or the claustrophobic vacancy of interiors, as the film consistently evokes the racialization of space only to obscure it. In this diegetic world, space truncates and supplants story or character, leaving the spectator to contemplate an aestheticized and distant view. Where narrative and character logics fail, the film covers the gaps with the shocks it delivers. But it also systematically makes leaps across relays of resemblance or repetition; mise-en-scène does the work of asserting connections that it cannot develop. In this strategy, the film powerfully recalls 1950s melodrama. It comes as no surprise, then, that the film's cinematographer, Roberto Schaefer, tells us in the DVD commentary that he deliberately wanted to cite *Imitation of Life.* But he might very well have been remembering *Guess Who's Coming to Dinner.* Or *A Patch of Blue.*

Plotting its course through rigorous parallel editing, *Monster's Ball* organizes a strong rhythm of mirroring and analogy among its characters. This technique first establishes a counterpoint between Hank and Sonny on the eve of the execution that launches the film's plot. Hank sits in the glaring light that illuminates the off-scale expanse of the vacant white diner he frequents throughout the film for chocolate ice cream and black coffee—his comfort foods. When the waitress inquires, "How's Sonny?" the film immediately cuts to a grim motel room. As the scene unfolds, it centers Sonny's reflected image in the middle of the frame. The painfully intense magnifying effects of the shaving mirror distort his features, while the quality of this image interrupts the visual cohesion within the screen's frame. Sonny's analogy to Hank's comfort food turns out to be bourbon and hasty sex with a hooker, Vera (Amber Rules). As this cordially affectless blonde removes her clothes and leans over a desk, Sonny takes her from behind. A cut takes us outside to view the scene through the window. In a move that becomes characteristic of *Monster's Ball,* the camera provides us with both excessive proximity, as in the mirror, and estranged detachment.

Parallel structure intensifies around the execution. One structural bridge connecting the anticipation that precedes this event to its aftermath comes in a sequence that mirrors Sonny's encounter with Vera. We find Hank meeting her in the very same room. His visit to her appears as a direct consequence of the chain of violence that has led from the execution to Sonny's suicide in response to Hank's threat to evict him. This time the mirror hangs empty, as a hole punched in the center of the frame. As Hank and Vera assume exactly the positions she and Sonny have taken, the film takes a creepily decisive oedipal turn. When Vera asks after Sonny, Hank abruptly withdraws. In retrospect, this moment of rupture over the dead son's memory will be constructed as Hank's personal turning point. Between these two sequences, which create a mimetic delirium, where father imitates son, down to the preferred sexual posture, the execution has intervened. Its structural consequences are definitive and multiple, but first among them is Sonny's suicide. Equally important, a second story has displaced and supplanted Sonny's, as the film brings Leticia into his place in its parallel structure.

Spatial Partitions

As its rigorous editing matches the troubled domestic and working lives of its two principals, the film establishes a logic that renders their eventual encounter structurally inevitable, though it is persistently underdeveloped at the narrative level. Equally important, this structure produces a powerful mirroring effect in the details of the characters' daily lives. But only an extraordinary event can bridge the radically partitioned spaces they inhabit. The fated "accident" that brings them together after Leticia's husband's execution is a literal one. Hank happens by just after Tyrell has been hit by a car. They meet, quite literally, over the bodies of dead black men, but they bond over the bodies of dead sons. In the intersection of these two series, Lawrence Musgrove becomes retroactively inflected with the innocence and victimization of the sons.

In the sequence that has reunited that condemned man with his family for the last time in the prison's vast, searingly white visiting room, it is Lawrence who functions as its visual and structural anchor, just as his execution anchors and propels the story itself. The filmmaker's own commentary indicates his care to maintain the father as the only figure who is held consistently in the middle of the frame. His wife and son shift places around him, pushed toward the edges, shown from oblique angles across the room. His structural centrality visually inscribes his emotional stability by contrast to the skewed, or disturbed, perspectives of mother and son. Significantly, the introduction of Sean Combs ruptures the film's realist frame, because the popular celebrity is known primarily as a rapper at this time, so he appears in cameo. He thus inflects Lawrence with an extra-diegetic charge, much as Poitier did his own characters. Similarly, rapper Mos Def, who plays Hank's uncannily resilient neighbor, also doubles his character. In this context of performers whose offscreen personas shadow their characters, Berry's own performance—like Poitier's but in a more troubling mode—must be read as depending upon, and playing upon and against, the real, biracial body of the actress herself. Holland describes the effect this way: "Berry and Leticia perform the evidence of excess: the actress is the product of miscegenation; the character she plays engages in the very act" (807). This shiftiness of actor and character echoes the camera's own unstable relation to its subjects, its troubling of the boundaries of inside and outside.

Consistent with the film's pattern of shooting its principals across barriers or screens, Lawrence functions in this scene as a visual obstacle, centered in the frame between his wife and son. Pulling focus, the camera blurs the father's body into a dark wedge encroaching in the frame and striking a sharp contrast with the crisper images of Leticia and Tyrell, who face him across the table. This kind of image—one body smeared out of focus and looming close to the camera while the other remains in sharp focus but held at a distance and contained by the blurred shape—returns repeatedly in scenes of "intimate" exchange.

Since this technique notably marks Hank's interactions with his brutally rejecting father, Buck, and with Leticia, it establishes both a counterpoint and a spatial analogy. In neither case can the characters inhabit the same plane. Nor can they establish a spatial balance within the frame. Each decentered scene exhibits the film's consistency in prohibiting characters from the center of the frame—always separating them by the dead zone it creates by confining them to opposite ends of the frame. But each scene also establishes the less literal—and therefore incalculable—distance that separates the two planes implied through the rack focus. A similar technique, we remember, marks key scenes in *Far from Heaven,* and to much the same effect.

If Lawrence, the black father, constitutes a visual center in the sequences in which he appears, he presents a sharp contrast to all the decentered, off-balance people who populate the rest of the film. Affectively, Lawrence emerges here as the good father, telling his son: "I'm a bad man. You ain't me. You're the best of what I am." Encouraging his son to identify with the "good object" and to split off the bad, Lawrence goes on to praise the drawing Tyrell shows him. His skill is inherited from the good father, whose own image he has rendered. This exchange of a drawing resonates with a later scene: as Lawrence awaits execution in his cell, he sketches both Sonny and Hank, who take turns guarding him. "It truly takes a human being to really see a human being," he tells Sonny as he sketches. Even as this scene establishes identification between Lawrence and Sonny it also inscribes Hank as the one who cannot see the other, who cannot produce the barest identification, and the one who needs enlightenment.

But if Lawrence, here exhibiting the Poitier figure's capacity to initiate contact, to really see and to truly educate the white subject, represents a cross-racial connection, his electrocution inaugurates a chain of ruptures and violence.[10] In this spectacularly theatrical death scene, the stable body that has centered the previous scenes now erupts convulsively. This con-vulsive body haunts the rest of the film, as the execution scene itself links its various sites and characters. Not only does Lawrence's photograph hang in Leticia's bathroom, but also his own drawings become her son's legacy. In the end, his portraits of Hank and Sonny, his gift to the latter, end up encrypted like relics in Sonny's attic room, now locked up and unvisited.

Moreover, this execution scene repeats the image of the supplement-ary mirror, or relay of mirrors, that introduces both excessive proximity and distance. In a grotesque superimposition, the film dissolves away from the electrocution. Lawrence's contorted image hangs suspended in the darkened glass through which the immobile witnesses observe his death. Reflecting two layers of image, the victim and his witnesses, this scene dissolves into a close-up of Leticia violently brushing her teeth, her image doubled by the large bathroom mirror and the smaller, magnifying one, like the mirror that has figured centrally in the motel room.

In an oblique repetition of the Poitier effect, Lawrence's death catalyzes the series of events—effects without causes—that make up Hank's trajectory for the rest of the film, his ersatz "redemption." That is to say, where Poitier's characters achieved their pedagogical goals and then passed on through, Lawrence must pass *away* to produce his effect. But his death's image also comes to haunt the film, returning as the repressed in both Leticia's and Hank's houses. Parallel sequences that frame the execution scene align Leticia and Hank as brutal parents: both physically and verbally abuse their sons relentlessly, and Hank charges Sonny with the epithet "pussy" for having collapsed to vomit while escorting their prisoner. Both spew their loathing for their sons in terms that feminize and abject them. But when Leticia pokes and grabs at her son's obese flesh and taunts him, this scene produces diegetic rupture, as the child's extradiegetic embodiment—his body's "realness"—obtrudes in the scene. His body doubles itself, as Berry's does, bringing its extradiegetic force into the fictional world. Yet all this extradiegetic freight cannot make the film's central plot and ending any more credible.

Dead Zones

As mirrors produce a mimetic relay and structure parallel spaces, they also introduce a series of implied identifications established through resemblances—real or imagined. For example, when Hank announces he has quit his job as a prison guard, Buck attacks him in the same terms Hank has applied to Sonny, saying, "You're reminding me of your mother. Your mother wasn't shit. I got more pussy after she killed herself than I did when she was living as my wife. She quit on me. You're doing the same." This brutal rhetoric of loathing locates Hank as another feminized son within a dizzying mimetic chain of paternal descent. Fathers and sons are haunted, not only by their inherited profession as prison guards and executioners but also by the disappearance of the mothers. A viewer may match Hank's absent wife, Sonny's missing mother, to the fate of Hank's own mother, since the film here suggests the men made analogous marriages. Most unsettlingly, as we see more than once, fathers and sons seem connected by sexual appetites.

While the Grotowski men construct their wives as disturbances, sources of shame, Leticia emerges as a "bad mother" by contrast to the dead father, the only "good" father in the film, Lawrence. Parental failure produces another analogy between Hank and Leticia. In this melodramatic universe, where generational strife becomes fatal, reproduction's extinction leads to interracial coupling. *Monster's Ball* presents a world structured by restless circulation of resemblances and substitutes: one thing or person in place of another. In such a universe, every scene and gesture is overdetermined, while Hank and Leticia's relationship remains *under*determined. Nowhere is this more apparent than in the film's notorious sex scene. Repeatedly cited for its graphic quality, this scene is hardly so realistic as all that: its naturalism is fractured by competing commitments to theatricality and to symbolism. After Hank has confessed that his sympathy for Leticia is born of an identification constructed through shared loss, Leticia's recollections of her dead son's obesity culminate in a tirade about the impossibility of being a fat black man in America. These are the memories that lead to her hysterical demand that Hank "make me feel good."

As the couple copulates, we notice that the space keeps mutating around them. Our gaze is continually relocated by the restless camera and by the jumpy editing, which truncates the sequence as if to contain its frenzy. Masking part of the screen, the film presents this sex in vignettes as it frames the couple in narrow vertical rectangles. Alternating between sharp verticals and the full horizontal range of the screen, this sequence also periodically introduces a rupture. Several times a cut introduces a completely alien shot: a hand reaching into a cage to grasp a fluttering bird. This interruption suggests a Sirkian estrangement and a retreat from the raw sexual flailing.

Combined with the tableaux of the couple in illuminated rectangles hanging within the black field, this image theatricalizes the scene, emphasizing its gestural quality and its layers of mediation. We simultaneously see too much and too little. When this sequence closes with the camera pulling back through two frames within the frame, it emphatically reminds us of the voyeuristic channel in which it has captured us, as it has captured its characters in this brutal intimacy, where raw violence cancels eroticism.

In the morning, Hank repeats the vomiting with which the film has opened. At this point, this "morning" sickness reads as "mourning" sickness, since it also recalls Sonny's vomiting at Lawrence's execution. Taking Leticia's place before her bathroom mirror, Hank suddenly becomes ill, apparently in response to her husband's image, which replaces his own as he lowers his head out of frame to vomit.

Evoking the most primitive and aggressive components of the psychic process of identification, *Monster's Ball* puts one character in another's place, establishing spatially identifications that it cannot explain narratively. Repeating the reverse oedipal scenario that sexualizes and spatializes the expression "Like father like son," in one of the film's more grotesque scenes, Leticia encounters Buck. When she shows him the cowboy hat she has bought as a gift for Hank, Buck tries it on and then begins to muse obscenely: "Hank's just like his Daddy. You're not a man until you've split dark oak." Perversely, Buck both literally and figuratively tries the son's place on for size. When Leticia recoils from Hank on account of his obscene father, he "evicts" Buck to a nursing home. And he then replaces his father with Leticia, who has literally been evicted from her home and now moves into Buck's room.

Claiming the father's space, Hank has completely transformed it, painting its drab, dark, aged wood paneling white. Space speaks, and it will continue to do so throughout the final sequences, even as the characters descend into muteness. But despite this abrupt spatial rearrangement, Buck's eviction does nothing to discredit his speculations about his son's sharing his own sexual fantasies or tastes, since the film resolutely fails to account for Hank's attraction to Leticia. Moreover, such a radical displacement pushes the conventional terms of racial melodrama, and the implications of the Poitier effect, to their breaking point. If we consider the father's eviction, it is as if the film imagines the racial past can be similarly evicted, disposed of, as Hank stows away his family's history of racism, now embodied in Buck, and attempts—like white characters in Poitier's films—to move on, as if newly innocent of that past.

Sharon Holland responds to critics' common complaints that Hank's "redemption" from his racist past through this sexual affair is unmotivated, or implausible: "Both time and history have proven that no amount of interracial sex will stave off racism's libidinal drive." "If racism is truly about defending racialized belonging and if it has its place within and without white bodies, therefore proliferating and moving throughout the culture at large," she asks, "then who owns the racism Hank is so steadfastly to reject? Where is racism's proper place?" (797). This film's answer seems to be that it goes underground, to leach through the foundational layers of its fantasmatic spatiotemporal zone, "the South."

The story of redemption and healing this film ambivalently proposes to tell is dramatically undercut in its final sequence of forced resolution. After Hank and Leticia make love, he announces his intention to go out for ice cream. She requests that he bring her some as well. These are the last words she speaks in the film. In Hank's absence, she discovers her husband's sketches of his executioners. Horrified by this proof of the history she shares with Hank, after wailing and flailing hysterically, she masters her reaction in a paralyzed muteness. Leaving the drawings encrypted in the locked attic room, the family archive where Hank has collected the residues of Sonny's and Buck's lives, she maintains her silence. Abandoning her husband's images, along with her own voice, she can end the film with Hank, but only in a stark asymmetry.

The attic contains the meaning of this asymmetry. Looking back at this amalgamated archive, we notice that where Hank's family is at the mercy of fathers, Leticia's is at the mercy of the state and the police. Yet at this point, both family histories seem to be encrypted in this locked and abandoned archive and thereby rendered equivalent. As an image, this reliquary strikes a pronounced echo with Hank's family graves, unmentioned and unvisited— except when he mows them to blend into the lawn. As losses pile up, the couple deposits them in crypts. But, by contrast to Hank, Leticia has been divested of everything. She has no place: no home, no community, no family, and no history. This asymmetry marks the film's unconscious, its failure to realize the promise Poitier's films so often made (even though they could not deliver on it): it has no place for Leticia in any imaginable future.

In the final sequence of "resolution," Hank and Leticia emerge from the house onto the back steps with their ice cream. But the camera tells a story that is different from the one the narrative would suggest. As it captures the couple in extreme long shot through an uneasy point of view that remains unattributed, the three family graves emerge obtrusively on the left side of the frame in front of us. It is as if we see for the first time what has been inhabiting the dead zones that the camera's framing has consistently suggested: the deceased sons and spouses. Thus, the film sutures the dead into the couple's exchange. But it also momentarily places us in the dead zone, stranded in a view from just "beyond the grave."

In a countershot that holds Hank and Leticia together in medium close-up, rack focus keeps the characters from inhabiting the same visual plane simultaneously. Hank's empty oblique gaze bisects Leticia's, and our look follows hers as she discovers the graves. We observe her blank gaze upward as Hank pronounces, "I think we're gonna be alright." In a literal moment of "uplift," the camera moves between the characters' heads, across their shoulders, to arc up in a view of the starry night sky. One cannot help recalling the conclusion of *Now, Voyager* (Irving Rapper, 1942), another wrenchingly hollow "happy ending," where Charlotte Vale relinquishes a future with her lover, claiming the stars as compensation: "At least, we have the stars."

But this impossible view from beyond the grave, the perspective this film offers us, seems perfectly consonant with the static *nowhere* this couple inhabits. If "healing" figures among the film's central tropes, at its conclusion this metaphorics seems to overlook Leticia entirely. Instead, the film drops her, and the spectator, in very much the kind of aporia that marks the endings of Poitier's films and, to a certain degree, the later civil rights nostalgia films that draw on this archive as well. In this case, the future emerges as a blank screen, and history has been reduced to the awful *mise en abyme* of intergenerational transmission in Hank's family that lies buried in his yard or locked in his attic.[11] Memory must be "evicted," banished to the archive like Sonny's and Lawrence's images, sequestered, like Buck, in a nursing home. History encrypted as relic—neither forgotten nor remembered—provides the only ground for this conclusion.

Suspended before this blank screen of the future, one might have hoped *Monster's Ball* would represent the ultimate impasse for racial melodramas of redemption and usher the Poitier effect's passage into obsolescence. But that was before the success of *The Help* demonstrated the continuing durability of its appeal. And that was before Lee Daniels's *The Butler* gave it yet another twist. Poitier returns stunningly in this later film to mark a decisive moment in the butler's family's ongoing generational struggle. In the late 1960s faithful White House butler Cecil Gaines (Forest Whitaker) and his wife, Gloria (Oprah Winfrey), are entertaining their militant son Louis (David Oyelowo) and his girlfriend, Carol (Yaya Alafia). The younger characters' hairstyles and dress mark them as adherents of the black power movement. Carol's insistence on belching at the dinner table, along with her noticeably unshaved armpits, indicate her resistance to middle-class/bourgeois norms. Because Louis has been somewhat estranged from his parents and Carol is a complete stranger, the atmosphere is tense. In an awkward attempt to engage the young people in conversation, Gloria ventures to Louis that she has seen a movie that reminded her of him: *In the Heat of the Night*. Louis erupts in a rage, shouting epithets and calling Poitier an "Uncle Tom," accusing him of providing precisely the black man that white people want to see. Cecil rails back at his son, asserting that Poitier's characters accomplish a progressive mission in displaying black dignity and achievement (arguably what his own character is doing in this film). These antagonists quite precisely describe the Poitier effect and the conflicted ways it registered for different—and sometimes for the same—audiences.

What is most stunning in this scene, however, is that it culminates in a definitive rupture between father and son, one that will be repaired only very late in the narrative. After Louis concludes his diatribe, insisting that Sidney Poitier is somehow "white," Cecil orders the young couple out of his home. In retaliation, Louis insults his father's profession of domestic service, and Gloria slaps Louis's face. So, in effect, the decisive—and violent—moment that precipitates the generational break is organized by the Poitier figure. In a conciliatory gesture after his brother has departed, younger brother Charlie (Elijah Kelley) offers a coda: "Dad, *I* like Sidney Poitier. What's that movie, *Look Who's Coming to Dinner?*" Then he adds, "Carol came to dinner," as if to invert the Poitier film's terms, casting the Gaineses as the Draytons and the female Black Panther as the Poitier figure. Amusing though it is, this last exchange also reminds us that this icon is just not going away. So, contrary to the confident assertions of his films of the civil rights period, he was not just passing through after all.

ACKNOWLEDGMENTS

I am in debt to many people, colleagues, friends, and family for support and sustenance during the long development of this project.

Camera Obscura has long remained the most exciting intellectual "home" I could have imagined. I am grateful to the members of its editorial collective—past and current—with whom it has been my privilege to work. For the consistent intellectual challenge, and for keeping me honest, thanks to Lalitha Gopalan, Amelie Hastie, Lynne Joyrich, Homay King, Constance Penley, Tess Takahashi, Sasha Torres, and Patty White.

Many thanks to the colleagues and friends who continue to make Rochester, New York, so intellectually and socially enjoyable—often over real feasts. Thanks to Steve Brauer and Joan Saab, Tom Dipiero, Georgia Eaves and Morris Eaves, Jennifer Grotz, Tom Hahn and Bette London, Rachel Haidu, Nigel Maister, and Ryan Prendergast.

The dynamic intellectual environment that surrounds me at the University of Rochester issues from close interdisciplinary collaboration among colleagues across numerous departments and programs. I am grateful for vigorous intellectual exchanges with colleagues who help to sustain the program in visual and cultural studies. I have benefited especially from participating in the Frederick Douglass Institute and the new program in American studies; each sponsors an invigorating research seminar series and rich programming.

Over the course of this book's development, I profited from regular exchanges with extraordinary colleagues: Janet Berlo, Joel Burges, Douglas Crimp, Paul Duro, Ken Gross, Sarah Higley, Larry Hudson, Rosemary Kegl, Cilas Kemedjio, Stephanie Li, James Longenbach, Katie Mannheimer, Jason Middleton, Nora Rubel, Joanie Rubin, Steven Schottenfeld, Ezra Tawil, and Jeffrey Tucker.

Special thanks to the friends who keep our conversations going over time and distance: Rajani Sudan and Chris Morris, Randall Halle and Mohammed Bamyeh, Paul Smith, Rachel Ablow and Ruth Mack, Jeffrey Geiger, Pat Gill and Richard Wheeler, Geoff Bennington, and, always, Elissa Marder.

I am grateful to Michael Awkward and the anonymous reader at the University of Minnesota Press for their generous and discerning comments on the manuscript. I owe Richard Morrison huge thanks for his keen intelligence, his writerly sensibility, and his willingness to take on an admittedly eccentric project.

I am deeply in debt to my sibling group—for sticking together, most of all, but also for the debates (sometimes heated) along with the boisterous festivities: Amy Willis and Matt Krupp, Beth Willis and Julie Wyman, Chris Willis and Lisa Nelson Willis, Julia Welton and (the late) Kenneth Welton, Meghan Willis and Larry Edelman.

Heartfelt gratitude to Marta Michael and Krysia Michael for the sharp wit and fierce intelligence that they share. No one is more fun to talk to, especially after dinner. Finally, to John Michael: more than I can ever say. His forceful intelligence, his subtlety, and his light touch with words mark every passage of this book, as they enrich my life. He animates my world, and I thank him for his very particular joie de vivre.

NOTES

Introduction

1. Jabari Asim, *What Obama Means . . . for Our Culture, Our Politics, Our Future* (New York: William Morrow, 2009).

2. Ta-Nehisi Coates, "Fear of a Black President," *Atlantic*, September 2012, http://www.theatlantic.com.

3. Colson Whitehead, *Sag Harbor* (New York: Random House/Anchor Books, 2010), 10.

4. David Marriott writes compellingly about *Pressure Point*'s contradictions in *Haunted Life: Visual Culture and Black Modernity* (New Brunswick, N.J.: Rutgers University Press, 2007). For Marriott, Poitier's character "appears to be both metaphor and metonym, cipher and symbol—as if there is something about him that the film can neither face nor address" (181). Marriott ends his analysis by considering the film's vexed—and vexing—conclusion: "The ending of the film again insists on placing Poitier into a startling vacuum. Not only must he forget his race, forget that he is a black man, if he is to stand for and symbolize that democracy; he must also be visibly punished by losing his job as a black psychiatrist" (202). "The ending of the film," he continues, "is still imagining the black man as a kind of cover, or metaphor—a way of referring to and discussing white liberal torment and anguish without addressing the growing refusal by blacks, to take—again and again—white hate. The film cannot legitimately address this tension because that would involve the liberal dream of integration, its sadistic fantasy, being called into question—left behind and revealed, as it were, in black and white" (202–3).

5. Thomas Elsaesser, "Tales of Sound and Fury: Observations of the Family Melodrama," in *Home Is Where the Heart Is: Studies in Melodrama and the Woman's Film*, ed. Christine Gledhill (London: BFI, 1987), 47.

6. Christine Gledhill, "The Melodramatic Field: An Investigation," in Gledhill, *Home Is Where the Heart Is,* 37.

7. Geoffrey Nowell-Smith, "Minelli and Melodrama," in Gledhill, *Home Is Where the Heart Is,* 73.

8. Steve Neale, "Melodrama and Tears," *Screen* 27, no. 6 (1986): 6–7.

9. Linda Williams, *Playing the Race Card: Melodramas of Black and White from Uncle Tom to O. J. Simpson* (Princeton, N.J.: Princeton University Press, 2001), xiv.

10. Robert Reid-Pharr makes such an argument about sentimental fiction, discussing Harriet Wilson's *Our Nig:* "I would suggest that what Wilson accesses through the representation of punches, slaps, lashes, and insults is the recognition not only that domesticity is founded upon and within systemic and historically entrenched modes of violence but also that it is itself one of these modes. Since the domestic is *the* primary vehicle by which bodies are brought into order, by which they are established as raced and gendered entities, it is necessarily violent because the process of racing and gendering subjects is always violent. That is to say, violence against bodies not only helps to establish a clean distinction between black and white but also does so precisely by foregrounding pain, hunger, freezing, and so on, none of which can ever be articulated fully. The very moment at which one expresses the most human of conditions—pain, for example—is the moment at which one announces an unbreachable gulf between self and other." Robert Reid-Pharr, *Conjugal Union: The Body, the House, and the Black American* (New York: Oxford University Press, 1999), 92–93.

11. Toni Morrison, *Playing in the Dark: Whiteness and the Literary Imagination* (New York: Random House, 1992), 7.

12. Robert Reid-Pharr, *Once You Go Black: Choice, Desire, and the Black American Intellectual* (New York: New York University Press, 2007), 129.

13. Herman Gray, "Remembering Civil Rights: Television, Memory, and the 1960s," in *The Revolution Wasn't Televised: Sixties Television and Social Conflict,* ed. Lynn Spigel and Michael Curtin (New York: Routledge, 1997), 353.

14. Aniko Bodroghkozy, *Equal Time: Television and the Civil Rights Movement* (Urbana: University of Illinois Press, 2012), 46.

15. Sasha Torres, *Black, White, and in Color: Television and Black Civil Rights* (Princeton, N.J.: Princeton University Press, 2003), 6.

16. Alan Nadel, *Television in Black-and-White America* (Lawrence: University of Kansas Press, 2005), 12.

17. Lynne Joyrich, *Re-viewing Reception: Television, Gender, and Postmodern Culture* (Bloomington: Indiana University Press, 1996), 45.

18. In his book on *American Bandstand,* American studies scholar Matthew Delmont explores Dick Clark's false claims—or false memories—that the show was integrated in 1957, when, in fact, it did not integrate until its move from Philadelphia to California in 1964. Throughout, Delmont is interested in the problem of false or distorted memory. Examining more recent fictional representations of *American Bandstand* as iconic of the civil rights period, the TV show *American Dreams* (NBC, 2002–5) and *Hairspray,* Adam Shankman's 2007 film version of the Broadway musical based on John Waters's 1988 film of the same title, Delmont finds that both texts offer "nostalgic stories of interracial unity and white innocence in the American

Bandstand era." Matthew F. Delmont, *The Nicest Kids in Town: American Bandstand, Rock 'n' Roll, and the Struggle for Civil Rights in 1950s Philadelphia* (Berkeley: University of California Press, 2012), 196. He invites us to remain suspicious of these representations, since, in his words, "these narratives can too easily be taken as endorsements of a color-blind racial ideology in which racism is strictly a problem of individual prejudice and in which this prejudice has disappeared since the 1960s" (222). Delmont's critical objects present much in common with the "civil rights nostalgia" films I examine here. Though Delmont does not really interrogate this, both *Hairspray* and *American Dreams* concern themselves quite centrally with budding feminism through their teenage heroines, who act as key agents in promoting integration of the television shows where they dance.

1. Passing Through

1. Jacqueline Rose, *States of Fantasy* (Oxford: Oxford University Press, 1996), 5.

2. Henry Louis Gates Jr., *Thirteen Ways of Looking at a Black Man* (New York: Random House, 1997), 169.

3. Nelson George, *Blackface: Reflections on African-Americans and the Movies* (New York: Cooper Square Press, 1994), 17.

4. Patricia A. Turner notes that *Driving Miss Daisy*, which won the Academy Award for Best Picture in 1989, and for which Morgan Freeman received a Best Actor nomination, has much in common with *Lilies of the Field*. Both films' male leads "portray benevolent, warm working-class men who go to work for aging, self-righteous, tough-minded white women who can't drive," she writes wryly. "Both films," she continues, "feature celibate heroes—lone African-American men—who, after passing a series of minor tests, advance to positions in which they are expected to fulfill the desires of older, chaste, white women." Patricia A. Turner, *Ceramic Uncles and Celluloid Mammies: Black Images and Their Influence on Culture* (Charlottesville: University of Virginia Press, 1994), 210.

5. Sidney Poitier, *The Measure of a Man: A Spiritual Autobiography* (New York: HarperCollins, 2000), 107.

6. James Baldwin, "Sidney Poitier," *Look*, July 23, 1968, 56.

7. Herman Gray, "Remembering Civil Rights: Television, Memory, and the 1960s," in *The Revolution Wasn't Televised: Sixties Television and Social Conflict*, ed. Lynn Spigel and Michael Curtin (New York: Routledge, 1997), 353. Aniko Bodroghkozy argues that the "civil rights subject" of Gray's analysis "is not merely a representation of a past remembered in a particular way to comfort contemporary viewers." This figure, she argues, "was already present in network television's representational strategies as a means to soothe and reassure the medium's white audiences about the worthiness of Southern blacks in their quest for equality and political rights." Aniko Bodroghkozy, *Equal Time: Television and the Civil Rights Movement* (Urbana: University of Illinois Press, 2012), 48.

8. José Esteban Muñoz, *Disidentifications: Queers of Color and the Performance of Politics* (Minneapolis: University of Minnesota Press, 1999), 182.

9. Sasha Torres, *Black, White, and in Color: Television and Black Civil Rights* (Princeton, N.J.: Princeton University Press, 2003), 14.

10. Richard Dyer, *Stars* (London: BFI, 1998), 26.

11. For an account of the trial's aftermath, including Huie's two articles on it, see Allison Graham, *Framing the South: Hollywood, Television, and Race during the Civil Rights Struggle* (Baltimore: Johns Hopkins University Press, 2001), 118–21.

12. Norman Mailer, "The White Negro," in *Advertisements for Myself* (New York: G. Putnam's Sons, 1959), 341.

13. Robert Reid-Pharr, *Once You Go Black: Choice, Desire, and the Black American Intellectual* (New York: New York University Press, 2007), 130.

14. Both Phillip Brian Harper, *Are We Not Men? Masculine Anxiety and the Problem of African-American Identity* (New York: Oxford University Press, 1996), and Gayle Wald, *Crossing the Line: Racial Passing in Twentieth-Century U.S. Literature and Culture* (Durham, N.C.: Duke University Press, 2000), have written compelling accounts of the desires and obsessions that shape Griffin's text. Crucially, as both authors point out, as Griffin undertakes his "ethnographic" journey disguised as a black man, he explains himself this way: "How else except by becoming a Negro could a white man hope to learn the truth? . . . The Southern Negro will not tell the white man the truth." John Howard Griffin, *Black Like Me* (New York: Signet, 1996), 1.

15. Slavoj Žižek, *Tarrying with the Negative: Kant, Hegel, and the Critique of Ideology* (Durham, N.C.: Duke University Press, 1993), 203.

16. Linda Williams, *Playing the Race Card: Melodramas of Black and White from Uncle Tom to O. J. Simpson* (Princeton, N.J.: Princeton University Press, 2001), 13.

17. Michel Chion calls such voices whose bodies are absent from view "acousmatic." For a sustained discussion of their effects, see his *The Voice in Cinema*, ed. and trans. Claudia Gorbman (New York: Columbia University Press, 1999).

18. As Alison Graham has argued, the question of class is central to representations of southern racism in U.S. culture of the period. "If the stubborn violence of . . . [the white southern working class] was 'in the blood,' . . . then class itself was an accurate gauge of sociopathology and the 'virus' endemic to poor whites was possibly containable." Graham goes on to describe this bad object's function in popular culture: "Bracketed—we might even say quarantined—as an almost allegorical figure, the ailing redneck would find a home in popular narratives as a chastened emblem of racial redemption, a scapegoat, in essence, for the sins of his betters." Graham, *Framing the South*, 121.

19. Michael Rogin describes *Home of the Brave*'s unforgettable image of the black soldier rocking the body of his dying white friend as "a black and white pietà," and he also notes its uncanny recurrence in *The Defiant Ones*. Michael Rogin, *Blackface, White Noise: Jewish Immigrants in the Hollywood Melting Pot* (Berkeley: University of California Press, 1996), 239.

20. In Poitier's own words, "The movie ended before viewers could question how long this comfort would last or where it would lead or how profound it was." Poitier, *Measure of a Man*, 105.

21. A notable exception to this compulsively repeated trope comes in *A Raisin in the Sun* (Daniel Petrie, 1961), the film adaptation of Lorraine Hansberry's successful Broadway play. Here Poitier plays Walter Lee Younger in a drama that centers on a working-class family's efforts to leave inner-city Chicago. This tightly claustrophobic

drama, set for the most part in the Youngers' cramped apartment, makes ample use of Poitier's smoldering affect and his anxiously coiled body to highlight the force of the angry eruptions to which he gives vent. Paradoxically, the greater the emotional range this film tolerates from the Poitier character, the more constricted his surroundings. In its cinematic incarnation, *Raisin in the Sun* seems to highlight Poitier's tight containment by the screen's frame. But this film's conclusion resonates oddly with the regular narrative arc of "passing through" that governs Poitier's other films. Here, once the family members carry out their resolve to occupy the home they have bought, despite the objections of white neighbors, they disappear from our view. Their residency in the new neighborhood passes beyond our view, utterly beyond to the film's horizon.

22. Quoted in Aram Goudsouzian, *Sidney Poitier: Man, Actor, Icon* (Chapel Hill: University of North Carolina Press, 2004), 217.

23. See ibid., 206–7; Poitier, *Measure of a Man*, 200–201.

24. For a fuller account of this landmark event, see Juan Williams, *Eyes on the Prize: America's Civil Rights Years, 1954–1965* (New York: Penguin Books, 1988), 213–18.

25. Goudsouzian, *Sidney Poitier*, 209.

26. Linda Williams, "Melodrama Revised," in *Refiguring American Film Genres: Theory and History*, ed. Nick Browne (Berkeley: University of California Press, 1998), 42.

27. Literary scholar Carol Mavor explores memories of her childhood viewing of this film in her recent book *Black and Blue: The Bruising Passion of "Camera Lucida," "La Jetée," "Sans soleil," and "Hiroshima mon amour"* (Durham, N.C.: Duke University Press, 2012). Her evocative memory captures something of this film's fantasmatic reservoir: "The character of Selina (played by Elizabeth Hartman) is helpless, white, blind, and adolescent, with a terrible mother who caused her blindness during a drunken scuffle. . . . The only color memory that Selina has from her world before blindness is a 'patch of blue.' . . . Blind Selina, with this bit of blue sky or blue ocean or blue cardigan or blue cup or blue nothing at all, falls in love with Gordon, Poitier's character: a gorgeous 'man of color.' Green could have made the film in color, but he was emphatic that it be in black and white" (4). Mavor goes on to reflect: "My adult memory of my childhood viewing of *A Patch of Blue*, where Poitier feeds the viewer and the blind girl with seen and unseen blackness, is hued blue and taboo" (8).

28. In this independent film, Roemer (born in Berlin in 1928) and his collaborator, Robert M. Young, directed Abbey Lincoln and Dixon in a story about the economic trials of a young African American couple and the impact of these difficulties on their relationship. Visually, the film maintains a documentary feel, as it focuses on the daily details of the couple and their family and friends. Unusually for its period, *Nothing but a Man* features no significant white characters.

29. The other Best Picture nominees were *Bonnie and Clyde* (Arthur Penn), *The Graduate* (Mike Nichols), and *Dr. Dolittle* (Richard Fleischer).

30. As Seth Cagin and Philip Dray observe, "This egregious oversight was an apt reflection of how both films were perceived: neither was truly about a black man, both were about the magnanimity of whites who overcame their racial prejudice." Seth Cagin and Philip Dray, *Born to Be Wild: Hollywood and the Sixties Generation* (Boca Raton, Fla.: Coyote, 1994), 24.

31. Quoted in Goudsouzian, *Sidney Poitier*, 271.

32. Richard Nixon, "What Has Happened to America?," *Reader's Digest*, October 1967, 53.

33. William Styron, *The Confessions of Nat Turner* (New York: Random House, 1967).

34. See Albert E. Stone, *The Return of Nat Turner: History, Literature, and Cultural Politics in Sixties America* (Athens: University of Georgia Press, 1982). Notable among the responses to Styron's book is John H. Clarke, ed., *William Styron's "Nat Turner": Ten Black Writers Respond* (Boston: Beacon Press, 1968). This collection is significant for, among other things, its "broad representation indeed of a new black intelligentsia," according to Stone.

35. Stokely Carmichael and Charles V. Hamilton, *Black Power: The Politics of Liberation in America* (New York: Vintage, 1967); Martin Luther King Jr., *Where Do We Go from Here: Chaos or Consent?* (Boston: Beacon Press, 1967); Eldridge Cleaver, *Soul on Ice* (New York: McGraw-Hill, 1967).

36. In *Once You Go Black,* Reid-Pharr argues that "the too heavy emphasis on the fact that Black American culture has deep roots in slavery and more generally in the life of the rural South" has tended to repress or exclude consideration of Black agency (12). His concern is that "all too often students of Black American literature and culture reproduce notions of a stagnant Black American history by insisting that the anguished cries of the slave are ultimately indistinct from the complicated musings of the contemporary artist" (37).

37. E. Ann Kaplan, *Trauma Culture: The Politics of Terror and Loss in Media and Literature* (New Brunswick, N.J.: Rutgers University Press, 2005), 74.

38. Jared Sexton, "The Ruse of Engagement: Black Masculinity and the Cinema of Policing," *American Quarterly* 61, no. 1 (March 2009): 44.

39. James Baldwin, *The Devil Finds Work* (1976), in *The Price of the Ticket: Collected Nonfiction, 1948–1985* (London: Michael Joseph, 1985), 591.

40. Susan Courtney, *Hollywood Fantasies of Miscegenation: Spectacular Narratives of Gender and Race, 1903–1967* (Princeton, N.J.: Princeton University Press, 2005), 254. Courtney argues compellingly that we should consider this film alongside Eldridge Cleaver's *Soul on Ice* as well as the Supreme Court decision. "While *Guess, Loving,* and *Soul* thus form a trio of authors, agendas, and implied audiences that could hardly be more different from one another, together they cut across a wide swath of popular culture to suggest that dominant American legacies of miscegenation were being confronted more directly than ever before" (250).

41. Sidney Poitier, *This Life* (New York: Alfred A. Knopf, 1980), 286.

42. Courtney argues that the film's frequent recursions to the image of Tracy and Hepburn together—in particular the expedition to the drive-in for ice cream—anchor its unfolding drama in a pronounced nostalgia for their "battle of the sexes" films of the 1940s. But, she notes significantly, "the sexual conservatism of the 1967 film thus not only works to stabilize gender relations for its own senior and junior couples, offering the revised portrait ultimately as a model for Joey and John, but in doing so goes so far as to deny and rewrite the gender discord of the 1940s and the 'classical' couple of the Tracy and Hepburn comedies." Courtney, *Hollywood Fantasies of Miscegenation,* 271.

43. Michel Chion, *Audio-Vision: Sound on Screen*, ed. and trans. Claudia Gorbman (New York: Columbia University Press, 1994), 5.

44. On the illusion of depth that sound provides, see ibid., 70–71.

45. Caryl Flinn, *Strains of Utopia: Gender, Nostalgia, and Hollywood Film Music* (Princeton, N.J.: Princeton University Press, 1992), 110–15.

46. The song's lyrics include these lines: "You've got to give a little, take a little / And let your poor heart break a little. . . . That's the glory of love. / You've got to laugh a little, cry a little . . . That's the glory of love."

47. Flinn describes one of the ways in which film music evokes anteriority: "Music establishes the means through which that nostalgic desire is activated in the first place; it appears as its very conduit. Music will also veil the jarring effects possible from such a break in chronological, linear narration, providing both the text and the spectator with a suturing illusion of fullness in the process." Flinn, *Strains of Utopia*, 109.

48. Another instance of contemporary musical obtrusion is Monsignor Ryan's (Cecil Kellaway's) brief performance of the Beatles song "We Can Work It Out." His off-key performance and unrecognizable phrasing seem to suggest that though he himself isn't "hip," unlike the Draytons he knows what *is*, since he supports the interracial marriage.

49. Baldwin observes that it distinctly replicates a scene between a maid and a black politician in *The Birth of a Nation*. "When our black wonder doctor hits San Francisco, some fifty-odd years later," he writes, "he encounters exactly the same maid, who tells him exactly the same thing, for the same reason, and in the same words." Baldwin, *The Devil Finds Work*, 602.

50. Courtney sets the final sequences from this point forward into the context of a visual analysis of when and to whom the film grants access to the view of the San Francisco Bay that the Draytons' house magnificently commands. Courtney, *Hollywood Fantasies of Miscegenation*, 277.

51. Baldwin comes to a terse conclusion about this film: "A black person can make nothing of this film—except, perhaps, *Superfly*—and, when one tries to guess what white people make of it, a certain chill goes down the spine." Baldwin, *The Devil Finds Work*, 600.

52. In *Once You Go Black*, Reid-Pharr argues that "the film's very syntax is dependent on the conceit that there is no real disconnect between the performers on screen and the lives they perform" (153).

2. Feminism as Alibi

1. *Crazy in Alabama* (Antonio Banderas, 1999) operates on a similar terrain. Melanie Griffith's character, Lucille Vinson, an aspiring television actress who will eventually realize her ambition by appearing on *Bewitched*, passes through her segregated southern hometown on her way to Los Angeles. She inspires her teenage nephew (Lucas Black) to defy white complicity and testify against a policeman who has murdered a black youth who dared attempt to enter a public pool. (Significantly, the film gives Lucille a crudely feminist discourse; she has murdered her husband because he prohibited her from pursuing her career!)

2. Jonathan Kaplan was born in 1947, and his screenwriter, Don Roos, was born in 1955. Richard Pearce was born in 1943 and Gary Ross in 1956. While Antonio Banderas was born in 1960, his screenwriter, Mark Childress, was born in 1957 in Alabama.

3. Notably, *The Help* repeats this effect for a younger generation, as both Tate Taylor, its director, and Kathryn Stockett, the author of the novel on which it is based, were born in 1969, a moment just beyond the civil rights movement's peak. It registers especially in the traumatic separation of the white child, Mae Mobley, from her caretaker, Aibileen (Viola Davis), a separation that echoes Skeeter's loss of her own childhood black caretaker, Constantine, which she commemorates with her account of the maids' working lives.

4. Linda Williams, *Playing the Race Card: Melodramas of Black and White from Uncle Tom to O. J. Simpson* (Princeton, N.J.: Princeton University Press, 2001), 300.

5. E. Ann Kaplan, *Trauma Culture: The Politics of Terror and Loss in Media and Literature* (New Brunswick, N.J.: Rutgers University Press, 2005), 74.

6. Steve Neale, "Melodrama and Tears," *Screen* 27, no. 6 (1986): 6.

7. Vivian Sobchack, "Introduction: History Happens," in *The Persistence of History: Cinema, Television, and the Modern Event,* ed. Vivian Sobchack (New York: Routledge, 1996), 2.

8. Robert Burgoyne, *Film Nation: Hollywood Looks at U.S. History* (Minneapolis: University of Minnesota Press, 1997), 107.

9. Robin D. G. Kelly, *Race Rebels: Culture, Politics, and the Black Working Class* (New York: Free Press, 1994), 57.

10. Significantly, in 1963 Betty Friedan published her groundbreaking book about the "problem with no name," another version of "not getting ordinary life," *The Feminine Mystique* (New York: Dell, 1963).

11. Mary Ann Watson, *The Expanding Vista: American Television in the Kennedy Years* (Durham, N.C.: Duke University Press, 1994), 105. Watson attributes some fairly far-reaching effects to Kennedy's position on civil rights: "The short-sightedness of entertainment television concerning the lives of black Americans underwent a rapid remission in the crucial summer of 1963. . . . It was as if, when President Kennedy firmly aligned himself with the righteousness of the cause, prime-time television did too. The voices of black advocates who had been agitating for increased media representation now fell on more attentive ears" (58).

12. Kelly remarks on the importance of this line and its instability: "On numerous occasions, black passengers paid their fare at the front door but before they had a chance to board the bus drove off. The rule itself was not only obnoxious but ambiguous: drivers were instructed to 'collect fares at the front entrance of all vehicles *when they are crowded*' (emphasis added). What was meant by crowded was always subject to interpretation, leading to immense confusion and, at times, intense disagreement." Kelly, *Race Rebels,* 59.

13. Freud asserts that the third-person perspective of such scenes marks a screen memory, since it displaces us from the original experience: "Whenever one appears in a memory this way, as an object among other objects, this confrontation of the acting self with the recollecting self can be taken as proof that the original impression

has been edited." Sigmund Freud, "Screen Memories," in *The Uncanny*, trans. David McClintock (London: Penguin, 2003), 20.

14. Sasha Torres, *Black, White, and in Color: Television and Black Civil Rights* (Princeton, N.J.: Princeton University Press, 2003), 27.

15. J. Fred MacDonald, *Blacks and White TV: African Americans in Television since 1948* (Belmont, Calif.: Wadsworth, 1992), 72.

16. MacDonald documents the repressive measures such fears provoked toward the media: "Many southern stations refused to accept syndicated and network movies because they felt such films would upset local social standards. . . . ABC refused for the 1962–1963 season to air *The Defiant Ones*. . . . One year earlier, the Alabama House of Representatives unanimously resolved to ask Alabama theater operators not to exhibit *Island in the Sun* . . . because, in the words of one legislator, 'the making of such films will be most pleasing to the Communists and other un-American organizations, and to all intents and purposes will amount to another tactic in their campaign to brainwash the American public into acceptance of race mongrelization.'" Ibid., 72–73.

17. According to MacDonald, "Talk show hosts like Mike Wallace on *Newsbeat* and David Susskind on *Open End* welcomed black leaders to their programs. Moderate leaders like Martin Luther King, Jr., Roy Wilkins, and A. Philip Randolph were engaged in insightful conversations intended to present their ideas to a broad audience." "Still, however," he points out, "the perimeters of television's black focus mitigated against blacks with radical positions." Ibid., 86.

18. On the "transient," or "itinerant," blacks on TV, see Robert Lewis Shayon, "Living Color on Television," *Saturday Review*, November 24, 1962, 25, cited in Phillip Brian Harper, "Extra-Special Effects: Televisual Representation and the Claims of 'the Black Experience,'" in *Living Color: Race and Television in the United States*, ed. Sasha Torres (Durham, N.C.: Duke University Press, 1998), 65.

19. Jennifer Fuller, "Debating the Past through the Present: Representations of the Civil Rights Movement in the 1990s," in *The Civil Rights Movement in American Memory*, ed. Renee C. Romano and Leigh Raiford (Athens: University of Georgia Press, 2006), 179. This documentation suggests that the film relies quite literally on the "feminist alibi."

20. Mimi White, "'Reliving the Past Over and Over Again': Race, Gender, and Popular Memory in *Homefront* and *I'll Fly Away*," in Torres, *Living Color*, 121.

21. Patricia A. Turner, "Dangerous White Stereotypes," *New York Times*, August 29, 2011, A21.

22. Kathryn Stockett, "This Life: Kathryn Stockett on Her Childhood in the Deep South," *Daily Mail*, July 18, 2009, dailymail.com.uk.

23. For a discussion of the uniform's function in both domestic and public spaces, as well as of maids' resistance to wearing uniforms in public, see Rebecca Sharpless, *Cooking in Other Women's Kitchens: Domestic Workers in the South, 1865–1960* (Chapel Hill: University of North Carolina Press, 2010), 144–45. The chapter in which this point appears, "Gendering Jim Crow: Relationships with Employers," also offers a detailed analysis of the mapping of domestic space and of white surveillance of black domestics, as well as of their anxieties about exposure.

24. Commentary on *Pleasantville* DVD.

25. As Dana Heller characterizes it, Nick at Nite's approach to TV "encourages a synchronic as opposed to diachronic method of perceiving television's social meanings," which "suggests that family sitcoms are best viewed with a cool, ironic detachment that structurally decontextualizes specific programming while reinforcing viewers' unity of experience and commitment to the dominant fantasies of the television dreamscape." Dana Heller, *Family Plots: The De-Oedipalization of Popular Culture* (Philadelphia: University of Pennsylvania Press, 1995), 41.

26. Sigmund Freud, "Family Romances," in *The Uncanny*, 37–41.

27. Alison Landsberg, *Prosthetic Memory: The Transformation of American Remembrance in the Age of Mass Culture* (New York: Columbia University Press, 2004), 19.

28. David Marc, *Comic Visions: Television Comedy and American Culture* (Boston: Unwin Hyman, 1989), 35.

29. A look at this show's "ideological fellow travelers," as Marc calls them (ibid., 65), confirms this coincidence: *The Donna Reed Show* (ABC, 1958–66), *Leave It to Beaver* (CBS, 1957–58; ABC, 1958–63), *Make Room for Daddy/The Danny Thomas Show* (various, 1953–65), *The Adventures of Ozzie and Harriet* (ABC, 1952–66).

30. Lynn Spigel, *Make Room for TV: Television and the Family Ideal in Postwar America* (Chicago: University of Chicago Press, 1992), 131.

31. Contemporary critic Robert Lewis Shayon advanced this position clearly in a *Saturday Review* column of February 9, 1963: "If Negroes were seen more frequently on TV—and in featured roles comparable to those played by white actors—their real-life employment picture might be favorably affected. Television's power to change mass habits and attitudes appears to be significant. An improvement in the Negro image on television might be a very important step toward real integration." Robert Lewis Shayon, "Living Color on Television—2," *Saturday Review*, February 9, 1963, 27, cited in Harper, "Extra-Special Effects," 63. On the sustained African American criticism of TV in the period, see MacDonald, *Blacks and White TV*, 65–100.

32. "Like previous communication technologies," writes Spigel in *Make Room for TV*, television "offered the possibility of an intellectual neighborhood, purified of social unrest and human misunderstanding" (111). It is in this context, she contends, that NBC's Pat Weaver could imagine the medium as "a cultural filter that purified the essence of an 'American' experience, relegating to another space the social conflict and struggle the 1950s form worked to hold apart from itself" (112).

33. As Spigel details Wylie's position, which coheres with popular anxieties of the period, it links "telephobia" with misogyny in identifying cultural threats to the "family" and to masculinity: "Indeed, the paranoid connections that Wylie drew between corporate technocracies, women, and broadcasting continued to be drawn throughout the 1950s. . . . Television was often shown to rob men of their powers and transform them into passive victims of a force they could not control." Ibid., 62.

34. Significantly, this classic novel became linked to civil rights issues in the 1950s. According to Jonathan Arac, the first discussion "in the public press concerning the racial offensiveness of *Huckleberry Finn* took place in New York City in 1957." And he notes this connection: "The discussion in the *Times* linked the controversy over

Huckleberry Finn with the events in Little Rock." Jonathan Arac, *"Huckleberry Finn" as Idol and Target: The Functions of Criticism in Our Time* (Madison: University of Wisconsin Press, 1997), 63, 65. My thanks to John Michael for reminding me of the important history of the novel's reception.

35. Think, for example, of J. D. Salinger's *Catcher in the Rye* (1951), also frequently banned, which foregrounds youthful alienation, sex, and profanity. Krin Gabbard points out the limitations of David's reading of this text: "in trying to get free, they see that they're free already." For Gabbard, "David conveniently defines freedom as something that is internal rather than as a right that can be granted or taken away by the state," thus ignoring "the legacy of slavery in the political and social life of Americans in the 1950s." Krin Gabbard, *Black Magic: White Hollywood and African American Culture* (New Brunswick, N.J.: Rutgers University Press, 2004), 99.

36. Ibid., 101. Gabbard analyzes this progression from white to black music through two directions in jazz initiated by Brubeck's album *Time Out* and Davis's *Kind of Blue*, both released in 1959. "The coffeehouse hipness that Gary Ross heard in 'Take Five,'" he writes, "still clings to the song and marks it as an artifact of the 1950s." On the other hand, he contends, "as black music, the Miles Davis recording carries with it an aura of the forbidden and transgressive that *Pleasantville* needs as it moves the narratives of the civil rights movement into a small town devoid of African American faces." Ibid., 98.

37. See Freud, "Screen Memories," 14–17. Notably, the central memory in this analysis features striking exaggerations of *color.*

38. This image evokes memorable cinematic moments: the scene in *Imitation of Life* (Douglas Sirk, 1959) when the mixed-race daughter, Sarah Jane (Susan Kohner), is beaten by her white boyfriend who has discovered that she is passing, and the scene in which white men pursue Pinky on a dark road in *Pinky* (Elia Kazan, 1949).

39. Significantly, the film's courtroom sequence also presents striking images that seem drawn directly from the civil rights era, mediated through contemporary representations in film, as the "colored" people all sit in the second-floor gallery while the remaining black-and-white characters occupy the main courtroom space. This scene produces a powerful echo with *To Kill a Mockingbird.* Released in 1962, Robert Mulligan's film details the struggles of a white southern lawyer (Gregory Peck) defending a black man accused of rape, and thus situates itself among the progressive "social problem" films that address civil rights issues.

40. In his commentary on the *Pleasantville* DVD, Ross discusses the commission, and he places the painter in a direct lineage with Diego Rivera. Romero was a member of the art collective Los Four, which mounted the first exhibition of Chicano art at a major museum in 1974 at the Los Angeles County Museum of Art.

41. Spigel reports that contemporary male dissatisfaction with the image of the sitcom husband in the period was considerable: "Television critics (most of whom were male) lashed out at the appearance of bumbling fathers on the new family sitcoms. In 1953, *TV Guide* asked 'What ever happened to men? . . . Once upon a time a girl thought of her boyfriend or husband as her Prince Charming. . . . Now having watched the antics of Ozzie Nelson and Chester A. Riley, she thinks of her man, and any other man, as a Prime Idiot.'" Spigel, *Make Room for TV,* 60.

42. Here we should recall an earlier film that Gary Ross cowrote, *Big* (Penny Marshall, 1988). Its thirteen-year-old protagonist gets his wish to be "big," grown-up, and he spends the rest of the film with a boy's consciousness in a man's body. His surprising success with women, then, suggests that this regressive position may respond perfectly to feminine desire. Tania Modleski comments on the film: "Thus, once again, we see a woman presiding over her own marginalization, participating in a nostalgia for a time in which human relationships are felt to have been relatively uncomplicated, although the cost of this simplicity is her own marginalization." Tania Modleski, *Feminism without Women: Culture and Criticism in a "Postfeminist" Age* (New York: Routledge, 1991), 98–99.

3. The Lure of Retrospectatorship

1. Film scholar Pam Cook characterizes this rereading aptly. "Whereas the lavish *mise-en-scène* of Sirk's melodramas is so over-the-top that it is said to produce an ironic distance that encourages the audience to criticise consumer culture," she writes, "the costume and production design of *Far From Heaven* is used to comment on the process of reconstruction itself, giving rise to a different sort of irony, one that recognises the gap between the source material and its representation with the knowledge of hindsight—Sirk's imitation of life becomes Haynes' imitation of art." Pam Cook, *Screening the Past: Memory and Nostalgia in Cinema* (London: Routledge, 2005), 14. .

2. Patricia White, *Uninvited: Classical Hollywood Cinema and Lesbian Representability* (Bloomington: Indiana University Press, 1999), 197.

3. We may note here that, in his recasting of Sirk, Haynes offers a kind of "second-generation" retrospectatorship. He follows the earlier independent auteur Rainer Werner Fassbinder, whose films frequently reread Sirk as a lens on 1970s German culture.

4. *Far from Heaven* emerges in a moment when media memory seems especially interested in imagining the confluence of struggles over social difference. NBC's contemporary television series *American Dreams*, for instance, which premiered in 2002, the year of this film's release, and ran until 2005, explores the cultural shifts of the 1960s in a family drama that opens onto the mother's incipient feminism, the father's workplace interactions with his black employee, and the children's confrontations with racial difference, centrally articulated through musical culture.

5. Mary Ann Doane, "Pathos and Pathology: The Cinema of Todd Haynes," *Camera Obscura* 57 (2004): 18.

6. For a different critical approach to the status and effects of *Far from Heaven*'s investment in melodramatic structure, see Salomé Aguilera Skvirsky, "The Price of Heaven: Remaking Politics in *All That Heaven Allows, Ali: Fear Eats the Soul,* and *Far from Heaven*," *Cinema Journal* 47, no. 3 (2008): 90–121.

7. Lynne Joyrich, "Written on the Screen: Mediation and Immersion in *Far from Heaven*," *Camera Obscura* 57 (2004): 190.

8. "The Continuity Script," in *"Imitation of Life": Douglas Sirk, Director,* ed. Lucy Fischer (New Brunswick, N.J.: Rutgers University Press, 1991), 100. In this connection, a casual remark by Sirk in an interview is striking; he commented that when his

film was dubbed into German, "all they got was the Negro angle." Quoted in James Harvey, "Sirkumstantial Evidence," in Fischer, *Imitation of Life,* 222.

9. To name just a few of these important interventions: Mary Ann Doane, Patricia Mellencamp, and Linda Williams, eds., *Re-Vision: Essays in Feminist Film Criticism* (Los Angeles: AFI, 1984); Christine Gledhill, ed., *Home Is Where the Heart Is: Studies in Melodrama and the Woman's Film* (London: BFI, 1987); Mary Ann Doane, *Femmes Fatales: Feminism, Film Theory, Psychoanalysis* (New York: Routledge, 1991); Mary Ann Doane, *The Desire to Desire: The Woman's Film of the 1940s* (Bloomington: Indiana University Press, 1987); Judith Mayne, *Cinema and Spectatorship* (London: Routledge, 1993); Tania Modleski, *The Women Who Knew Too Much: Hitchcock and Feminist Theory* (New York: Methuen, 1988); Constance Penley, ed., *Feminism and Film Theory* (London: Routledge, 1988); Annette Kuhn, *Women's Pictures: Feminism and Cinema* (London: Routledge & Kegan Paul, 1982); Fischer, *Imitation of Life.*

10. Barbara Klinger, *Melodrama and Meaning: History, Culture, and the Films of Douglas Sirk* (Bloomington: Indiana University Press, 1994), xi, xiv.

11. Lynne Joyrich, "Epistemology of the Console," *Critical Inquiry* 27 (Spring 2000): 445.

12. It would be interesting to consider *Far from Heaven* in light of two other contemporary films that center on the maternal. Pedro Almodóvar's *All about My Mother/Todo sobre mi madre* (1999) presents as its generative moment a mother and son watching *All about Eve* (Joseph L. Mankiewicz, 1950). The son's death prompts his single mother to revisit figuratively the "moment of his birth," bringing news of the tragedy to the father whose identity he never knew, a transvestite homosexual. *The Hours* (Stephen Daldry, 2002), based on Michael Cunningham's 1998 novel of the same title, features Julianne Moore as the 1950s mother whose remote indifference and ultimate abandonment of her child—maternal lack—generates the whole story and connects its three female protagonists.

13. Quoted in Juan Williams, *Eyes on the Prize: America's Civil Rights Years, 1954–1965* (New York: Penguin Books, 1988), 107.

14. As television scholar William Boddy notes, "The FCC's Office of Network Study heard testimony in New York in June 1961 from a number of prominent writers and producers from the era of live television." "The witnesses," Boddy reports, were "in virtual agreement that at about the 1957–58 television season, much of the diversity in entertainment programs disappeared from network schedules and that such schedules tended to become disproportionately loaded with action-adventure type film programs and other film series programs of a 'stereotyped nature.'" William Boddy, *Fifties Television: The Industry and Its Critics* (Urbana: University of Illinois Press, 1990), 194.

15. Sasha Torres, *Black, White, and In Color: Television and Black Civil Rights* (Princeton, N.J.: Princeton University Press, 2003), 19.

16. Lynne Joyrich describes the couple's relationship to TV in the following way: "The problem may not be that the Whitakers are too absorbed into television, but that they are not absorbed enough; or, maybe more accurately, that they are absorbed in the wrong way, framed only as televisual spectacles and not as spectators, posed with (and against) the television set, and so set into place themselves, rather than

positioned as engaged and enthusiastic readers of the texts." Joyrich, "Written on the Screen," 200.

17. My thanks to Randall Halle for calling my attention to this effect.

18. Lynne Joyrich has explored similar patterns of vacillation in "knowingness"— between enigma and enlightenment—in the positions of "queer sidekicks" who have recently emerged on network TV. "Television's queer characters," she writes, "may not necessarily play the (still often common) role of obscure objects, loci of mystery, scandal, and uncertainty; instead they may be figured as devoid of all mystery (and thus potentially of all dramatic interest), more pedagogic than puzzling. But whether enlighteners or enigmas, knowing readers or riddles to be known (however impossible this task is taken to be), TV's gay characters are constructed as epistemological nodal points." Joyrich, "Epistemology of the Console," 456. *Far from Heaven* provides a much more nuanced treatment of its epistemological nodes, but, nonetheless, as a figure Raymond consistently shifts between mystery and mentor.

19. Dana Heller analyzes what she calls the "de-oedipalization" of popular culture in the 1950s through readings of "post-family romances": "What is brought to light in post-family romances, however nervously, is that the plot for origin need not inevitably lead us to the discovery or invention of paternity, the privileged trope of Freud's family romance. Nor does it necessarily lead to the reclamation of an alternative romance centered on a unified myth of maternity." Dana Heller, *Family Plots: The De-Oedipalization of Popular Culture* (Philadelphia: University of Pennsylvania Press, 1995), 19.

20. This uneasy scene recalls Haynes's disturbing 1995 film *Safe*, which also stars Julianne Moore. Carol White flees her home and family, retreating into ever more stark isolation to escape toxic elements in her domestic environment. Whether these are chemical, organic, marital, familial, or neurotic remains undetermined. One possible reading of the film is that the suburban nuclear family itself is toxic and psychotogenic. Significantly, Carol's first symptoms appear when she collapses at a particularly cute—and chaotic—children's birthday party attended only by other mothers and kids.

21. Historian Ellen Herman tracks the shift in clinical opinion about homosexuality from World War II into the postwar period. "Because it involved psychological identity," she writes, "homosexuality ought to be treated with compassionate psychotherapy rather than with criminal penalties. Sexual deviance was no simple matter of wicked behavior; hence, punishment could not fix it. Only experts with a grasp of the personality as an integrated whole could hope to illuminate—let alone alter—the psychological processes implicated in the production of homosexuality." "Belief in the possibility and desirability of reforming the self, although not necessarily applicable to sexual preferences and behaviors deemed deviant, was nevertheless at the core of most of the self-help effort," Herman continues, concluding that the name of this effort is "adjustment." Ellen Herman, *The Romance of American Psychology: Political Culture in the Age of Experts* (Berkeley: University of California Press, 1995), 109.

22. Cultural studies scholar Andrea Slane describes the "pathologies" that the Cold War period brings together: "The . . . postwar practice of drawing analogies

between vastly different experiences encouraged the homology between fascism and homosexuality, as the theory of family dynamics and identificatory structures thought to produce homosexuals indeed matched the template of social pathologies of many sorts, including those of Nazis and other racists." "Through the collapse of these 'pathologies,'" she continues, along with "the postwar expansion of fears of momism, and heightened surveillance of both individuals and families, homosexuals came to represent the most publicly vilified 'un-American' sexuality, ranking with, and sometimes conflated with, communists in their threat to the Cold War nation." Andrea Slane, *A Not So Foreign Affair: Fascism, Sexuality, and the Cultural Rhetoric of American Democracy* (Durham, N.C.: Duke University Press, 2001), 169.

23. Indeed, Cathy's wardrobe links her to that other feminine proto-type of the 1950s, Barbie, who came on the market in 1959. We might say that she functions as the film's very own fantasy Barbie doll, and thus she strikes a forceful intertextual reference with Haynes's short film *Superstar: The Karen Carpenter Story* (1987).

24. Exploring the functions and meanings of lesbian bars in the midcentury urban environment, film scholar Kelly Hankin cites Jack Lait and Lee Mortimer's *New York Confidential!*, which suggests that the laissez-faire attitude of the police toward lesbian bars in Greenwich Village rests on "the theory that [as long as] you can't do away with [lesbians], and as long as they're with us, it's better to segregate them in one section, where an eye can be kept on them." Jack Lait and Lee Mortimer, *New York Confidential!*, rev. ed. (New York: Crown, 1948), 75, quoted in Kelly Hankin, *The Girls in the Back Room: Looking at the Lesbian Bar* (Minneapolis: University of Minnesota Press, 2002), 10.

25. This is the moment when Frank attempts to move from the zone of the criminal—"loitering" that the police survey and punish—to that of therapeutic remedy. But it is in the therapist's office that Frank encounters the expert assessment of this newly constituted "distinct clinical syndrome," which Herman explores, citing the assertion of the *Diagnostic and Statistical Manual of Mental Disorders*: "Attempts to reform such men are almost always futile." Herman, *Romance of American Psychology*, 109. This is precisely Dr. Bouman's position, contending as he does that there is only a 15–30 percent rate of "heterosexual conversion." Frank himself asserts his embrace of a pathological definition: "I'm going to beat this thing; I know it's a sickness because it makes me feel despicable."

26. In an early commentary that contributed to Sirk's revival as "auteur," film scholar Fred Camper examines the "flatness of the frames": "Flatness is perhaps a better word than unreality or falseness, both of which have negative connotations which should be avoided, and it also suggests another method by which Sirk creates his style. On the deepest expressive level, his frames never possess anything remotely resembling three-dimensional perspective, but rather they all operate in a kind of pre-Renaissance flatness." And this effect is related to distance and point of view in general, as he suggests: "There are many points of view that the camera, or a character, can take; but rather than contributing by simple addition to a total picture each remains separated from the others; and it is their very multiplicity that renders hopeless the possibility of real seeing." Fred Camper, "The Films of Douglas Sirk," in Fischer, *"Imitation of Life,"* 257.

27. Eve Kosofsky Sedgwick, *Epistemology of the Closet* (Berkeley: University of California Press, 1990), 4.

28. Lynne Joyrich reminds us that Frank has chosen the film about "reintegrating yet medicalized cure" over *Miracle in the Rain* (Rudolph Maté, 1956), a melodrama about a woman "wasting away from desire" for a lost lover, suggesting that his choice inclines toward "good domestic urges versus bad sexual appetites." Joyrich, "Written on the Screen," 192–93. Joyrich goes on to propose that Frank's own later pursuit of medicalized "reintegration" serves to highlight this film's refusal of medical melodrama's tight closure in the cure.

29. Allison Graham, *Framing the South: Hollywood, Television, and Race during the Civil Rights Struggle* (Baltimore: Johns Hopkins University Press, 2001), 40–41.

30. In the words of Dr. Thigpen, one of therapists who wrote the case history on which *The Three Faces of Eve* is based: "When Eve Black is 'out,' Eve White remains functionally in abeyance." Because of the asymmetry in their relations to the conscious ego, Eve Black, as Graham reminds us, frequently "comes out" and "passes" as Eve White, even with her husband. Significantly, she contends, "the ability of the Black twin to 'pass' as the White one pitches the film precariously close to the edge of Hollywood's gender and racial representational boundaries." Ibid., 48.

31. Salomé Aguilera Skvirsky questions this claim, but she does not examine or discuss the visual strategies on which I base it. Instead, her argument relies primarily on evidence drawn from the film's dialogue. See Aguilera Skvirsky, "The Price of Heaven," 106–8.

4. Black Authenticity and the Ambivalent Icon

1. That no such incident ever occurred in the life this film fictionalizes speaks powerfully, I think, to *Talk to Me*'s alertness to the shaping impact of media representation—and access to such representation—on American culture's divisions and intersections.

2. Herman Gray, "Remembering Civil Rights: Television, Memory, and the 1960s," in *The Revolution Wasn't Televised: Sixties Television and Social Conflict*, ed. Lynn Spigel and Michael Curtin (New York: Routledge, 1997), 353.

3. Quoted in Aram Goudsouzian, *Sidney Poitier: Man, Actor, Icon* (Chapel Hill: University of North Carolina Press, 2004), 275.

4. Thelma Golden, *Black Male: Representations of Masculinity in Contemporary American Art* (New York: Whitney Museum of American Art, 1994), 20. Golden structured the exhibit around several "cultural signposts," the first two of which were black power (1968) and the rise of blaxploitation film with the release of Melvin Van Peebles's *Sweet Sweetback's Baadasssss Song* (1971). This film, of course, participated vigorously in making myths visual.

5. Charles Kronengold suggests that in black action films of this period, "identity—of both persons and groups—is radically under construction." He writes, "Rather than endorse one stable identity, these films enact the conflicts among competing notions of identity—the same conflicts as are worked through in the critical literature." Charles Kronengold, "Identity, Value, and the Work of Genre: Black Action Films," in *The Seventies: The Age of Glitter in Popular Culture*, ed. Shelton

Waldrep (New York: Routledge, 2000), 103. On anxiety and struggles over black male identity in the Black Arts Movement, see Phillip Brian Harper's excellent analysis in *Are We Not Men? Masculine Anxiety and the Problem of African-American Identity* (New York: Oxford University Press, 1996), in the chapter titled "Nationalism and Social Division in Black Arts Poetry of the 1960s" (39–53). Harper explores the assertion of authenticity through structures of address that establish a "we" opposed to "you."

6. Donald Bogle, *Toms, Coons, Mulattoes, Mammies, and Bucks: An Interpretive History of Blacks in American Films* (New York: Continuum, 1989), 234.

7. Commentary on *Talk to Me* DVD, Universal Studios, Focus Features, 2007.

8. This exclamation of course recalls Mr. Señor Love Daddy, the disc jockey in Spike Lee's 1989 *Do the Right Thing*. It does not seem a stretch to suggest that this character, who observes the community continuously and comments often sharply on its behaviors, might be modeled on Petey Greene, especially since his final injunction, with which the film ends, is "Wake up!"

9. "It's a Man's Man's Man's World," written by James Brown and Betty Newsome, performed by James Brown.

10. Cedric the Entertainer, comedian, actor, and frequent voice-over artist, achieved special notoriety for his performance in *Barbershop* (Tim Story, 2002) as Eddie, a cynical older barber who makes Rosa Parks and Martin Luther King Jr. the subjects of a controversial routine.

11. Jason Loviglio, *Radio's Intimate Public: Network Broadcasting and Mass-Mediated Democracy* (Minneapolis: University of Minnesota Press, 2005), xv.

12. Susan Douglas describes radio as a technology that "has worked most powerfully inside our heads, helping us to create internal maps of the world and our place in it, urging us to construct imagined communities to which we do, or do not, belong." She goes on to argue that "radio hastened the shift away from identifying oneself—and one's social solidarity with others—on the basis of location and family ties, to identifying oneself on the basis of consumer and taste preferences." Susan Douglas, *Listening In: Radio and the American Imagination* (Minneapolis: University of Minnesota Press, 1999), 5.

13. Kobena Mercer, *Welcome to the Jungle: New Positions in Black Cultural Studies* (New York: Routledge, 1994), 107. Mercer characterizes the Afro this way: "By emphasizing the length of hair when allowed to grow 'natural and free,' the style countervalorized attributes of curliness and kinkiness to convert stigmata into emblematics of pride" (106). But he also emphasizes the way the Afro straddles a nature / culture divide, as it figures in debates that speak through and struggle over ethnic signs (105).

14. Following Thomas Kochman, Henry Louis Gates notes that, among other things, "signifying can also be employed to *reverse* or *undermine* pretense." Henry Louis Gates Jr., *Figures in Black: Words, Signs, and the "Racial" Self* (New York: Oxford University Press, 1987), 240.

15. Mercer, *Welcome to the Jungle*, 118. Mercer includes among these stylized forms and forms of style verbal virtuosity. "In speech and language," he writes, "games like signifyin', playing the dozens and what became known as jive-talk, verbal style effected a discursive equivalent of jazz improvisation. The performative skills and

sheer wit demanded by these speech-acts in black talk defied the idea that Black English was a degraded 'version' of the master language" (118).

16. Mercer suggests that "at one level, this alternative political orientation of Black Power," away from "the Civil Rights demand for equality within the given framework of society," "announced its public presence in the language of clothes." "The Black Panthers' 'urban guerrilla attire,'" he writes, "encoded a uniform of protest and militancy by way of the connotations of the common denominator, the color black." "The Panthers' berets," he continues, "invoked solidarity with the violent means of anti-imperialist struggle, while the dark glasses, by concealing identity from 'the enemy,' lent a certain political mystique and a romantic aura of dangerousness." Ibid., 106–7.

17. Kronengold, "Identity, Value, and the Work of Genre," 101.

18. Kronengold notes the strength of black action films' sound tracks, demonstrated by their crossover into the mediascape of popular music. He notes a similar pressure of music on the visual, but characterizes it somewhat differently: "These movies clear a great deal of space for the soundtrack, and what they receive in return is a sense of depth—consciousness, even a conscience—that the image and dialogue cannot themselves provide." Ibid., 83. Where he emphasizes what music *adds* to image and speech, I would stress the interaction of the musical with the visual, the space of speech and action.

19. We might characterize Dewey's performance as a kind of "backstepping or "loud-talking," which Harper describes as "a verbal device, common within many black-English-speaking communities, in which a person 'says something of someone just loud enough for that person to hear, but indirectly, so he cannot properly respond.'" Harper, *Are We Not Men?*, 7, quoting Roger Abrahams, *Talking Black* (Rowley, Mass.: Newbury House, 1976), 19.

20. Gates, *Figures in Black,* 240. Gates also quotes Claudia Mitchell-Kernan's economical characterization of the term's elasticity: "Complimentary remarks may be delivered in a left-handed fashion. A particular utterance may be an insult in one context and not another. What pretends to be informative may intend to be persuasive. The hearer is thus constrained to attend to all potential meaning carrying symbolic systems in speech events—the total universe of the discourse." Claudia Mitchell-Kernan, "Signifying," in *Mother Wit from the Laughing Barrel: Readings in the Interpretation of Afro-American Folklore,* ed. Alan Dundes (Englewood Cliffs, N.J.: Prentice-Hall, 1973), 313.

21. In an essay on the astonishing racial vocabulary of Shirley Temple films, as well as that vocabulary's contribution to the films' cultural force, Anne Du Cille offers a similar perspective on authenticity, contending that "the real power of whiteness . . . is how readily many African Americans have accepted the notion that *authentic* blackness is first and finally vernacular, impoverished, illiterate." "I want to *insist*," she writes, that this institutionally validated definition of authentic blackness depends on an essentialism as pathological as the ridiculous blackness used to affirm Shirley Temple's whiteness, beauty, and superiority more than half a century ago." Anne Du Cille, "The Shirley Temple of My Familiar," *Transition* 73 (1997): 29.

22. Quoted in Goudsouzian, *Sidney Poitier,* 275.

23. Performance as this film's central trope, of course, echoes at the level of its very actors. Cedric the Entertainer began in stand-up comedy. Don Cheadle's career has been marked by protean transformations: from the psychotic, sometimes homicidal, rages of Mouse, Easy Rawlins's comical sidekick and best friend in *Devil in a Blue Dress* (Carl Franklin, 1995), to Paul Rusesabagina in *Hotel Rwanda* (Terry George, 2004) to his roles in *Ocean's Eleven* and *Ocean's Twelve*. Chiwetel Ejiofor, a British actor, impresses for his seamless performance of two American idioms.

24. Ralph Ellison, *Shadow and Act* (1964; repr., New York: Random House, 1994), xvi–xvii.

25. Like Nighthawk, Sunny Jim is a historical figure.

26. "Knock on Wood," written by Steve Croper and Eddie Floyd, performed by Eddie Floyd.

27. This laugh-out-loud moment will echo later on in a segment that depicts Greene's television show, in which he introduces a guest clearly modeled on Mayor Marion Barry this way: "My next guest is a hustler and a pimp who I wouldn't trust to wash my car. But you all elected him city official."

28. The term is Mel Watkins's. See his *On the Real Side* (New York: Simon & Schuster, 1994), 271.

29. William Barlow, *Voice Over: The Making of Black Radio* (Philadelphia: Temple University Press, 1999), 1.

30. Les McCann and Eddie Harris recorded the song at the Montreux Jazz Festival in 1969, and it came out on the album *Swiss Movement* (Atlantic Records, 1969). The same year, Roberta Flack recorded a version on her album *First Take* (Atlantic Records).

31. Wahneema Lubiano, "'But Compared to What?': Reading Realism, Representation, and Essentialism in *School Daze, Do the Right Thing,* and the Spike Lee Discourse," in *Representing Black Men,* ed. Marcellus Blount and George P. Cunningham (New York: Routledge, 1996), 175.

32. "I Want to Take You Higher," written by Sly Stone, performed by Sly and the Family Stone (Epic Records).

33. Writing of the effects of early radio, transmitted from fixed home consoles as well as car sets, Jason Loviglio cites Saul Bellow's anecdote of walking down the street and listening continuously to one of Roosevelt's Fireside Chats as car radios on the Chicago Midway were all tuned in to it. "You could follow without missing a single word as you strolled by. You felt joined to these unknown drivers, men and women smoking their cigarettes in silence, not so much considering the President's words as affirming the rightness of his tone and taking assurance from it." Loviglio, *Radio's Intimate Public,* xiii. Reflecting on the range of such anecdotes, Loviglio writes: "Accounts such as these emphasize radio's ritual power to transform the anonymous spaces of towns, cities, the nation itself into a new site of reception, a momentary extension of the private space of the family home or car." He continues: "The domestic space of reception becomes more public even as feelings about its intimacy become heightened" (xv).

34. Quoted in Barlow, *Voice Over,* 195. Barlow relates the origin of his book project to his own surprise at discovering "that black radio had played a far greater role in the

shaping of urban black culture—and the popular culture as a whole—than I had first surmised. Especially since the late 1940s, when it emerged as African Americans' most ubiquitous means of communication—surpassing the black press—black radio has been a major force in constructing and sustaining an African American public sphere" (xi).

35. "Tainted Love," written by Ed Cobb, performed by Gloria Jones.

36. "'Petey' Greene: Pioneering Shock Jock, D.C. Icon," *All Things Considered*, NPR, July 13, 2007, http://www.npr.org.

37. Cited in Goudsouzian, *Sidney Poitier*, 217.

38. On the relationship of spectacle to forgetting, see Marita Sturken, *Tangled Memories: The Vietnam War, the AIDS Epidemic, and the Politics of Remembering* (Berkeley: University of California Press, 1997), esp. chap. 4.

39. Petey's remarks sound similar to those of the real Bob "Nighthawk" Terry on the night of the assassination, as reported by Barlow: "Terry was openly outraged—not only by the assassination but also 'at the brothers on the block,' whom he challenged: 'Why ya burnin' down your own communities, brothers? Don't see no riotin' and lootin' at the White House and the Congress, no siree, everybody up on U Street lootin' and shootin' your own!'" Barlow, *Voice Over*, 218.

40. The single was released by RCA Victor. Cooke performed it on *The Tonight Show* during an appearance in February 1964.

41. Commentary, "Recreating P-Town," on *Talk to Me* DVD.

42. Siegfried Kracauer calls the camera "a rag-picker" and cites cinema's proclivity for objects that generally go "unnoticed": "Most people turn their backs on the garbage cans, the dirt underfoot, and the waste they leave behind." "Films," he writes, "have no such inhibitions." Siegfried Kracauer, *Theory of Film* (Princeton, N.J.: Princeton University Press, 1997), 54. He also emphasizes cinema's commitment to the "evanescent," to "fleeting impressions." "It may be anticipated," he remarks, "that the street in the broadest sense of the word is a place where these sorts of impressions are bound to occur" (52).

43. "The Revolution Will Not Be Televised," written by Gil Scott-Heron, released on the album *Small Talk at 125th and Lenox* (Flying Dutchman Records, 1970).

44. Lynn Spigel and Michael Curtin, "Introduction," in Spigel and Curtin, *The Revolution Wasn't Televised*, 1–2.

45. Henry Louis Gates Jr., *Thirteen Ways of Looking at a Black Man* (New York: Random House, 1997), 155.

46. A lecture delivered by Sasha Torres at the Symposium on Visual Memory, University of Rochester, May 6, 2008, reminded me that Wexler filmed in Resurrection City.

47. Commentary on *Talk to Me* DVD.

48. John Limon, *Stand-up Comedy in Theory, or, Abjection in America* (Durham, N.C.: Duke University Press, 2000), 3.

49. W. E. B. Du Bois, *The Souls of Black Folk* (1903; repr., New York: Penguin/Signet, 1969), 45.

50. The real-life Hughes purchased WOL-AM in 1980 with his then wife, Cathy. Cathy Hughes shifted from "WOL's traditional soul music soundscape for a talk-radio

format—a bold move at the time." She also relocated the station "from the upscale white Georgetown section to the heart of the black community." Cathy Hughes owns the station to this day, and it forms part of her nine-station Radio One Network, "the largest and most prosperous black-owned radio chain in the country." Barlow, *Voice Over*, 276, 278.

Conclusion

1. In a contemporary iteration of the force of moral authority that the Poitier figure still seems to wield in the white cultural imaginary, during an interview on NPR's *Fresh Air* on February 20, 2013, Quentin Tarantino repeated to Terry Gross a story he was regularly telling in the media as he was promoting *Django Unchained* (2012). At a certain point as he was preparing to make the film, he became worried about the subject of enslavement and the extreme and sadistic violence of the cinematic treatment he was planning. So he went to dinner with Sidney Poitier, who, Tarantino reported, told him that he "shouldn't be afraid of [his] movie." Still an authority on racial "correctness," on white–black relations, Poitier remains, as he was at the height of his acting career, poised somewhere between the real world and the cinematic one.

2. Jabari Asim, *What Obama Means . . . for Our Culture, Our Politics, Our Future* (New York: William Morrow, 2009).

3. Barack Obama, *Dreams from My Father: A Story of Race and Inheritance* (1995; repr., New York: Three Rivers Press, 2004).

4. Frank Rich, "Guess Who's Coming to Dinner," *New York Times*, November 1, 2008, http://www.nytimes.com.

5. Manohla Dargis and A. O. Scott, "How the Movies Made a President," *New York Times*, January 18, 2009, Arts and Leisure, 1, 9.

6. Jared Sexton, "The Ruse of Engagement: Black Masculinity and the Cinema of Policing," *American Quarterly* 61, no. 1 (March 2009): 41.

7. Sharon P. Holland, "Death in Black and White: A Reading of Marc Forster's *Monster's Ball*," *Signs* 31, no. 3 (2006): 788.

8. Aimee Carrillo Rowe, "Feeling in the Dark: Empathy, Whiteness, and Miscege-nation in *Monster's Ball*," *Hypatia* 22, no. 2 (Spring 2007): 128.

9. Holland notes that "the word *implausible* became a sort of mantra in the negative reviews of the film." Holland, "Death in Black and White," 796.

10. Interestingly, Combs appears in Poitier's role as Walter Lee Younger in the 2008 television remake of *A Raisin in the Sun* (Kenny Leon).

11. The image of a blank screen recalls the ending of John Sayles's *Lone Star* (1996), which much more self-consciously leaves its central interracial couple, who have recently learned they share a father, contemplating their future possibilities before the decrepit screen at an abandoned drive-in movie theater.